The Germans Who Never Lost

To my wife

Also by Edwin P Hoyt, Jr

THE LAST CRUISE OF THE *EMDEN*
THE GUGGENHEIMS AND THE AMERICAN DREAM

THE GERMANS
WHO NEVER LOST

Edwin P Hoyt, Jr

LESLIE FREWIN : LONDON

First published in Great Britain 1969 by
Leslie Frewin Publishers Ltd,
1 New Quebec Street, Marble Arch, London W1

Set in Scotch Roman
Printed by Anchor Press
and bound by William Brendon
both of Tiptree, Essex

09 096400 4

Contents

1
Dar es Salaam

IN THE EARLY months of 1914 one major topic of conversation dominated the meetings of little groups of white-clad
Germans sitting on the stone verandas of the big bungalows
in Dar es Salaam, a matter that quite transcended the
usual gossip about the prices of sisal, tea, rubber, and
cinchona, or even the progress of the new railway line being
built between the harbour and Kigoma on the eastern
shore of snaky Lake Tanganyika. The subject was the
coming to German East Africa, almost at any moment it
was said, of the German light cruiser Sein Majistate Schiff
Königsberg, one of the most modern of the Imperial German
Navy's war vessels. With the colonists of East Africa this
interest was a matter of pride as much as anything else;
the Germans in far-off Tsingtao had their German East
Asia Squadron, half a dozen sleek, silvery ships which
graced the half-moon harbour of that China port, and it
was a matter of constant chagrin to East Africans that the
Reichsmarinamt had never felt it necessary or proper to
dispatch more than two old worn-out naval vessels to this
best established of the German colonies. Dar es Salaam was
the starting place of the brave German effort to match
their English cousins in the acquisition of territories across
the sea; it was to this place that Karl Peters, the father of
German colonisation, had come originally. Well – not
quite – but almost: in 1884 Herr Peters had arrived at
Bagamoyo a few miles up the coast from Dar es Salaam,
and at that time the city was nothing, a ruined wreck of the
town of old Sultan Majid of Zanzibar. The sultan had

selected the beautiful little harbour as the site for his palace and had begun building a capital there, but in 1871 he had died and his successors were of different mind, so Dar es Salaam had languished until Peters came along.

Herr Peters was quick to impose his ideas and the will of his German backers on this part of Africa. A year after his coming he had obtained an imperial charter, guaranteeing the Kaiser's protection of German lives and property in the interior of Africa. The idea of his union for German colonisation had appealed very much to the crown prince's son, young Wilhelm, and old Prince Bismarck saw nothing wrong in acquiring a few colonies as long as nothing was allowed to interfere with Germany's growth and burgeoning power on the European continent. Kaiser Wilhelm I had agreed, and in 1886 a joint commission of German, British, and French members had defined the territorial limits of the Zanzibar sultans so that the vast interior of the land – south of British East Africa, east of the Congo and the land that would be Rhodesia, and north of the Portuguese possession of Mozambique – would belong to Germany. It was granted that the sultan should have suzerainty over a strip of land ten miles wide, extending inland along the coast from his islands, but it was not granted for long; Germans found themselves fighting the troublesome Arabs almost immediately. The trouble really began when Peters persuaded the sultanate to let him have the deserted palace at Dar es Salaam as a trading post. Within a year the Germans were taking over the coastal lands as well. When the Arabs struck back with a raid on Dar es Salaam, the Kaiser decided it was time to establish a permanent military base there for protection of German interests, and to accomplish this the original *Kreuzergeschwader*, the German Cruiser Squadron, was created as the nucleus of the German navy.

Young Wilhelm had something to do with this plan, for he was a naval buff and its simplicity appealed to him. Germany was not strong enough to match mighty Britannia ship for ship, or for that matter to match France or Russia;

but Germany could build a squadron of cruisers, fast ships with strong engines and big guns for their size, which could absolutely devastate any savage flotilla in being and whose presence in a colonial area was the equivalent to a division or two of troops on land.

The late 1880s had been the years when German might was felt along the coast of East Africa. In 1888 the squadron in Dar es Salaam had been something to see: the flagship *Kreuzerfregatte Leipzig* with 12 guns and a crew of 434 men, the *Kreuzerkorvetten Carola* and *Olga* with 12 guns and 267 men each, the *Kreuzer Schwalbe* with 8 guns and 114 men, the *Kreuzer Möwe*, with 5 guns and 127 men, and the *Aviso* or dispatch boat *Pfeil* with 5 guns and 127 men.

The squadron had been a mighty force in the development of German East Africa, and there were old men and women who still frequented the clubs of Dar es Salaam in 1914 who could remember the days when men from the squadron had landed and marched through the countryside, burning villages and destroying crops when the Chaga or the Nyamwezi refused to behave themselves and do the German bidding. The cruiser squadron and troops from the homeland in 1905 and 1906 had put down that bout of bloodshed known as the Maji-Maji Rebellion, and there were more men and women who came to the club terraces every evening to sip their *spritzers* who could recall those days.

There was one root of colonial discontent: too many of the older settlers could recall the bad old days, and they also could recall the old-fashioned gunboat *Geier* and the even older *Möwe*, which seemingly had been hanging around the East African coast with no more military efficiency than the gull after which she was named. Every German in the colony resented the humiliation of being so feebly represented at sea, and as the mighty ships of the British Navy stood out from the headlands of the East African coast, cruising up and down in reminder of Albion's naval power, the Germans complained. Why could not Berlin maintain the same balance of power here in Africa that she insisted on in the North Sea? Had not the High Seas Fleet been built simply to counter Britain's Grand Fleet? And if this were so, why should Africa be blighted with inattention? Germany, after all, had four colonies in Africa: Togo, the Cameroons, German Southwest Africa, and German East Africa. The importance and value of these colonies was obvious, and the colonists of East Africa were quietly confident that of all the African possessions of the Kaiser, theirs had the greatest potential.

So it was with mingled pride and anticipation that the planters and traders looked forward to the arrival of the *Königsberg* to German East Africa. She was the answer to the incessant pleas of business and shipping interests for power and prestige along the northwest corner of the Indian Ocean, and for once Berlin had listened, even after the Reichstag had played deaf and refused the appropriations.

In March, as the *Königsberg* refitted at the German naval base in Kiel, Dr Heinrich Schnee, the governor of German East Africa, was already making plans with the naval authorities for use of the *Königsberg* to further national ends. He counted on holding open house aboard the ship; native chiefs and village headmen would be brought from all over the interior to examine the shining cruiser, the evidence of Germany's military might which made her a power to be feared and thus obeyed even on the banks of Lake Tanganyika. Every week Governor Schnee indicated his impatience to Berlin as he urged the rapid dispatch of the cruiser.

The timing of the German naval command could not have been better as far as the officers and crew of the *Königsberg* were concerned: as they fitted out for sea the southeast monsoon blew over the coast of German East Africa, bringing the autumn rainy season (for this land is below the equator, where the seasons are reversed) and when the *Königsberg* would be ready for sea in May the rains would have ended and the sunny bright weather of the cool season be about to begin.

On 1st April Fregattenkapitän Max Looff was piped over the side of SMS *Königsberg* as she lay at dock and took command of the ship. His first action was to raise the ship's pennon and war ensign as his new crew cheered and to remind the men of their ship's motto:

To be strong before the enemy, to be the upholder of your country, and to remain faithful until death and through battle and all trials; that will always be the supreme rule of your crew.

The arming of the little cruiser continued apace with scarcely a day off for captain or crew until their sailing date. Day after day carts and wagons trundled up to the dockside bearing all the modern instruments of war that the *Königsberg* would carry. There were shells for the ten big guns in one cart and hogs for the ship's butchers in the other, rifles for the *matelots* in one wagon, and sheets of leather soling for the ship's cobbler in the next. There was coal, nearly a thousand tons of it, good hard German coal that would burn hot and nearly smokeless when tended by the black gang under the watchful eyes of Engineer Bockmann. There was the dirty job of coaling, for which the navy hired porters in the harbour, but still the men had to don their oldest fatigue uniforms, cursing as they saw what the black dust did to their shining ship even with all blowers going.

In the officers' club at Kiel the slender, square-faced Max Looff was chaffed a good deal by his fellow captains when the word was out that he was going to Africa.

'Are you a hunter?' they asked him, for the minds of German naval officers in the spring of 1914 were turned to matters of the chase, the hunt of boars in the forests of Germany, the hunt of gazelles and bushbucks and even lion for the daring in Africa.

A little timidly Captain Looff adjusted his steel-rimmed spectacles and said yes – for in recognition of the major avocation that awaited him at his new station, Max Looff had gone out to purchase a 9-mm hunting rifle just a few days earlier and had taken one day off to go rabbit hunting. In fact he was an excellent shot, because to be an excellent marksman was a part of his naval discipline, but he had never been hunting before – at least, hunting wild animals. Since his cadet days aboard the old sailing ships he had been trained to hunt, but in quite a different way – to hunt the enemies of his emperor.

Amid the responsibilities of fitting out and loading, Captain Looff was briefed on the strategic reasons for his assignment to German East Africa to replace the *Geier*, which would go to the Far East to join Admiral the Graf von Spee's East Asia Squadron. German East Africa was becoming increasingly important to the homeland, and the flag should be shown properly in Africa lest the natives forget that Germany was every bit as important in the world as Great Britain.

During April, once the stores were taken aboard and the ship was pronounced ready for sea by the captain, time was taken out for intensive gunnery practice and torpedo drill in the waters of the North Sea, then towards the end of April the *Königsberg* was inspected by the admiral in charge of the Kiel base, and early on the morning of 25th April Captain Looff took the bridge and gave the order every man aboard had been waiting to hear:

'Cast off all lines!'

Passing between the lanes of the great battleships of the High Seas Fleet, the silvery *kleine kreuzer* – little cruiser – *Königsberg* set out for sea and the high adventure that every man of the three hundred and twenty-two in the crew expected in his next two years on foreign duty. It was a handpicked crew; not all the men of the German navy either wanted to serve in the tropics or were fitted for the duty. Captain Looff had checked the records of every man, for he insisted that they be strong and healthy and that they have the proper temperament for duty so far from home.

It was a day of exhilaration, this departure day. The sun

had come out bright and the sky was clear and blue, an unusual state of affairs for April in the North Sea, so unusual that it might have been a day made in honour of the *Königsberg's* sailing. Through the lines of the fleet they went, the crew of the *Königsberg* cheering each ship as they passed and being cheered in turn, while signal flags flashed up the masts and ensigns dipped to wish the captain and his crew good sailing and good fortune in the months to come.

Good weather was with them all the way. Captain Looff put in at ports in Spain and Italy, combining good-will visits with his mission; there was no particular hurry to get to East Africa except that Governor Schnee and the colonials were itching for his arrival. At Naples there was a grave exchange of visits between Captain Looff and the Duke of Aosta, admiral of the Italian fleet and a distinguished Alpine mountain climber. The duke was all amiability, and he spoke several times of the grand alliance of Germany, Austria, and Italy which in his opinion (he said) preserved the peace of all the world.

Königsberg steamed steadily at ten and sometimes twelve knots through the warm blue Mediterranean; she was quite capable of making twenty-four knots but there was no point in broadcasting this fact to the British ships that coursed these waters, and at ten knots she obtained her maximum economy in use of coal, which was an important matter in peacetime. At Suez she entered the canal and at Aden she came to anchor while Captain Looff paid a visit of state to the English governor and was honoured at a dinner by this friendly but vague official. Where was *Königsberg* bound, the governor asked, making conversation. Dar es Salaam? Oh, yes, he knew it – the Far East. So much for English knowledge of geography in the spring of 1914. It would not be many months before the governor's sense of direction was firmly corrected.

They steamed through the Gulf of Aden, the roasting Arab sun beating down on them all the way; but when they reached Cape Gardafui and turned south, the weather changed remarkably. They entered the southwest monsoon and the enormous swell of the Indian Ocean, which the slim little cruiser cut through with the precision of a carving knife. After days of hot winds blowing off the deserts of Africa and Arabia, a fresh sea breeze swept through the cabins and the forecastle and made it possible once more to sleep and even to sleep below.

A steamer of the German East Africa Line passed so close to *Königsberg* that the crews of the ships could exchange cheers and badinage, the bands of both ships struck up German songs, and the crews sang lustily: '*Deutschland, Deutschland über alles in die Welt . . .*' and the great hymn of travellers: '*Wem Gott will rechte Gunst erwiesen, den schicht er in die weite Welt. . . .*'

Then she was gone, the great white steamer that carried the German commercial flag so proudly from Africa to the homeland, and *Königsberg* steamed on south through the sparkling sunny sea, alone, out of sight of land.

Suddenly the land loomed up and, nestled in it, the small, perfectly sheltered harbour of Dar es Salaam – the Haven of Peace where old Sultan Majid had sought his rest – palms on the shore waving welcome above the white sands of the wide beach, and, beyond, the friendly rambling white houses with red roofs beckoning in the sunshine. Navigation officer Kapitän-leutnant Hinrichs was to be congratulated: he had made a perfect landfall on the Makatumbe lighthouse before dawn, on 6th June, and at the precise moment predicted.

Königsberg entered the roadstead and moored at the buoy which had been prepared for her. Of course, for several days *Königsberg* had been in touch with Radio Dar es Salaam and her coming was expected, so the town was alive with unusual activity, from the tips of the church steeples to the minarets of the mosques. Europeans in cork topis, white-clad, and women in loose prints carrying parasols walked down the main street under the acacia trees to the harbour or rode in rubber-tyred rickshaws pulled by slender

14

black men past the broad yards of houses, each with its wide veranda to keep the African sun away from the windows. In the adjoining native city lived twenty thousand blacks, and it seemed that nearly all of them had deserted their clay huts with corrugated iron roofs to come to the harbour. Mingled with the white and the silk prints of the ladies were the newest in African fashions: the frizzle-headed native women wore gold leaves in the sides of their noses and were draped in robes of cotton newly imported from the Fatherland; nearly every robe came from the new bolts for sale in the drapery shops of the traders. How could one tell? By the ever-repeating patterns, prints of parlour lamps and prints of the Graf Zeppelin's marvellous new airships. The men wore loincloths, and, as symbols of their well-being and in deference to the sensibilities of the whites of the cities, they had adopted the long white shirts of the Hindus which they wore over their loincloths, tails flapping in the breeze as they walked. One could tell the importance of this day, for the town also was filled with natives from the bush, black men in loincloths only, many of them carrying their spears, who had come to town to trade and to see the *Mano-wari-ya-bomba-tatou* whose coming Governor Schnee had broadcast across the jungle telegraph.

As *Königsberg* moored, the chattering of the town was suddenly drowned out by the thundering of the harbour guns in welcome to the symbol of His Majesty's might; the *Geier* and the *Möwe* added their salutes to the cacophony, and then *Königsberg* responded with her own salute.

A few minutes later the harbour itself came alive as a hundred bumboats milled around the naval anchorage, passing through the disorderly tangle of the inner harbour with its clots of rakish-masted dhows, flatboats, and caiques, to cluster around the largest German man-of-war that most of these natives had ever seen. They admired her silvery grey colour, her projecting cut-water and ram, her low sleek lines, her three sturdy smoke-stacks, the ten plugged guns sitting so calmly in turrets fore and aft and on her upper works to port and starboard, the pompoms and machine guns, the flags flying so gaily from the main-mast rigging. Governor Schnee came aboard, smiling broadly, and pumped Captain Looff's hand, then introduced him to the commander of the colonial troops, Oberstleutnant von Lettow-Vorbeck, resplendent in his high-collared uniform with its red and white piping, heavy white belt, and gold braid, wearing the heavy felt safari hat of the German colonial officer corps with the right side pinned up tight against the crown, and a toothbrush moustache against his long upper lip.

There was a brief reunion of the officers of *Geier* and *Möwe* with those of *Königsberg*, and there was much gossip about affairs at Kiel and in Berlin and a good deal of talk about the posting of senior officers to points around the world; and then, with true Teutonic efficiency, *Geier* was gone. She simply had been waiting for the arrival of *Königsberg* to steam east towards her new Asiatic station, and *Königsberg* and *Möwe* were left in the harbour alone with the Arab sailing craft that had not changed their lines or ways in a thousand years; then *Möwe* was off to continue her assignment: she was charting the waters of German East Africa, spotting reefs and shoals and channels along the coast and, less openly, keeping an eye on events north-ward, the naval comings and goings in British East Africa. Oberstleutnant von Lettow-Vorbeck paid his compliments and returned to his basic task, which was to survey his military domain – the two thousand troops ashore – the Protective Force whose duty it was to keep order in the vast hinterland of the colony. He went upcountry to Iringa and Rugeno, inspecting the Askaris, the native troops who were his first line of defence, coming back to Dar es Salaam to plead for modern weapons for them, to replace the old-fashioned rifles of 1871 that fired black powder with a roar and a cloud of smoke. Von Lettow-Vorbeck's representations to Governor Schnee and the governor's rep-resentations to Berlin were not much more effective than the old pleas for a strong naval force had been. The army got new weapons, but not enough of them; Berlin grumbled: had it not done quite enough by detaching one of its most modern naval vessels to be put at the service of this blasted colony?

2

The Eve of War

JUNE PASSED QUICKLY and pleasantly. Captain Looff went big-game hunting and bagged an oryx much to his surprise and pleasure. But in Berlin the German chief of staff, General Helmuth von Moltke, was after bigger game; von Moltke was ready, able, and simply waiting for the right time to go to war, and had been since April. Grand Admiral von Tirpitz, the German naval secretary, might know some of Moltke's plans and suspect more of them, but a mere fregattenkapitän knew no more about Germany's world strategy than he could deduce from gleaning around the headquarters of the Reichsmarin, and Captain Looff had not been one to hang around headquarters sniffing the wind. As the word of the assassination of Archduke Franz Ferdinand of Austria-Hungary was flashed around the world on 28th June, Captain Looff was surprised and concerned, but only because of the senselessness of the murder and the difficulties it brought to several small nations in the Balkans; he realised that the assassination might bring about the 'possibility of international complications' but he worried no further than that.

The captain's concern was still over showing the flag and impressing the natives of Africa with the strength of Germany. Hundreds – thousands – of natives were taken on conducted tours of the silvery warship in the harbour at Dar es Salaam, and when the flow of visitors slackened, the governor asked Captain Looff to take his ship to Bagamoyo and Tanga, so the cruiser could be displayed to whites and blacks in both ports. Before the end of

June most of the six thousand Germans in the colony had somehow managed a glimpse of the warship if not an actual visit to her decks, and a good share of the black population of eight million at least knew of her coming to East Africa's shores; her purpose had been achieved and the results were all that Governor Schnee and the settlers could wish.

July was given over to training the crew. *Königsberg* went to sea and Captain Looff put the men through hour after hour of dry runs, doing everything but shooting guns and launching torpedoes; he authorised some gunnery practice but he knew that almost as valuable as shooting practice was the readiness and familiarity with every motion and every piece of equipment that a man might be called upon to use in battle.

By mid-July the naval high command was warning its far-flung captains that they might expect war; the danger was serious and imminent; Captain Looff was kept informed daily by coded wireless messages passed along from Radio Dar es Salaam, and he knew exactly what was happening in Berlin, so far as the Admiralty was aware of the train of events. He was surprised, then, when he came ashore to visit the governor's great square white palace, to learn that Governor Schnee knew almost nothing of the events occurring in Europe in July. Even at the end of that tortured month the governor continued to argue with the captain: there was no danger of war, the captain was simply overwrought; and if he did not believe it, Captain Looff ought to see the message the governor had just received from the Ministry of Foreign Affairs. Captain Looff picked up the message and looked at it, first idly, then with interest, then with surprise.

'Reassure the colonists, there is no danger of war for the colonies.'

All the while, Captain Looff was receiving constant additions to his instructions, information about the disposition of German naval forces around the globe, and, particularly, advice about coaling supplies, munitions, and foodstuffs in case of war.

If war broke, the *Königsberg* was to conduct *Kreuzerkrieg*, what the French called *la guerre de course*, which was privateering or hit-and-run warfare against enemy shipping. Primarily the *kleine kreuzer* of the German navy were built for just such action; they outgunned anything but a modern armoured cruiser and they were swift and could be elusive in an area as large as the Gulf of Aden and the Indian Ocean.

Theoretically Captain Looff's *Kriegsbuch* called on him to protect German commerce in time of war and make war on the commerce of his country's enemies. The high command in Berlin was under no illusions about the fate of German commerce in the Red Sea and Indian Ocean, however, and while *Königsberg* certainly had the 'book' responsibility in theory, in fact her value would be twofold: she could raid enemy commerce and do millions of pounds' worth of damage (or francs or rubles, depending on the nature of the enemy); she also could move swiftly and very quietly about a huge hunting ground, and thus would force her enemies to dispatch several capital ships to hunt her down.

The British Admiralty was as conscious of this German strategy as was Berlin, so much so that during these last tense days in July London wanted to know where *Königsberg* was and would be. The Admiralty's interest was obvious enough: there had been only two effective German warships in an area that extended north as far as St Helena, and all around East Africa – the gunboat *Eber* and the *Königsberg*. Fortunately, in the eyes of the British Admiralty, the *Eber* was known to have left African waters for the South Atlantic; the British knew because she had called in at Cape Town on her way west.

But *Königsberg* was another matter entirely. In case of war she offered a grave threat to British security in all East Africa, which included the ships coming up the east side of Africa from Cape Town and Durban to the Suez Canal. The whole Indian Ocean could be her hunting ground, too, which meant she threatened the shipping lanes to Australia, Singapore, Java, Calcutta, Bombay,

Colombo, Hong Kong, Shanghai, Mauritius, and every other British port of call in the east. When the admirals in London had nightmares, the *Königsberg* might be lying hidden just off Aden, guns trained, in their dreams, ready to murder the ships of the merchant fleet as a spider murders flies.

A staff admiral may have awakened sweating from such a nightmare one night in mid July; in any event the word was passed that *Königsberg* must be located. By wireless on 27th July the word came to Rear Admiral Herbert King-Hall, commander of the cruiser division stationed at the Cape of Good Hope. The admiral and his three cruisers were on routine mission when the word reached him by wireless: he was to look out for *Königsberg* and shadow her in the grim days of tension. Then, if war broke out, the admiral and his three cruisers could certainly abort the *Königsberg*'s potential career as a commerce raider one way or another; she would surrender or she would be blown out of the water.

The lords of His Majesty's Navy expected a great deal of the men they sent to sea; Rear Admiral King-Hall was at Mauritius with his fleet when the secret orders reached him. Luckily all three ships of the squadron were in attendance on the cruise, for they were old, tired ships by *Königsberg*'s standards, and not one of them would be a match for her in single combat.

Königsberg was built in 1905, which meant she was nine years old this year, with her ten modern 105-mm guns and two dangerous torpedo tubes. She was longer and slimmer than any of the British ships she might face hereabout; although she was nearly 126 yards long she displaced only 3400 tons; whereas the English admiral's flagship *Hyacinth*, about 117 yards long, displaced almost 5700 tons. The British light cruiser HMS *Astrea* was also short and fat, 107 yards long and weighing 4400 tons. Only the little HMS *Pegasus* was lighter than *Königsberg*: she weighed 2170 tons but was only 100 yards long.

Lengths and tonnages hardly told the whole story.

21

Hyacinth was already sixteen years old, wheezing in her tubes, and at her best she had never done more than twenty knots to match *Königsberg*'s twenty-four. *Hyacinth*'s armament looked good – on paper – for she boasted eleven 152-mm guns, and eight 7·6-mm guns, but they were old-fashioned, slow-loading, slow-firing, and their projectiles did not pack the wallop that Captain Looff could boast for those of his silvery cruiser. And *Hyacinth* was the newest and the best of Britain's Cape of Good Hope squadron, for *Astrea* was twenty-one years old and *Pegasus* was seventeen. As for torpedoes, only *Pegasus* was armed with torpedo tubes.

Together these ships set out on 27th July to find *Königsberg* and execute their orders. How to look for a needle in a haystack? They set out west for Zanzibar and then to Dar es Salaam harbour, in case their quarry might be lurking at her base there. As they went the crews were busily scraping paint; the handsome white enamel of the squadron's upper works was coming off to be replaced by a coat of naval grey.

Admiral King-Hall had good reason to believe he would find *Königsberg* in her parlour, so to speak; from the beginning of the crisis the British had been well served by their consul, a young man named King, who lived at Dar es Salaam, taking care of British commercial interests and spending most of his waking hours, it seemed, sitting around the local clubs, treating whoever might come by to whisky and soda on the largesse of His Majesty. Consul King came to the German officers' club, where the naval and military men met, and was the most jovial of friends to all. He played a good game of bridge and was always available for a rubber. He was a careful man, he visited the *Königsberg* only once as any European was almost bound to do out of sheer curiosity about the ship, but he knew almost everything about her that was worth knowing, and on 26th July he had the gall to ask Captain Looff what the *Königsberg* would do in case of war – with Russia.

Looff was shocked by this brazenness and would not

reply; he began adding up all that he knew of Consul King as of that moment, and he came to the conclusion that the consul had been an excellent espionage agent for the British government all the while. Captain Looff issued orders to his own officers to beware of Consul King, and he passed the word ashore to Governor Schnee and the colonial troops, but it was too late; Consul King's work had all been done, and as the Germans warned each other of him, Rear Admiral King-Hall steamed steadily for German East Africa.

During the last two days of July, *Königsberg* was a hive, with hundreds of men scurrying up and down her sides and inside her; she was making ready for sea. The basic responsibility devolved on Korvettenkapitän Koch, the first officer, who was also the 'maid of all work' aboard the ship. Mountains of supplies were piled on deck and in lighters that came alongside, and they had to be transferred to their proper places: every bag of potatoes, every sack of coal, every box of cartridges.

As First Officer Koch sweated over his stowage, Captain Looff went ashore to confer with the governor and the military authorities. The first matter was to secure the supply of coal in case of the outbreak of war, and Captain Looff's instructions covered the problem as Berlin expected it to develop. Dar es Salaam had its coal dump and had been building a supply for several weeks. Captain Looff and the authorities ashore sent out instructions by radio to all German freighters in the area, ordering them to bring their coal or pick up coal at neutral stations and bring it to Dar es Salaam.

The survey ship *Möwe* could not be expected to serve any useful purpose in war, but her crew and her armament could be used. Captain Looff made arrangements for the *Möwe* to be blown up if war came, but before she was blown up her armament was to be removed, as was her wireless station. These instruments and the crew of a hundred men would be transferred to the first suitable steamer that arrived in Dar es Salaam; the steamer then would be rechristened as 'auxiliary cruiser' and would be armed with *Möwe*'s two 88-mm guns, two hundred shells, three 37-mm guns, and four machine guns.

Ashore, Captain Looff also tried to discover all he could through the wireless station as to the whereabouts of his possible enemies. All he could learn was that the Cape of Good Hope Squadron was away from base. And as to the whereabouts of his other potential enemies, he knew little. From French Madagascar the old French gunboat on the African station, the *Baucluse*, in drydock at Durban, could be quite well disregarded; so could the three old French torpedo boats, but the British had more than the Cape Squadron to worry Captain Looff. His zone of operations in case of war would extend into the Indian Ocean, and there the British East India Squadron was located at Bombay. This group of warships included HMS *Dartmouth*, with eight modern 152-mm guns and a speed of twenty-six knots, very definitely a threat to the *Königsberg*.

Lieutenant Colonel von Lettow-Vorbeck was at this moment engaged in a thorough tour of his defences inland, and so Captain Looff worked out the questions of harbour defence and liaison between land and sea forces with Major Kepler, the commander's deputy. The Protective Force, as it was called, consisted of only 216 Europeans and 2540 Askari, or native soldiers, plus 45 European police officers and 2154 Askari police; not many men, but then no one really expected much trouble between the various African colonies of the European nations, no matter what happened at home.

So 30th July saw Captain Looff ashore nearly all the day, moving from one meeting to another while his ship was made ready for sea. The next day proved how right Captain Looff had been to insist on readiness; Captain Gauhe arrived in the steamer *Tabora*, bringing news from the German consul in Zanzibar that the British Cape Squadron was expected there on 1st August. It was sobering news, for if war were to come in the next few hours, there was serious danger that *Königsberg* might be bottled up in harbour, and then all her speed and superior gun-power would not save her from three enemies who might roam back and forth outside the harbour at will and smash her as she came steaming through the narrow channel between the protective coral arms of the opening.

Hastily Captain Looff transferred the command of naval forces at Dar es Salaam to Captain Zimmer of the *Möwe*, and ordered First Officer Koch to make the grey ship ready for sea. At 4.30 in the afternoon the bow anchor buoy was cast loose and *Königsberg* steamed slowly out of Dar es Salaam harbour, under the tearful eyes of a thoroughly worried German population, many wondering if they would ever see her or their homeland again. No flags flew, no bands played, there was no time for sentimental songs; *Königsberg* had work to do, and her first task was to assure her own safety by being on the high seas if trouble came.

In port that day were the German East Africa Line's *Somali*, an eleven-knot steamer of 2500 tons, which brought 1000 tons of coal – one good cruising load for *Königsberg* if she stripped down and took on a deck load; *König*, a 5000-ton steamer good for twelve knots, which had brought 600 tons of coal to the port; and *Tabora*, also of the German East Africa Line, an 8000-ton liner capable of 13·5 knots. *Tabora* was singled out as one of the auxiliary cruisers that would be dispatched from Dar es Salaam to help win the war if it came. Ashore, Governor Schnee shook his slender head, blinked his baggy eyes, fingered his pencil moustache, and deplored these warlike preparations, for he had it on the best authority that all the colony need do under any conditions was observe the rules of neutrality and there would be no trouble in East Africa. But Captain Zimmer had his orders, and the work of unloading the steamers and making ready for a war condition went on apace in the harbour, as *Königsberg* steamed out through the entrance that afternoon.

Königsberg crept out through the coral, and then slowly increased her speed as she passed Makatumbe lighthouse until she was cruising at ten knots. The short twilight of the tropics was lowering even as the blood-red sun dropped like a falling plate into the sea, and behind the *Königsberg* the palms were blotted out into an indistinct grey mass. She had left harbour in perfect light, and she was not yet ten miles off the coast and it was nearly dark.

As *Königsberg* emerged from the harbour, her men were called to action stations, for the political situation was so delicate, so undecided, that Fregattenkapitän Looff did not know if Germany was at war or not. Every man aboard the ship was certain that war with Russia and France was inevitable. The constant flow of messages from Station Windhuk in German Southwest Africa indicated that it was a matter of hours away, and this state of affairs quite suited the men of the *Königsberg*, but there was a question in their minds: what would England do?

Suddenly, in the gathering darkness, the officer in the foremast crow's nest called the bridge – there was a ship in sight – two ships – three ships!

Captain Looff trained his night glasses from the bridge around 180 degrees to starboard and from the port side the officer of the watch did the same. The captain ordered the guns loaded and ready to fire, the torpedo tubes cleared for firing, every division ready for action.

Königsberg had been travelling without lights, and so had the British cruisers, for here they were! The flagship *Hyacinth* had come up on the starboard bow headed on an intersecting course that would have caused German and British ships to cross at a 90-degree angle. The *Astrea* was moving in from port, and almost directly ahead, slightly off the port bow, came the third cruiser, *Pegasus*. Captain Looff could see the British ships quite clearly in the light from the horizon, for they were easterly of him. Were they enemies or not?

Lowering his glasses, Captain Looff told the officer of the watch to keep steady on his course, and keep the speed at twelve knots, and then he raised his glasses once again to follow the movements of the British cruisers. *Pegasus* came on, travelling almost on a collision course;

Astrea was two points off the port bow; *Hyacinth* was six points off the starboard. Then, when they were not three thousand yards away on either side, the British cruisers turned, and paralleled *Königsberg's* course, matching her speed.

The game then became apparent. Captain Looff was being followed, and if the British ships were able to keep him in sight, and if they suddenly received the news that war was declared, he would be far worse off than had he been caught in Dar es Salaam harbour.

On the bridge, Captain Looff looked around. The eyes of every officer on the bridge and every enlisted man were fixed on him. He smiled absentmindedly, considering his next step, then walked to the speaking tube that led to the engine room and issued some terse instructions to Engineer Schilling three decks below. He wanted steam for twenty-two knots just as quickly as the engine room could provide it for him but he did not want any sign of activity or any excess smoke.

The captain then moved back to the rail, and stood looking out at *Astrea* on *Königsberg's* port beam. The British ship had matched her speed to that of the German, and seemed to be standing alongside. *Hyacinth* had dropped back to a position well astern of *Königsberg*, and *Pegasus* had pulled ahead of her. It was as if *Königsberg* were a bad little boy being escorted to school by his sisters, one ahead and one grasping him firmly by the arm, while the truant officer marched along behind.

The captain's steward, Schussel, came up on deck and gave him a cup of tea which he drank absently. Then the steward handed him a packet of cigarettes. There had been no word about the smoking ban, but when the captain lit up, so did every other officer on deck, and then the men began to smoke too.

The bridge was silent. All that could be heard was the gentle clicking of the wheel as the helmsman moved it a point to starboard, then back to port, to keep her on her course, and, faintly, the sound of the trackers as they sounded off, recording the course and speed of the 'enemy' for the gunners.

The gunnery officer, Oberleutnant Apel, looked across at the *Astrea*, and, spotting his opposite number there, broke into a wide grin.

'Look there,' he said, 'at her guns. Standing right beside the starboard battery – just like on the school ship.'

A laugh on the bridge relieved the tension for a moment, but only for a moment. The swish-swish of the ship travelling through the gentle night sea came back immediately to dominate the sounds on the bridge, and the men stood stiffly, looking at the three shapes out beyond. No sound of the clanging in the boiler room came up to the bridge, no indication of the rising heat below, as the temperature in the boilers drove the pressure even higher, no one topside could hear the increased tempo of the shuffling of the feet of the stokers as they moved between bunker and firebox.

For forty-five minutes they travelled thus, the unreal foursome, three escorts and an unwilling companion, heading towards the tip of British Zanzibar. At the end of that last minute, the speaking tube whistled, and, going to it, Captain Looff heard the words he had been waiting to hear. Marinoberingeneuer Schilling reported that he had steam for twenty-two knots. The captain stepped across deck to where the officer of the watch was standing, next to the engine telegraph, and spoke a few words.

Still the captain did not make his move, but continued onward at twelve knots without a break, waiting for the advantage that must come sometime, moving back to the port side of the bridge where he could watch *Astrea*, standing quietly and waiting, but smoking one cigarette and then another.

Then came what the captain waited for. Out of the southwest the monsoon was blowing, and now she blew a squall across the paths of the four ships. One moment Captain Looff could see all three British cruisers, the next moment he was engulfed in the warm rain and the wind was pelting at his right cheek.

Here was *Königsberg*'s chance.

'*Hart steuerbord,*' Captain Looff commanded, then turned to the officer at the telegraph. '*Beide maschinen ausserste Kraft voraus!* (Both engines full speed ahead).'

As *Königsberg* swept around in a 180-degree turn, her propellers began to quicken, and she left a great swirling wake behind her. She headed back towards *Hyacinth*, which had been a thousand metres to starboard, and perhaps a half-mile off her stern. For ten minutes Captain Looff held the course, and as he held it and left the safety of the squall, he passed *Hyacinth* going the other way, the British ship now on his port and making heavy smoke, which meant she, too, had increased her speed. The two ships drew away from one another at a combined speed of perhaps forty knots, a very satisfactory speed for Captain Looff. Two minutes after passing *Hyacinth*, as she disappeared in the darkness, Captain Looff turned 90 degrees to port, heading due south, and steamed steadily at 22·5 knots for an hour towards the northern point of Mafia Island. Then the captain turned east and sped out to sea until 0600 on 1st August, when he ordered the engines cut back to the twelve-knot cruising speed at which *Königsberg* was most economical. The course then was set for the ship's chosen station off Aden, where the British shipping lanes crossed from far and near.

During the night Captain Looff ordered the radio officer to send a message to Dar es Salaam, warning Governor Schnee and Captain Zimmer that he had eluded the English, and that they might well come to the capital of German East Africa in search of him.

Admiral King-Hall was furious and frantic that the German cruiser had eluded him, yet there was no one to blame save the gods of the winds and storms, or the Admiralty which sent slow ships to take a faster one, and the Admiral would never have thought of blaming his superiors' strategy in a matter of this sort. He set out to make the best of a bad situation, knowing that *Königsberg* had escaped him and that the certainty of putting one

German ship out of action was gone forever. Early on the morning of 1st August Admiral King-Hall arrived at Zanzibar to take on a badly needed load of coal for *Hyacinth* and then set out hastily for Cape Town where he had left only two thirty-year-old torpedo boats to protect his rear. When the Admiral had steamed off for Mauritius in July there was no real worry; a week later there was everything to worry about. The Admiral left *Astrea* and *Pegasus* behind him, to start at the bottom of German East Africa's coastline and to search each bay and harbour northward to the British East African border. The search began, with the cruisers standing offshore at every inlet where an anchorage might be concealed, while cutters and pinnaces moved in to shore, clearly violating German territorial rights. In Dar es Salaam Governor Schnee soon heard of the British searching and was infuriated but could do nothing about it.

Not many hours after Governor Schnee received the warning from *Königsberg* he also received grave news from Berlin, official dispatches announcing the mobilisation of Germany's total military force and other official dispatches warning of danger of war in Europe. On 2nd August the governor began to realise what the word 'war' meant when the British cable stations around the German colony deliberately held up his messages and attempts were made to jam his radio communication with German Southwest Africa and Togo. That day the big white steamer *Feldmarschall* came into Dar es Salaam; she was a 6000-ton ship which made thirteen knots, a very welcome ship at this time for she brought foodstuffs and supplies for the civilians of German East Africa, tinned goods and materials from the homeland whose like they might not see for a long, long time.

Almost immediately after *Feldmarschall* came in, the harbour went on day-and-night work, with prams surrounding the freighters to unload their coal and provisions.

The next three days were frantic ones inside the port. Korvettenkapitän Zimmer had no mines to lay in the harbour, no shore guns to protect Dar es Salaam or his ships from any enemy warships that wanted to come prowling, so everything that could be done to save cargoes and prepare the port for war was done at that time. On 3rd August the governor had news from Zanzibar, by way of Bagamoyo, that an Arab dhow had run across the strait carrying dispatches from German Consul Kuentzer, the last he ever would send to Dar es Salaam. The consul warned that his dispatches were being delayed by the British government and that Britain was mobilising, so war could be expected any moment. On 4th August there was no news at all, and at six o'clock on the evening of 5th August came the word from the German radio station at Kamina in Togo that war had been declared. Post Office Director Rothe, who was in charge of wireless as well as posts, immediately telephoned Governor Schnee, and the governor dropped everything to send the word of war throughout German East Africa.

Königsberg was on station a thousand miles from Dar es Salaam, and already, even before he knew about the beginning of war, Captain Looff was beginning to be dogged by the worry of warship captains everywhere at that time: his coal supply. *Königsberg* had eaten coal as a hungry lion eats a buck on that high-speed flight from the three British police cruisers, and the long voyage to the Aden crossroads had noticeably emptied her bunkers. Captain Looff had only two hopes of securing coal in these waters: one was to have it brought to him by colliers out of Dar es Salaam; the other was to take it from ships at sea in the Aden area, whether they be friendly or unfriendly, whether it be good German coal or Cardiff coal.

On the evening of 5th August, *Königsberg* was running in heavy weather, the southwest monsoon was blowing again, and while she was rolling deeply from port to starboard water splashed in her scuppers from the seas that swept over her as her bow plunged and then tossed the spray far behind her. Tall, blond Leutnant zur See Richard Wenig, one of the younger officers of the *Königsberg*, was leaning on the rail of the bridge, gossiping with the officer

31

of the watch and with Oberleutnant Apel, the gunnery officer. Although the weather was sloppy the ship was still not cool, and the other officers kept popping up from below, complaining that they could not sleep in the infernal heat. The sea was running so heavy that the helmsman had to move the wheel a few points to starboard and then back a few points to port to keep her steady as *Königsberg* wallowed in the troughs, and the click-clack of the wheel's movement punctuated the conversation of the officers.

Just before 11.30 Oberleutnant Freund, who had the watch, dispatched Wenig to the radio room to see if any dispatches were stacking up there. Lifelines had been rigged on the middle deck for safe passage fore and aft, and the normal curiosity of the senior officers still was not great enough to persuade them to go themselves instead of sending their junior to get wet.

Leutnant Wenig trotted down the ladder with the ease of a strong young man who had plenty of experience on that stair, and at the bottom was rewarded for his over-confidence by being slapped head over heels by a wave and skidded halfway along the waist of the ship. He picked himself up, soaking, and jerked open the door of the cabin, then moved back next to the wardroom to the cubbyhole of the radio officer.

'Any news?' he asked.

Oberleutnant Eberhard Niemyer, the redheaded wireless officer, nodded, and indicated the signal book that stood before him, open on the desk. Inside, most recently transcribed, was the word Egima, repeated several times.

EGIMA

Seemingly a perfectly meaningless group of letters, Egima was filled with meaning this night. Here was the code word for which every man on *Königsberg* had been waiting, the word that Germany was at war with Britain, France, and Russia. There it was, the bad news that the Fatherland would have to fight a war on two fronts; but even the bad news was a relief, for now the men of *Königs-berg* knew who their enemies were and what they must do.

Bursting with excitement Leutnant Wenig rushed to the bridge and reported the stirring news to Oberleutnants Apel and Freund. The officer of the watch then went below and awakened the captain and First Officer Koch.

Königsberg was at war, and of one thing her captain and crew could be sure: cruising off Aden the hand of every man they might meet was likely to be turned against them.

3

Commerce Raider

IN DAR ES SALAAM Captain Zimmer pushed his crew and that of *Somali* in order to get that steamer ready for sea – she was to become *Königsberg*'s collier. The wireless taken from the *Möwe* was installed in *Somali*, the radio technicians from the survey ship were assigned to her crew, and on the night of 3rd August she was sent out of the harbour to hide in the south for a few days and then make her way to meet *Königsberg* at a rendezvous far to the north. Captain Zimmer did not want *Somali* in the harbour in case war was declared and the British cruisers suddenly appeared to stop sea traffic.

By 5th August when East Africa learned that war had actually come, *Somali* was safely out of the way and ready for Captain Looff's call which would bring her to the meeting place.

The men of *Königsberg* were up late that night of 5th August. As they learned that war had actually come, they appeared on deck in shirts and trousers, sleepy and heavy-eyed, but eager to have all the news. There was no elation, no cheering, aboard *Königsberg*, for one might say the crewmen of the cruiser already had been 'blooded' in their exciting escape from the British cruiser squadron five days before. Officers and crew were patriotic and enthusiastic, but their enthusiasm was tempered, too, by their complete understanding of their dangerous positions. *Königsberg* was the only German warship in all these waters, in the millions of square miles of the Indian Ocean and the Gulf of Aden, and they could expect that while they were hunting they would be hunted by all the might Britain could assemble to protect her far-flung merchant navy.

As the middle watch began, the captain ordered Lieutenant Niemyer to begin calling up German ships that might be in the area to warn them of the war. The ships were to seek neutral ports if they could not make German ports, he said. So that night, as the little cruiser bucked her way through the heavy seas south of Cape Gardafui, the radiomen were busy talking. They made contact with *Zieten*, a North German Lloyd steamer coming from the South Seas with a hundred navy men from the survey ship *Planet* who were going home on leave; the steamer *Reichenfels*; the liner *Hansa*. The *Reichenfels* could have been very useful to Captain Looff, because she was carrying six thousand tons of coal from Colombo to Aden, but she was too far away for Captain Looff to order her to come to him.

Coal was already a problem, as Captain Looff had known it would be eventually. It was taking more coal than he liked to stay on course this night, heading west towards the cape, the monsoon driving a heavy sea against his port side, giving the *Königsberg* a noisy passage to mark the beginning of the war. Her port anchor chains clanked heavily against the bow, and as her masts described great ellipses in the air the rigging banged against them. The sea was running so heavy that the portholes were kept dogged down and the air in the ship was dank and sticky with sweat and staleness.

On the morning of 6th August, however, the weather took a turn much for the better; after they rounded the cape and were protected from the monsoon by the land of northeast Africa, day dawned cool and calm, at least, calm enough that ports could be opened on the starboard and on the upper port decks. Yet as the divisions made their reports to the captain on the forenoon watch, one problem above all others dominated his thoughts and drove such minor considerations as the weather from his mind: his coal supply had been reduced from the 830 tons he was carrying when he left Dar es Salaam to 200 tons; in the flight from the British cruiser squadron alone *Königsberg* had burned 120 tons in one night. It was a miserable way to begin his task of raiding commerce, and it was also a very quick and very good lesson to him that the chairborne sailors of the *Reichsmarin* in Berlin, playing with their paper boats, could cover the world with German cruisers and cripple British shipping in theory, but in practice the five-thousand-mile cruising radius given ships like *Königsberg* did not take into account chases by British cruisers that could use up a fifth of their fuel in one night.

The afternoon watch had scarcely begun when the forward lookout sang out:

'*Drei Strich an Steuerboard eine starke Rauchwolke!* (Smoke, three points off the starboard bow!)'

The captain ordered the ship cleared for action, and headed towards the smoke. Soon the smoke became two masts sticking up above the horizon, and the masts were joined by a gold funnel. Here it was – the *Zieten* – not an enemy at all but a German ship. Almost simultaneously the lookout spotted another plume of smoke, and that one proved to be *Hansa*, another German ship; a few minutes later a third smoke trail was seen and Captain Looff charged after that one too, having detailed the two German steamers to follow in his wake. With the *Zieten* and the *Hansa* there had been no difficulty at all because they had known of the presence of *Königsberg* in these waters and half expected to see her this day. This third ship did not behave at all in the same fashion – she headed towards Aden. When Captain Looff put his helm hard over to starboard to give chase, the steamer quickly veered away and tried to escape. Captain Looff frowned, for the attempt to escape meant he must steam at full speed to overtake his ship, whatever she was, and he was reluctant to expend any more coal than necessary until he found a new supply.

As he gave chase, Captain Looff used his radio – a sure sign that he was not very much afraid of the presence of any British warships in the immediate area.

'What ship is that?' tapped out the telegrapher, in German.

There was no answer.

Again the question was asked, also in English.

Again there was no answer.

Stop! demanded the wireless from *Königsberg*.

No answer. Or, to be exact, there was an answer, but it was not delivered by wireless: the captain on his bridge could see the smoke smudge from the ship ahead blacken and grow larger, and he could detect an increase in his quarry's speed.

There was nothing to do but increase *Königsberg*'s speed to full ahead, and catch her – so the race was set, even though the cruiser's coal supply was so badly affected by it. It was half an hour before Captain Looff overtook the strange ship and came close enough to make flag signals to her, in case she had no wireless or her wireless was out of order. He ordered the stranger to stop; she did not and, finally, he put a shot across her bow. Then she stopped.

As the ship stopped and the men of *Königsberg* stared across the narrowing gulf of open water between the ships, the merchantman hoisted his flag – the red, white and black flag of the Fatherland.

All that chase for nothing! All that coal wasted! Captain Looff could hardly be blamed for the thoughts that passed through his mind when he considered the captain of the merchant ship. She was the Hamburg steamer *Goldenfels*, she had thought the *Königsberg* was a British cruiser, and now that the merchantman was stopped and could be expected at least to restore to Captain Looff what it had cost him to catch her, he discovered that she was bound for Aden, and that she had only a four-day coal supply left in her bunkers with which to escape the British now that Aden was out of the question. He could scarcely take her last drop of blood and turn her over to the enemy; he must swallow his chagrin and send her on her way, Godspeed!

Nor were *Königsberg*'s other friends much more productive; *Hansa* was bearing a surplus of coal, but it was poor quality Indian coal and Captain Looff did not want to chance it – better to wait than to clog his boilers with that dusty stuff. *Zieten* was able to do more, she gave up a few days' supply of good hard lump coal; *Zieten* was kept back by *Königsberg* until a time and place could be found for transferring the coal, and the other ships were sent away. There was no hurry. Something special must be done with *Zieten* anyhow, for she could not go through the Suez Canal where she had been heading – those hundred German naval sailors could not be put so easily into the hands of the enemy.

At about nine o'clock on the evening of 6th August on the eastern horizon two smoke smudges came in sight, both of them heading for Aden. When *Königsberg* stopped the first ship, and for safety's sake questioned her in English, Captain Looff was pleasantly surprised to discover that he had here a passenger ship of the Nippon Yushan Kaisha line, and the very steamer on which he had made a very pleasant cruise to the Far East a dozen years before. She was a neutral, on her way to Europe, and he did not detain her. While questioning, he had kept her bridge in the glare of his searchlights, and her captain went away secure in the belief that he had been stopped by a British cruiser.

The second smudge on the horizon that evening was something else again: the British steamer *City of Winchester*. She gave the *Königsberg* no trouble at all, because she stopped obediently when signalled and prepared to welcome aboard the officers and boarding party of the British cruiser-she believed *Königsberg* to be; she was a 6600-ton freighter, heavily laden with a cargo of tea valued at 5·1 million marks, and in this easy capture, *Königsberg* marked an important 'first': *City of Winchester* was the first ship to be captured by a German man-of-war on the high seas during the war. (Also, she carried the lion's share of the best Ceylon tea crop of 1913–14, and when the news of her capture hit the London tea market it brought about a panic.)

Captain Looff was delighted to have captured a large English steamer, to meet his need for coal. He put a prize crew aboard her (twenty of the hundred men from the South Seas who were aboard *Zieten*) and kept the British ship alongside, cruising slowly between the African and Arab coasts, but without seeking further action that day. In the night the little squadron steamed through squally weather towards the South Arabian coast, arrived before daybreak in the bay called Bender Barum, and moved well into the bay to anchor at four o'clock in the afternoon behind an island. By radio, Captain Looff then called up the German steamer *Ostmark*, with whom his radio man had been in contact all day, hoping that she might have extra supplies of coal and food to give him, but again he drew a blank: *Ostmark* was to be diverted to Mozambique in Portuguese East Africa, and she would have just enough fuel to make the trip, so she too was sent away.

Captain Looff now sought the safety of the Churja-Murja Islands, a group so little known that it did not appear on most charts (and he devoutly hoped it appeared on no British charts at all). He was growing weary of asking friendly captains for supplies and receiving the same negative, if understandable, answers. Why could not these merchant captains have had a little foresight, to realise that a war might break out at any time and to provide themselves accordingly? There was no reasonable answer to that question and so asking it helped very little; what was to be done was to investigate the value of his prize. He moved to the protection of Hallanija, the largest of the group of islands, and in its little bay he anchored, safe from prying eyes.

Investigation showed that the *City of Winchester* carried four hundred tons of coal, but what coal! *Ach und was!* It was more of that cheap Bombay dust, sheer poison to the boilers of *Königsberg*, which had never been subjected to such tortures. Quite aside from his Teutonic pride in German coal, Captain Looff's sailor's instinct told him he would be better off taking the chance of running out of coal altogether than wrecking his power plant with this inferior product. He realised only too well how far he was from a dockyard where he could go for a major overhaul. There was no place closer than Germany herself. He passed up the inferior coal, and from all his efforts managed only to secure some eighty tons of good coal from various German ships.

The trouble was that *Somali* was now long overdue at the rendezvous; if she would only arrive with her twelve hundred tons of good German coal all *Königsberg*'s problems would be solved. Had *Somali* been sunk? Had she been captured? Both were possibilities, but they were not possibilities that Captain Looff could afford to face. He must proceed as if his collier was just around the corner.

On 11th August, the civilian crew of the *City of Winchester* was transferred to the *Zieten* and the prize crew of German sailors from the South Seas went back there too; additional supplies of coal and fresh water and provisions were taken aboard the *Zieten* from the British ship, and the next morning *Zieten* left for Mozambique, to stop off at the Rufiji Delta and drop the hundred sailors of the navy for the defence force of East Africa. That day Captain Looff sent a demolition party aboard the *City of Winchester*; they opened the sea cocks and placed time bombs where they would do the most good. The crew came back aboard the cruiser, and Gunnery Officer Apel put a few 105-mm shells into the Englishman's side just at the water line. She sank quickly, until only the tips of her masts were showing in the shallow water of the harbour, and *Königsberg* then went back to sea to search for victims.

That Japanese ship the Germans had encountered on 6th August had not been as bewildered as Captain Looff had believed, it seemed, for things began to happen on 12th August. On the middle watch, the airwaves were filled with strange transmissions in code, and they were close transmissions, apparently between Aden Radio and some unidentified ship or ships nearby. Late in the day Oberleutnant Niemyer put his hat firmly down over that flaming red hair and marched to the captain's cabin to wake up Captain Looff and give a welcome message, a report from the *Somali* that she had finally reached the rendezvous and was waiting for her cruiser there behind Hallanija Island. *Königsberg* came in and found her, and prepared to anchor next to her and coal. But suddenly the captain was nearly blinded by a sweeping searchlight that came poking out of nowhere, from the sea beyond the island. Out there, somewhere, was a ship large enough to carry a pair of searchlights – which meant she was at least a light cruiser, and more probably something bigger; at least so it seemed in the middle of this night.

Again the weather saved *Königsberg*. The searching, probing fingers of the lights moved around the bay and passed directly across the ship, but they never stopped. It was a dirty night and that was all that could be said for the British tars who manned those lights; the rain was coming down in sheets, the sea was rising thirty feet or so out on the bay before the island, and the wind was whipping the spindrift into the eyes of the lookouts and the men on the bridge. Then she was gone, that ship outside, and suddenly Captain Looff and his officers found that they had not been breathing well for the past few minutes, and that now they were gulping in breaths of wet, salty air without a thought to the wet and the salt.

All that night the transmissions hummed about the radio room, and Captain Looff asked for constant reports on them. Obviously a large force of foreign ships was in the region, and this fact made *Königsberg*'s continued presence there most unwise. The captain had been looking forward to the meeting with *Somali* as much as any man, because he knew she carried the mail that had been brought in by the last courier from home, but now he ordered Lieutenant Niemyer to cancel the rendezvous and set one up for quite another area, across the gulf, next to the African coast.

How right Captain Looff was to move out – and fast! Rear Admiral Pierce, commander of the East India Squadron, had moved into these waters to be sure that the

41

Bombay-Aden and Colombo-Aden sea-lanes were swept clear of enemy forces, and the searchlight that frightened the men of the *Königsberg* was a result of that probe.

Königsberg moved out, away from *Somali*, away from coal, fresh provisions, and even a supply to replace the drinking water that was falling low in the tanks.

The new rendezvous would be far away, on the northeast coast of Africa, near Cape Ras Hafoun, south of Cape Gardafui, where there was a little bay that offered a safe anchorage. But getting there was something else again. It was a miserable voyage for *Königsberg* from the very beginning. The wicked monsoon wind hurled the sea at her, built up its thirty-foot waves and slashed off their tops and threw them in the faces of the men of the ship, built up new waves to smash against her port bow, and come charging across the main deck, foaming and pushing at anything so foolhardy as to stand in their way. What a night to go out of harbour, but both vessels had to leave, for who knew but that some lowly seaman aboard the probing ship might not have seen more than those entrusted with the task? It was out into the night for the *Königsberg*, and even for the coastal steamer that was now her slave.

The next day dawned bright and cheerful, and the men of *Königsberg* came up to appreciate the sun. Where *Somali* had gone was anyone's guess. It would be a week before they could even expect to find her at the rendezvous. The task now, short on coal, even short on provisions, and growing short on water, was to carry on the cruiser warfare to which *Königsberg* had been assigned.

Cruiser warfare meant *Königsberg* had to have victims. Here she was, at the crossroads of Asia and Africa, at the place where the ship-lanes of twenty countries met and crisscrossed, at the busy centre of Europe's most lucrative traffic, and she found nothing. Day after day she cruised, up and down, across and back, to the very edge of Aden harbour and she found – nothing.

There was, of course, a reason for her finding nothing, although Captain Looff and his men were not aware of the reason: the Japanese ship *had* recognised them, and before he was stopped altogether, the captain of the *City of Winchester* had managed to get out a message indicating his predicament. When he failed to arrive in Aden, the authorities knew that a commerce raider was in the middle of their British lake – it was much as if a farmer had discovered a den of foxes underneath his henhouse; his first act would be to evacuate the hens and bring in dogs – and this was exactly what Britain was doing. The shipping lanes were closed and the merchant ships were warned to stay off the Aden route until it could be cleared of this raider by the warships of Admiral Pierce's squadron.

As much as she searched for the enemy, then, *Königsberg* cruised in vain. As the days went on and there were no prizes, as the sea became a huge, wet desert to her, *Königsberg* began to be concerned about her own problems of life and headed for the rendezvous, which was to be behind the island of Socotra in the bay. But when Captain Looff arrived, with less than fourteen tons of coal in his bunkers, and anchored on 19th August – there was no trace of *Somali*.

Captain Looff and his officers considered their grave plight. They could not possibly reach Dar es Salaam with their supply of coal. They had been totally unable to supply themselves by capturing coal; if *Somali* did not show up it was very likely that the career of the *Königsberg* would end here on the northeast coast of Africa or somewhere in the Gulf of Aden.

The most serious immediate problem was that of drinking water. *Königsberg* distilled her own drinking water by turning sea water into steam in her boiler system; but to distil water took coal, and there was practically none left for the more than three hundred aboard the little cruiser. Engineer Schilling estimated that he had enough coal to supply them for three days – no longer.

A few days earlier they might have had a greater margin of safety – they could have burned the panelling in the wardroom and the extra chairs, tables, and other wooden objects that a ship accumulates in peacetime. But before leaving Dar es Salaam the officers and men had sent ashore everything they owned that was not regulation, panelling had been stripped, the overstuffed furniture in the ward-room had gone, and now in their hour of need there was absolutely nothing burnable left aboard the ship to help them.

It was a desperate situation, demanding desperate measures. First Officer Koch went to the captain, suggesting that he be allowed to take a party ashore and search for water. It was possible; Captain Looff knew of occasions when ground water had been found within a dozen feet of the surface, particularly in desert areas along the coast. He gave permission for Koch to assemble a landing party and try to dig a well.

Koch called for Lieutenant Wenig, and ordered him to make the landing party ready; they would take the star-board cutter, he said. The officers and petty officers would carry Mausers, and the men would be armed with carbines and boarding belts. The two officers would go ashore with ten men to search the area and attempt to dig a shallow well; they were to do all possible to avoid discovery by any human beings, and if they were approached they were to fight only if attacked.

Even though the *Königsberg* was anchored in the lee of Socotra Island, the wind was kicking up the water of the bay between the ship and the African shore a mile away, and when the men of the cutter began to row they found themselves in the grip of a strong current and heavy waves. It was a long, hard trip to shore and when they arrived they found the coast so rocky and so steep that it seemed they would never find a place to put in the boat. They did find a place eventually; it seemed to be a more gentle slope between two huge rocks, but when they went into land, the surf caught them and spilled the crew out on to the shore just as the boat hit the rocks, wetting every man. Disgustedly they dragged themselves and the cutter into shore, secured the cutter on dry land as best they could, and began climbing the rocky cliff and the sand dunes beyond.

How would one go about finding a place to dig for water?

First Officer Koch selected a spot that seemed more likely than any other in this sandy waste, a declivity at the base of a rocky pile, and here the men unshouldered the shovels and began to dig. They dug for an hour until the trench reached their shoulders, but each time that Koch scrambled down inside to feel for telltale liquid, he felt only cold, dry sand.

Suddenly Leutnant Wenig heard a sound off to the west of them, and at that moment the guard they had placed on the nearest dune sang out the warning:

Da kommen Eingeborene (Natives are coming).

Scrambling up to the high ground, First Officer Koch could see a line of black specks against the lighter desert sand and as they came closer the Germans could see that the men were armed. They were distinctly outnumbered, and there was nothing to do but retreat as quickly as they could to their stranded ship. The sailors rushed back to the shore as the blacks approached silently and steadily, and the Germans strained and puffed to shove the cutter into the water against the pushing of the surf. Finally they had it afloat, the men scrambled over the sides and the first officer took the tiller as the men pulled on the oars. Soon the black shapes on shore were lost in the vague dimness, and they were alongside *Königsberg*, where men were waiting to man the davits and pull the cutter back aboard.

The first officer reported to the captain, who was not surprised that their mission had been unsuccessful. Captain Looff took the measure now that he had been dreading: the water ration for each man was reduced to a quarter of a litre per day, hardly enough for one good drink, and not a drop to spare to wash sand or salt from a man's face.

Captain Looff had his easy leather chair moved out on to the bridge, and there he sat, lips tight, a thousand miles away in his thoughts, plunged in gloom. Every other German cruiser in the world had begun its war with adequate facilities. All the others had plenty of auxiliary ships to supply them with coal and water, food and ammunition. Not one of them faced the problem that had bedevilled him since the day he steamed out of Dar es Salaam. Before the war began, even, he was troubled with the knowledge that he had no real supply of coal – *Königsberg*'s daily bread, as he called it – a care which denied him freedom of action. The coast of East Africa was obviously the most unfavourable in the world for a ship left to its own resources. And of, course, it all came clear to him now; the British had been fiendishly clever and had realised exactly his situation, so they had simply cut off traffic through the Red Sea and were bent on starving him out. (In fact Captain Looff was exactly right, and even as he sat in his brown chair, musing so bitterly, the newspapers of Aden and the Middle East were referring to him as 'the plague of the Indian Ocean'.) Little did they know how close *Königsberg* was to becoming a derelict, powerless, with only her anchors to keep her from being cast up on a lee shore, and only her guns to keep off the fierce black tribesmen of Italian Somaliland, who were controlled by no government in existence.

Two days after their arrival at the rendezvous, early on the morning of 21st August, the foremast lookout suddenly contacted the bridge.

'*Schiff in sicht,*' he said, and it was bearing from the southeast.

Southeast?

Somali was to come from the northeast, not the south. The smoke perceived by the lookout might well represent another British cruiser. The captain gave his orders. On the German light cruisers under war conditions the captain took the starboard watch, the first officer the port, but of course in any action the captain automatically came to take charge and conned his ship and issued orders directly, the light cruisers operating with much more of the easiness of destroyers than with the tight formality of the bigger battle cruisers.

'*Klarschiff zum gefecht*,' the captain called, and the bugle blew the call to action stations throughout the ship.

For ten minutes Captain Looff stood at the bridge rail, peering through his glasses at the smoke; then the lookout from his higher post could make out masts and other features, and the ship was identified as the *Somali*.

In two hours she was at the rendezvous, anchoring next to *Königsberg*; as she came up the captain could see why she was so late. *Somali* obviously had taken a battering from the sea; her starboard plating was badly dented.

Then began the infusion of new lifeblood into *Königsberg*. She took on tons of supplies, fresh water, and eight hundred and fifty tons of coal to feed her hungry boilers. The mail – the last post from the Fatherland – was brought out and delivered that first day, and Captain Herm of the *Somali* told Captain Looff of the terrible storm that had driven his ship fifty miles south of Cape Guardafui and kept him busy beating back for two days, making only two knots against the howling wind and beating sea.

Now for two more days the ships lay together, and then it was time to go, to be about the Emperor's business. Captain Looff ordered Kapitänleutnant Hinrichs to lay a course for the east, to pass Cape Guardafui, and then to turn south. The captain of the *Königsberg* had done all he could to carry the war to the British on the edge of the Red Sea, and fate had worked completely against him. Now he would travel south, still within his zone of operations, and see if he could not inflict some damage on his country's enemies in the French waters of Madagascar.

It was easy enough to see why the Admiralty had for so long resisted the importunations of the colonial office in regard to dispatching modern vessels of war to the waters of German East Africa; it was the old story of too little and too late. Had the war at sea been considered as a *weltkrieg* by the German general staff, more might have been done for the German navy in the important years since 1900, but, as everyone knew, the imperial general staff thought only in terms of land warfare, and all the work of

47

the admirals had been the concentrated development of a single great fleet to challenge Britain at home. *Königsberg* was alone, the most alone and most neglected of all Germany's many ships of war, and there was no chance in the world that anything could be done for her, except perhaps to get some supplies to lonely rendezvous in her war zone. Otherwise she faced the might of England all alone.

4

The Return to East Africa

HAVING FIXED A new rendezvous with Captain Herm for the Isles of Aldabra, northwest of Madagascar, on the morning of 23rd August Captain Looff parted company with the *Somali* before Cape Guardafui. *Somali* travelled so slowly that it would be a waste of *Königsberg's* valuable coal to try to keep geared down to her seven- or eight-knot cruising speed.

Königsberg rolled miserably in the heavy monsoon seas because the addition of a deck load of coal had changed her centre of stability; Captain Looff became very much aware of the change on the first night out when suddenly the ship gave a great lurch to starboard and he fell out of his hammock on to the deck, with great injury to his prestige but nothing else. Yet the bad weather was welcome to the captain of the *Königsberg*, because he had no wish to meet Rear Admiral King-Hall and his Cape squadron or any other British cruisers, save those his own size, and he wanted to deal with those one by one.

Radio Officer Niemyer and Radioman Gotzinger came to the captain with an idea designed to further this end, and when he accepted it enthusiastically they returned to the radio room to concoct false messages for the consumption of the British. The first of these was sent out before the ship cleared Cape Guardafui, and it established a rendezvous with an imaginary ship. *Königsberg* would meet the other, the messages said, on the eastern coast of the Arabian peninsula, and then would proceed deep into the Indian Ocean to attack British ships bound to and from India.

Messages of this kind were sent out for several days, alternating the use of the *Königsberg*'s own sending set with that of the *City of Winchester*, which had been taken aboard the cruiser for exactly such a useful purpose.

Somali, with *Möwe*'s wireless set aboard, played the part of several German ships, replying meekly – in English – to the orders of the *Königsberg* to meet the warships on the coast of Arabia. Soon the airwaves were filled with British warnings to Aden, Bombay, Karachi, and Colombo. The British said nothing openly, but ships were dispatched to the pretended rendezvous – which meant fewer ships to be dispatched for the area where *Königsberg* intended to operate.

Königsberg was also in touch with the Italian radio station at Mogadiscio, pretending to be a Dutch ship that wanted the news of the war. The Italians by this time had refused to go to war with the other members of the Triple Alliance and were changing their sympathies, so the news received by the 'Dutchman' was all about British and French victories over the evil Huns, enough to make the Germans' hair stand on end if they believed it (which they did not). This interchange was rapidly broken off when a real Dutch ship came into the conversation one night, extremely curious as to the identity of her fellow countryman.

Soon the *Königsberg* approached the equator, and it was not long before she was opposite German East Africa, whose affairs were a complete mystery to her since she had steamed out of Dar es Salaam on the afternoon of 31st July. Had the British attacked the town? Did they occupy the port? What had happened to Radio Dar es Salaam? Something had happened, because it was completely silent, while Radio Zanzibar sent out a constant stream of messages in code, obviously destined for the British navy. Measuring the strength of the transmissions, Radio Officer Niemyer could assure his captain that the British who had chased him back in July were still lurking somewhere near.

Much had happened at Dar es Salaam since the *Königs-*

berg sailed away, and Captain Looff was quite right in believing that his capital city's radio station was out of service; it had been out of service since almost the first day of the war, destroyed as a result of British activity.

Early in August Lieutenant Colonel von Lettow-Vorbeck was on his way from Kidodi to Kilossa in the interior, when he received a special telegram from Governor Schnee ordering him back to Dar es Salaam. Von Lettow-Vorbeck caught a freight train at Kilossa and was back in the capital on 3rd August, immediately to fall into argument with the governor. Dr Schnee believed that German East Africa could stay out of the war, even if England and Germany began to fight at home. He firmly intended to keep the colony neutral. Lieutenant Colonel von Lettow-Vorbeck did not believe it would be possible to maintain neutrality, and while he was called back to reassure the settlers about the future, he began immediately to mobilise his forces for the war he firmly expected. He pointed out to the governor that if they tried to remain neutral they could not even give shelter to *Königsberg* if she showed up in the colony; Dr Schnee shrugged and said that *Königsberg* was long gone from German East Africa, and that, besides, her job was to raid commerce in the Gulf of Aden and the Indian Ocean. The military officer was conscious then of a basic difference in viewpoint between himself and the governor – a very serious difference because the governor held supreme military power in case of war.

Lieutenant Colonel von Lettow-Vorbeck began collecting all the troops in the colony and concentrating them on the heights of Pugu, a day's march west of Dar es Salaam. The governor began doing what he could to maintain neutrality, telling the crews of the ships of the East African Line, for example, that there was no room for them in the Protective Force, and persuading them to sign declarations of neutrality during the war. Von Lettow-Vorbeck was unconscious of this move because he was busy at Pugu setting up a supply system for the war.

War was announced on 5th August, and three days later

the British cruisers *Pegasus* and *Astrea* steamed into Dar es Salaam harbour, looking for *Königsberg*. They did not find her, but the *Astrea* opened fire with her eight guns on the radio station tower, until someone there hung out a white flag which caused the British ship to cease firing. The British sent a landing party ashore and Governor Schnee concluded an agreement of neutrality with them, which bound the Germans to do nothing to help their country but did not bind the British either at sea or on land in this area.

Lieutenant Colonel von Lettow-Vorbeck sent a man down to Dar es Salaam to see what was happening, and discovered to his chagrin that the governor had been in treaty with the enemy. He ordered the radio station tower blown up so it would not fall into British hands, and began to march toward the city twelve miles away. The next morning he marched into Dar es Salaam, sending Captain Tafel ahead to warn that von Lettow-Vorbeck was taking power, and that no negotiations were to be conducted by anyone else. The governor had negotiated the surrender of Dar es Salaam to the British without firing a shot.

Von Lettow-Vorbeck did not choose to accept the governor's decision. He went to the port and ordered Korvettenkapitän Zimmer to blow up the *Möwe*, keeping her out of British hands, and then to bring his men to join the force at Pugu. Oberleutnant zur See Moritz Horn was dispatched with a small contingent west to Kigoma, and there he took over the small lake steamer *Hedwig von Wissmann* and put aboard her some of the armament intended for the auxiliary cruisers which had never materialised because of the quickness with which war came. Lieutenant Horn was ordered to secure command of Lake Tanganyika and to hold the lake against all comers. Von Lettow-Vorbeck sent a force against Taveta, a small British outpost in British East Africa, and captured the place on 15th August. On 23rd August, when Captain Looff set out for Madagascar, Lieutenant Colonel von

Lettow-Vorbeck was bicycling down a road in the interior to catch troops and divert them to Bagamoyo, where a British cruiser was lying offshore and threatened to attack if the Germans did not destroy the radio station there. The commander telegraphed his officer in charge, Lieutenant von Chappuis, who sent the British cutter back to her ship with a warning that a landing would be repelled, and then the *Pegasus* (for it was she) shelled Bagamoyo, but without visible result.

So as Captain Looff passed by the shore of German East Africa, although far at sea, and gazed inward, wondering what had occurred there, Lieutenant Colonel von Lettow-Vorbeck was gaining his way in the struggle for power with Governor Schnee. German East Africa was committed to the war. Looff had no intention of putting in at Dar es Salaam, not knowing that now he could not put in anyhow, since an obstruction had been placed in the channel and *Möwe* had been blown up in the middle of the port.

Captain Looff steamed steadily south toward Madagascar, to carry out cruiser warfare against the French merchant vessels he hoped to find in those waters. He reached his target zone and slowly moved across the north of the island and then down the west side. He found nothing; the French had done exactly as the British: they had interdicted all ships from moving in or out of Madagascar until the whereabouts of *Königsberg* was established. The big liners of the Messageries Maritimes, which Looff had hoped to find, keeping one as a collier and sinking the rest – these were nowhere to be seen. Oh, Captain Looff knew where to find them all right, they were locked up in the harbour of Diego Suarez, behind the big guns of the fort there. Foiled in his attempt to find targets, Captain Looff decided to take a look inside the harbour at Majunga on the west coast of the island and on the night of 29th August he slipped inside, so that at daybreak he was under the headlands of the port and steaming away. He had expected to find a fort there, but there was none; instead a lighthouse showed the way into the inner harbour. As the light of day came streaming from the east, the watchers on *Königsberg* could see houses, trees, towers, and no fort. They glided in over a dead calm bay, and as they came in the lighthouse signalled the port, happily:

'A British cruiser has entered the harbour.'

Captain Looff could not have been more delighted.

They were ready to fight, and Captain Looff's secret instructions indicated the fort was on the waterfront inside – but there, above the only large building in sight, fluttered the flag of the International Red Cross. The harbour was shut down; he had expected to be able to requisition coal here, but there was no coal. There were no ships in the harbour; there was nothing there to interest Captain Looff. Disgustedly he made a circle of the inner port and then turned out, without incident except that as the ship left harbour and the French realised that they had been invaded by a German cruiser, the radio station set up such a racket that Radio Officer Niemyer was forced to jam its transmissions.

The spectre of the cold hearth again began to haunt Captain Looff, as days went by without seeing a funnel that could supply him with coal. There was not a single ship for them to capture in this vast ocean, not a single friendly or neutral harbour into which they might run; even the Portuguese were unfriendly and soon would declare war; all the rest of the African coast belonged to Germany's enemies. *Königsberg* had nothing but the coal remaining on board *Somali*, two hundred and fifty tons of it, so small an amount it seemed hardly worth worrying about, but there was no other, so Captain Looff headed back for the rendezvous at the Aldabra Islands.

When the rendezvous was made, Captain Looff had known little about the islands except that fine tortoises were to be captured there. What he had not known – the important thing – was that the anchorage was tiny and nearly unsheltered from the swell of the sea, and that coaling here was very nearly impossible. Yet it could not be impossible – *Königsberg* must have its coal – so the fenders were brought out, the coal sacks were brought up from below, lines and hawsers were secured between the ships, and gangways were run across. The always dirty but now dangerous work began in the face of a swell, a high wind, and a current that ran directly counter to the wind right through the anchorage. So heavily did the two hulls strain in their attempts to grind together that the fenders were mashed and battered in nearly no time at all, and others had to be improvised. The coaling did not take long, but the swell grew worse and so did the wind, and by the time *Königsberg* had taken on four days' supply Captain Looff was thoroughly worried about the safety of his ship and broke off the work.

Now where should they go? Captain Herm, commander of the *Somali*, knew every inch of the East African coast and the adjacent islands, and he suggested that the *Königsberg* and *Somali* head for the delta of the Rufiji River, where they would find protection from the sea. *Möwe* had recently charted the waters and had found the river to be unexpectedly deep. Captain Looff agreed, and the two ships headed northwest that day. Captain Looff needed a quiet place where the engineering department could do some needed work on the ship's engines, and there was no better, safer haven for him in all Africa than the delta of the Rufiji, so he sailed.

On 3rd September, at high tide, the *Königsberg* passed over the bar of the mouth of the Simba-Ouranga branch of the Rufiji Delta in five metres of water, which was just enough for Captain Looff to clear satisfactorily, and began the slow voyage up the channel that had been charted by *Möwe* that year. Ten miles up the river lay the village of Salale, a customs and forest service station, the only one in the Rufiji Delta. The warship's coming was noted with much concern by the natives, who had only just heard of the bombardment of Dar es Salaam by the British cruisers and believed that the ship they saw was either *Pegasus* or *Astrea*, not knowing that *Astrea* had been recalled to South Africa for convoy duty, not knowing that *Pegasus* was in

Zanzibar, not knowing that *Königsberg* was still afloat.

Director Dankert of the forest service did not know what might be expected of him, but he and his wife sat, he in his khaki shorts and shirt and she in her white dress, on the veranda of their bungalow on the banks of the river at Salale, waiting for the appearance of the ship, two loaded rifles and an old-fashioned pistol at their side. His native runners had told him to expect the coming of a *Wangeresa mano-wari* – English warship – and so he was pleasantly, delightedly surprised when he recognised the silhouette and three smoke-stacks of the *Königsberg*.

In half an hour he was aboard, on the bridge, shaking hands with Captain Looff and the senior officers, congratulating them on their coming, and asking what he could do to be useful. Captain Looff outlined his plans: he had come to refuel and repair, and he did not want to be discovered by the enemy. Were the blacks reliable? he asked forester Dankert, and being assured that they were completely loyal to the Emperor, Captain Looff demanded that they be sworn to secrecy about the presence of the *Königsberg*.

The first thing to be done was to send messages to Dar es Salaam and see what help might be obtained from that quarter. Dankert called up his messengers, while Captain Looff prepared the telegrams he wanted sent to the capital, and then the messengers were dispatched by dugout canoe to the delta station with instructions to speed all the way. Captain Looff was working up a bad case of claustrophobia in this delta, where only a single spy could make the difference between success and failure, where he might be trapped, but now he found two sources of reassurance. First, Radio Officer Niemyer managed to rig up a field telephone, attached to the telegraph line, so they could monitor the telegraph traffic and if necessary send clandestine messages to Dar es Salaam. Second, forester Dankert brought out a chart of the Rufiji Delta and showed the captain how he could navigate within the six channels of the Rufiji and that he had at least two avenues of escape. Actually, claustrophobia or not, Captain

Looff had no real choice, the Rufiji was the only sensible haven for the *Königsberg*.

Immediately the reason became clear: in response to the call for help, Korvettenkapitän Zimmer took a handful of men and made a forced march to Kigoma and then travelled by dhow to Kissidju to find coal and lighters for the *Königsberg*; only a few hours after the ship anchored, up the river came a huge canoe laden with mangoes, bananas, and oranges, and bearing Oberleutnant de Reserve Hauser, commander of the Rufiji district under the defence force of von Lettow-Vorbeck, accompanied by senior government counsellor Dr Fraenckel. Immediately they began making plans to supply provisions for the cruiser.

From these officials, Captain Looff learned some of the news of the war – at least as it was given out in British and French radio broadcasts monitored by the Germans. He learned that *Königsberg* had been sunk by a squadron of British cruisers, and he had sunk a dozen allied ships before he was caught off the Arabian coast (how he wished that were true) and that he had shelled the railroad line leading from the *Somali* coast to Addis Ababa.

A few days later he learned of more sinkings by the *Königsberg* and began to disbelieve the foreign broadcasts altogether. But there was a reason for the confusion. In August, the *Kleine Kreuzer Emden* had been detached from the German East Asia Squadron in the Pacific and Captain von Müller had made his way into the eastern end of the Indian Ocean to carry on the *Kreuzerkrieg* planned by the German Admiralty. *Emden* was far luckier than *Königsberg*: from the beginning she had had all the coal she needed, for her very first capture was a Greek collier, and besides that she had her own German supply ship lurking in the background. Then, within three days, *Emden* took half a dozen ships in and around the Calcutta-Rangoon sea lanes, causing a complete panic that reached from Burma to England. The British thought the sinkings must have been the work of *Königsberg* for she was the only German ship known to be in the Indian Ocean, and the belief that *Königsberg* had somehow made her way from Madagascar to Rangoon in less than two weeks gave a frightening unreality to every report of sinking in Far Eastern waters. The British were weeks in discovering what had happened (that *Emden* had broken into the Indian Ocean), and even with the first reports from survivors the Admiralty believed *Königsberg* and *Emden* must have joined forces in a two-ship plot against the British fleet.

On 19th September, Captain Looff also learned of another development which interested him more: a coast watcher north of Dar es Salaam reported that a British cruiser with two smoke-stacks had entered Zanzibar harbour alone, after having anchored for several days off the German coast, ostensibly either to pick up or deliver spies on to the enemy mainland. It was not impossible that the British were already informed of the coming of the *Königsberg* to the Rufiji; in any event the news of the German cruiser's movements emphasised to Captain Looff his own danger, and also appealed to his sense of daring.

The news was brought by the watcher himself, who came in a dugout canoe, first having destroyed everything behind him in expectation that his report would be tracked down and bring about immediate counteraction by the British. Somehow within five minutes everyone aboard had the news; the captain decided in the sixth minute that the time had come for action and that the crew should be informed.

'All hands to the poop,' was the command, and the officers and men began shuffling their way aft, excited because they knew something was afoot.

'Men,' said the captain, 'you have done your duty up to now, although we have had no luck. We are going out now to take an English cruiser in the harbour at Zanzibar, either the *Pegasus* or the *Astrea*.

'There is the enemy. The victory will be ours. We will not turn back. . . . With God for Kaiser and for Reich.'

Captain Looff was under no illusions about the danger he

ran in the course he was to follow; he would steam into the lion's mouth, into Zanzibar harbour itself, and attack the enemy.

A last lighter filled with coal arrived from Dar es Salaam that day, and the fuel was swiftly transferred to the *Königsberg*'s bunkers. On the afternoon tide the *Königsberg* set out, steaming slowly out of the mouth of the Rufiji and setting course between Thumbe Island and the Nyange Reef. Captain Herm of the *Somali* had been called up as a reservist and now found himself to be chief pilot of the *Königsberg* and *Oberleutnant zur See de réserve*. Carefully he guided the ship between lighthouse, buoy, and lighthouse. The crew was quiet but excited, obviously pleased to be going into action, and that night no one seemed to be able to sleep; it had been difficult to keep the four hundred young men of the *Königsberg* under control there in the Rufiji Delta, eager for action as they were, but now there was no trouble on the ship. Only one man was unhappy, Bwanamanganga, German-trained native doctor of the Utete district, who had volunteered for service and had been taken aboard as an under-surgeon. Poor Bwanamangaga! All night long he stood at the lee rail, paying his tributes to Neptune, rueing the moment he had decided to come to sea, but there was no escape; *Königsberg* was on her way into battle.

5

Attack

UP THE AFRICAN coast they went for a way, Africa on their
port side, the mountains blue-grey against the blue sky,
far to the west. Against the mountains they could see
occasional long, stringy columns of smoke – the usual
brush fires – either lighted by the natives to fertilise their
fields or trap some animal, or set by the sun itself. In
daytime the smoke curled up lazily, then darkness fell
with the unbelievable rapidity of the tropics, and the fires
stood like candles against the black western sky.

The night grew blacker, and Captain Looff reduced
speed, because when *Königsberg* travelled above her
cruising speed of ten knots, flames that could be seen for
several miles came out of her stacks, and this night he did
not wish to be seen. Half the crew was at battle stations,
half the crewmen were in their hammocks, sleeping or
dreaming idly of the fight to come. The ship moved on,
rolling slightly in the swell, steaming with steady vibrations
towards Unguyu, as the Arabs called the city of the sultan
of Zanzibar.

Captain Looff, Kapitänleutnant Hinrichs, and Pilot
Herm were all on the bridge; the officer of the watch and
his lookouts stared steadily at the horizon through their
night glasses, guarding against any unpleasant surprises.

Suddenly, off the port bow, lookouts and bridge at once
saw a white light blinking. All glasses were trained on it and
around the ship the gunners began readying their guns,
without orders. No orders were needed; each man knew
what was to be done. The *Königsberg* approached the light

and passed less than half a mile to port; it was a British picket boat, and so silently had *Königsberg* come up in the darkness that she was not seen, or at least not recognised for what she was. No radio messages split the quiet of the air, no lights were shown, no sirens sounded. And *Königsberg* moved on.

At two in the morning, to the east, off the starboard beam, a land mass came up; Captain Looff saw it first and joked quietly with his officers on the bridge that the old man's eyes still were better than theirs. What he saw was the southern tip of Zanzibar, their landfall; Pilot Herm confirmed it and said that from there on they would be travelling constantly through coral reefs and submerged rocks. The ventilators were stopped, so the noise would not drown out the sound of surf on rock, and the bridge was suddenly so still that each men could hear the footsteps of the others as they shifted position on the deck. *Königsberg* steamed on in a gentle following sea, millions of tiny creatures boiling in her wake to create a long phosphorescent trail of *Kielwasser*.

Just before five o'clock in the morning, the dawn began to bring a rosy glow in the eastern horizon, and they saw that they had reached the middle of the island. The horizon was masked by a long low band of land, and in its shelter the sea had become as calm as a deserted bath.

Now they were before Unguyu. The capital of Zanzibar, the city of white minarets, lay on starboard, and to port they were soon passing the lighthouse on Tchumbe Island. This was dangerous water. The current drove them steadily in the direction of the reef, and the helmsman had to keep turning the wheel a few points to port, then coming back – straightening out – to keep the ship's relative position steady. For three solid hours the bridge had been silent, no man wishing to be the cause of disaster through an unheard order from the captain. But all this tension and stillness suddenly evaporated, for just after five o'clock the lips of the harbour seemed to open as they came around the point and the officers on the bridge of *Königs-*

berg could see into the interior of the harbour of Zanzibar, enveloped in a blanket of early morning mist. The morning fog obscured the buildings and the vessels in the harbour; all that was visible immediately were softly blinking lights which grew dimmer moment by moment as the dawn came up over the harbour, and then the sun's rays peeped into the harbour and the fog began to lift.

Tubby Steward Schussel chose this moment to bring Captain Looff a cup of cocoa. (Schussel had an unerring instinct for the exactly wrong moment – he had brought Captain Looff a cup of bitter tea just at the time when the landing party in Somaliland reported that they could *not* find water.) If there was anything that Max Looff did not want at that moment it was a cup of chocolate, but he forced himself to keep his temper and drink it casually, for he had never shown excitement or tension in the face of his crew, and here again was a need to play the part of the calm, cool captain.

So it was that the captain's keen eye was not the one to search the harbour and find their objective; he was confident anyhow that one of his men would soon see the target, and he was right. The range-finder sang out the words he was waiting for:

'Cruiser with two smokestacks in sight.'

The bridge sprang into noisy action. Captain Looff increased speed to bring the *Königsberg* closer to her enemy; he gave the orders to ready the guns and torpedoes. They could see the ship with the naked eye, but they were not yet close enough to make out her identity. Then, immediately behind the silvery grey hull of the cruiser they saw the form of another hull, but could not see it well enough to establish its identity or type. On the bridge the captain and his officers conferred: did they have anything to fear from this second vessel? Was it perhaps another cruiser that would blow them out of the water as they came in to attack? This second hull was anchored in such a way that they could not see her profile and could not decide just what she was, but time was wasting, the men's hands were itching to get at the guns, and if they did not attack soon they would lose the element of surprise.

Captain Looff ordered the helmsman to turn the ship slowly to starboard, in order to bring the port guns to bear on the cruiser.

Poor *Pegasus*! – for it was she who lay at anchor in Zanzibar harbour, anchored in front of the offices of the Eastern Telegraph Company. Commander J A Ingles, her captain, had been nervous for weeks lest just this chance meeting occur in just this fashion. For nearly two months *Pegasus* had been engaged in the search for *Königsberg*, but always before the British ship had searched together with *Astrea*, the two old-fashioned cruisers still at least a match for the more modern German warship. After Rear Admiral King-Hall had been recalled to the cape by a worried Admiralty to protect shipping there with his *Hyacinth, Pegasus* and *Astrea* had searched up and down the East African coast for their quarry, without success. Then *Astrea* too had been recalled in the flurry of excitement about the paralysis of shipping in Indian and Burmese waters, and *Pegasus* was ordered into port at Zanzibar for some necessary work on engines and boilers fouled by too much powder coal. Admiral King-Hall had given the order that she was to have at least enough of a refit to regain her twenty-one knot speed, and recalling to London the three-knot superiority of *Königsberg* he had argued to the Admiralty against the separation of *Pegasus* and *Astrea*. But the Admiralty saw a different picture, of the Seven Seas beset by German cruisers, and so certain were the admirals in London that *Königsberg* was thousands of miles to the east that they termed the risk as negligible, and the Admiral and Captain Ingles had no recourse but to obey and lay aside their fears.

Captain Ingles had not been remiss in setting a protective screen about his little cruiser, even though he was assured that *Königsberg* was thousands of miles away. He had sent the armed tug *Helmuth* to patrol the waters to the south of Zanzibar (it was she who had missed *Königsberg* in the night). He had anchored near the Admiralty collier *Banffshire* (it was her hull, bow-on, that gave the officers of *Königsberg* so much concern when they could not identify her). But he had anchored broadside to the shore, two hundred yards from the land, and he had banked his engine-room fires, believing himself secure in the safety of the harbour.

At 5.10 Captain Looff ordered the battle flags run up the masthead, and while still more than four miles from the British ship, he opened fire with a salvo of five shells from the 105-mm guns.

Gunnery Officer Apel stood in the fire control station, directing his guns.

Salve, Feuer!

The first five shells were in the air.

Auffschlag! (Over!)

The aimers adjusted their instruments.

Feuer!

Five more shells rose in the blue morning sky.

Kurz! (Short!)

The gunners again adjusted, now also making allowances for the increasing speed of *Königsberg* as she swept closer in to shore.

Feuer!

It was not until this third salvo that *Pegasus* began to reply, her first shots falling in front and behind the ship, some fragments breaking on the bridge but without injuring a man.

Lieutenant Apel continued to direct his salvos, with the calm of a man shooting tow targets off Heligoland for the Kaiser's Cup, the most prized prewar possession of the fleet.

Königsberg swept in, her port guns blazing until they were hot, and then turned to bring the starboard guns to bear and rest those of the port, without losing the cadence of her firing.

At the forward hatch, very close to the forward turret, there suddenly appeared the head of a stoker, a young

Hamburg boy, covered from forehead to waist with black soot; he came up to the gun captain and whispered, 'Captain, let me take a shot,' then turned and ran back down to his post amid the laughter of the gun crew. It was a happy occasion, remarkable as it might seem, and it was also an indication of what a tight ship the *Königsberg* was – for under other conditions of battle the first lieutenant of the German cruiser *Gneisenau* was to shoot down a stoker who deserted his post for a moment to get a drink of water.

In twenty minutes the *Königsberg* had fired a dozen salvos and *Pegasus* was enveloped in a cloud of black and grey smoke, so heavy amidships that much of her outline was obscured, and through smoke came lashing red and yellow tongues of flame. She was firing very slowly, perhaps one salvo to every four of the German ship. From time to time a hit within the smoke would cause a new cloud of greasy black to rise above the British ship – another hit on some vital point. The British cruiser's decks were pitted with shellholes, twisted, smoking, and littered with debris. Below she was an inferno. On the afterdeck some sailor began waving a white flag, but when Gunnery Officer Apel called it to Captain Looff's attention he knew it was but the work of some single sailor, that British captains did not raise white flags no matter what their fate, and he gave the orders to continue firing.

Soon the forward turret of the English ship was out of action, and still the *Königsberg* rained shells on her. The British ship's fire became weaker and weaker and finally stopped altogether. Then the officers of the *Königsberg* could look around to discover the nature of their other enemy: she was a collier, they saw, and not worth wasting shells on; but, oh, how they wished they could steal in and cut her mooring lines and take her out with them.

The clouds of smoke, lanced by jets of flame, continued to rise above and around *Pegasus*, and the water seemed to be boiling near her. The Germans could see that one gun was off its mounting, that the bridge had been hit and twisted, one smokestack had broken off and lay on its side, and the mainmast had fallen across the port side of the ship.

Pegasus was silent. She was beaten.

Cheering the first naval victory of the war between a German cruiser and a British cruiser, the captain and crew of *Königsberg* swung out of Zanzibar harbour, searching for other ships to fight. From the beginning of the battle *Pegasus* had tried to send signals for help, but Radio Officer Niemyer had worked his hardest to jam them and had been successful.

Now the *Helmuth* came up, unfortunate as it was for her, just at the right moment to receive the full attention of *Königsberg*. Lieutenant Apel pumped three shells into her. One of them must have hit her in the boilers, for she blew up, and the crew and captain leaped overboard as she sank, trying desperately to swim ashore in the shark-filled waters.

Somewhere in Zanzibar harbour there was a new wireless station – and it could be heard now sending out the word of the British disaster. Captain Looff, hoping to destroy the radio station but, not knowing the results, did not know exactly where to find the station, but he finally located it behind a grove of palm trees, its mast half concealed behind the hill.

Then the ship set out to accomplish a last gesture – a joke on the British. No, not a joke, but a stratagem to deceive the enemy and cause him pain.

At Salale the *Königsberg* had found a number of old gasoline drums. First Officer Koch and Torpedo Officer Angel dreamed up a plan to discomfit their enemies:

All the naval lists of fighting craft showed the *Königsberg* as a mine-laying cruiser, although she had not brought any mines out from Germany with her when she came to East Africa. The drums from Salale were stored on the quarter deck of the *Königsberg*, in plain view of the shore, and as the Germans turned to steam out of Zanzibar harbour, with a flourish they began throwing the 'mines' overboard, then put on speed as the last one sank, and turned south, away from the coast.

Behind him, as they left the harbour, Captain Looff could see the smoke rising from the wreck of the *Pegasus*, and around her twenty or thirty small boats which had put out from shore to help. Then they were gone, and the loudest sound in the harbour was the roar of flame, the hissing of hot steel in the water, and the explosion of small shells and ammunition.

There was no hope of saving the *Pegasus*, although men from the collier and the *Pegasus* tried manfully. She had taken three hundred hits from the guns of the *Königsberg*, her forecastle was a bloody abattoir, her hull was riddled with shellholes, thirty-one of her men were dead or dying, including two officers, and fifty-five men were wounded. The action ended in the late morning. Efforts were made to move wounded and survivors ashore and then to save the ship, but at two o'clock she began to stir and in a few moments slipped over and capsized.

At the radio station, unknown to the Germans, their bombardment had been as effective as they might have asked: the station was destroyed. Even their 'joke' succeeded: the British in the harbour warned all ships at sea that they must not come into Zanzibar until a minesweeper had made its appearance, because the *Königsberg* had left its infernal calling cards.

And as for *Königsberg* herself, the only unhappy man aboard was Undersurgeon Bwanamanganga, who felt quite useless because not a single German sailor had been scratched, and the one sign that she had been engaged in a fight was a parted mainmast backstay on her starboard side, the souvenir of one lonely British shell.

6

Counterattack

CAPTAIN LOOFF HAD chosen as his next objective the British shipping off the coast of South Africa, where he fully expected to be able to capture enough coal-bearing ships to feed the hungry maws of his engine room for weeks to come; he would wreak havoc with his enemies off the Cape of Good Hope as *Emden* was doing in the Indian Ocean, and then, when the British least expected it, he would move north in the Atlantic, raiding as he went and making his way home until he reached the waters of Europe, where he would stop raiding and travel a predetermined secret route back to the Fatherland.

But a ship is only as good as its machinery, and it was the machinery which caused the *Königsberg*'s next complication, not the captain or the crew. The effort made to travel at high speed through Zanzibar harbour had taken its toll of the ship's boilers, so long in need of dockyard attention, and one of them broke down altogether when the high pressure steam valves collapsed – which meant that *Königsberg* could go nowhere until the repairs were made. The repairs could not be made at sea; new parts were needed, and the only place they might be made was in the machine shops at Dar es Salaam.

So the charts of South Africa waters were put aside, and *Königsberg* headed again for the Rufiji Delta, where Captain Looff expected she would be forced to remain for about ten days while the old parts were sent to Dar es Salaam and new ones were made to match them. That very day – 20th September – *Königsberg* was back in the delta, and at high tide she crossed the bar, steamed upstream to Salale, and moved slowly to her anchorage. The ship had scarcely come to anchor when Engineer Bockmann and his crew were dismantling the affected boiler. A safari train of blacks was found to carry the heavy steel parts and the long trip began, along the arms of the river, across the sandy desert to Dar es Salaam.

Why had Captain Looff twice chosen the delta? There was very good reason to choose this particular hiding place, quite aside from its relative proximity to Dar es Salaam. The delta was very much like a man's misshapen left foot, with the short big toe on the south pointing out east into the Indian Ocean and there separated from the first toe by the Msala Nindung, or mouth; the first toe separated from the second by the Kiomboni mouth; the next two toes separated by the Ssuninga branch, the next two by the Simba-Ouranga branch, and the small toe set off from all others by the Kikunja branch of the river. In between these major branches, creeks and streams coursed back and forth in the swampy mangrove and palm land, providing a haven for crocodiles, hippos, and great mud-coloured fish, and above all a breeding place for the mosquitos which carried the scourge of the tropics: malaria. It was not the kind of country Max Looff would choose for a weekend or for a hunting excursion, or for any other purpose, save perhaps smuggling, but its very unpleasantness provided the delta with assets of its own. Until 1914 no white man knew much about the delta although David Livingstone had passed by here half a dozen times in his explorations. The whites were interested in the Nile, the big lakes of Victoria Nyanza and Tanganyika, the Zambesi and the Rovuma – but not the muddy, serpentine Rufiji, which was not even believed to be navigable for anything much more modern than an Arab dhow. Consequently when the survey ship *Möwe* came to East Africa, she was the first vessel to make a thorough charting of the channels of the Rufiji, and Captain Zimmer had discovered not only that the mouth of the Rufiji was navigable, but that three of the mouths were navigable and two were suitable for deep-draught vessels, and that they intersected at several points. Max Looff knew, when he sought shelter this September day, that his enemies did not have this information, and the knowledge was a treasure to him.

To protect the crippled cruiser from surprise by the British, landing parties were put ashore, armed with machine guns and field guns, and sent to establish posts at the entrances to the two most important arms of the Rufiji Delta. Signalling stations were set up between the posts and the warship. Along the coast shore watchers were stationed in the palm groves.

Several days went by, the broken pieces of valve and piping arrived at the marine repair shops in Dar es Salaam, and the machinists shook their heads dolefully, not really believing that they had the equipment to do the job properly. What Captain Looff demanded was almost impossible, given the equipment the shop had managed to acquire and hold together. But somehow the job was done and perfect new pieces were sent back to the ship over the same road that the broken ones had travelled.

The word that the pieces had been made arrived before them, and Captain Looff brought out his charts once again; it would take only a few hours to remount the tubes when they arrived, and then he could be at sea in less than a day. The captain was optimistic – not so Kapitänleutnant Hinrichs, who kept quoting Schiller to him to the effect that man was the creature of his fate.

The new parts arrived on 30th October and the enthusiastic captain put the engineers to work without wasting time. They were clanking and banging away below when one of the shore watchers reported an armed launch from a cruiser, which appeared to be the four-stacked light cruiser *Chatham*, anchored behind an island out of sight of the Germans. The launch was approaching the Kiomboni arm of the Rufiji, three and a half miles north of the Simba-Ouranga branch where *Königsberg* lay. The enemies came to shore at a point where the Germans had not expected them and where there were no fortifications or even troops to stage a delaying action, so there was no way of stopping them. Ashore, an English sailor climbed a tree, and from his vantage point could see the masts of *Königsberg* and *Somali* rising above the palm trees a few miles away. The *Königsberg* was found out! As it had developed, the pessimistic Hinrichs was right and the optimistic Captain Looff was wrong.

The Germans hastened to try to cut off the British sailors from their ship, but they were unable to move so quickly through the jungle, and an hour later the British landing party was back aboard the *Chatham*, reporting its findings. *Chatham*'s radio began to chatter, and aboard *Königsberg* Radio Officer Niemyer bent his red head over his desk and puzzled over the strange sounds coming through his earphones. The call signals were in the clear: Bombay, Aden, Cape Town, London, but the messages were secret, so Lieutenant Niemyer and then Captain Looff could only guess what Schiller's fates had in store for them.

Captain Loof and his officers had no real idea what effect their surprise attack and total destruction of the *Pegasus* had created in London, but consider this: only two days after *Königsberg*'s attack on Zanzibar harbour the German light cruiser *Emden* had steamed up to the harbour of Madras, in India, and bombarded the town, setting much of the port afire. The Admiralty, which had been concerned about these two German raiders, now became doubly, trebly concerned because the destruction of the *Pegasus* and the bombardment of an Indian city struck serious blows at British prestige in Africa and Asia, and because the continued presence of these two dangerous ships meant that every possible British warship must be on guard against them, yet not knowing where they would turn up next, singly or possibly together. Every valuable cargo must be convoyed from one port to another, the transportation of supplies was slowed immeasurably, and shipowners and merchants throughout Eastern waters were becoming leery of sending their vessels and cargoes abroad.

HMS *Chatham* was the first ship to be called up to search out and destroy the *Königsberg*. The Admiralty found her the day after the *Pegasus* disaster in the middle of the Red Sea, on her way to the Indian Ocean to join the dozens of ships searching for *Emden*.

Chatham was a modern ship, even newer than *Königsberg*; she was built in 1912, armed with eight 152-mm guns and four 47-mm guns. She displaced 5400 tons, 2000 more than *Königsberg*, and at twenty-six knots she was two knots faster. This time the Admiralty had sent a man to do a man's job.

Chatham stopped in at Aden and Captain Sidney Drury-Lowe went ashore to learn the news of his quarry. He heard a half-dozen stories: *Königsberg* was in Sabang; she was off Madagascar; she was rushing to India to join the *Emden*. But he did not believe a word of the stories. He reasoned that if he was captain of the *Königsberg*, and if he had just destroyed the only British warship in East African waters, he would stick tightly in the area for a while and see how much British and French shipping might come his way near Zanzibar and Mombasa. So Captain Drury-Lowe began to search for the *Königsberg*.

The British captain was to be helped in this search, the Admiralty said, by two more cruisers of the same style, strength, and city class as *Chatham:* the *Weymouth*, built in 1910, and the *Dartmouth*, built in 1911. Obviously the Admiralty was willing to go to great expense and great lengths to destroy Max Looff and his men.

By constant attention to the airwaves, the radio officers of *Chatham* soon learned that the call sign of *Königsberg* was AKO, and as early as 25th September they heard coded radio conversations between AKO and another ship called DTM, which they took to be a German steamer. So they were certain *Königsberg* was still in East African waters, at least. The next step of the British was to seek out and identify the various German steamers in German

72

harbours. They knew that in Dar es Salaam at this time were the steamers *König*, *Feldmarschall*, and *Tabora*, and in Tanga lay the *Markgraf*.

Soon the three cruisers were operating as an independent task force with the sole object of finding and sinking the *Königsberg*. *Chatham* had run aground on a reef early in October, and then had been forced to put into Mombasa harbour for repairs. *Dartmouth* and *Weymouth* had searched unceasingly in the sectors assigned to them, but *Königsberg* was not there. When *Chatham* was repaired she put in at the port of Lindi, where she saw the German East Africa Line's ship *Präsident*. When Captain Drury-Lowe inquired into the *Präsident*'s situation he was told that the Germans had converted her to a hospital ship, but on checking the Red Cross records in Geneva he found no mention of her, and he boarded *Präsident*, to discover that the Germans in Lindi were planning to put her at the disposal of *Königsberg* as a supply ship.

So, all this time that Captain Looff was sitting anxiously in Salale, fretting and waiting for his boiler parts, the ring had been closing on him. His instinct had been exact: the British really did not expect him to travel around the Cape and up the west coast of Africa.

Captain Looff did not know that it would have made no particular difference if the British sailor who climbed that palm tree on the afternoon of 30th October had not seen the masts of his ships. The British already knew that he was in the Rufiji, for in their searches of the delta they had come upon natives who had seen the ship there and had pointed it out to British interrogators when shown pictures of various warships with one, two, three, or four smokestacks. Captain Looff and his crew were indeed in the hands of fate. The question was what fate would offer them.

On the afternoon of 30th October the *Weymouth* arrived off the Rufiji, and the next day the *Dartmouth* also came up. On that morning of 31st October, the *Chatham* opened fire from off-shore on the German signal post established on Mafia Island, which guarded the Rufiji Delta. Later that day the *Chatham* sent boats to ascertain the depth of the channel and found less than seven feet of water – which made it impossible for *Chatham* to enter (she drew more than sixteen feet). That afternoon, the range-finders concentrated on the masts of *Königsberg* and *Somali*, and the captain prepared his plans for offensive action.

On 1st November, Captain Drury-Lowe moved *Chatham* to a point eight miles from the masts of *Somali*, and early in the afternoon began firing at her. The range-finders had done their job well, it was not long before the 152-mm shells were hitting the cargo ship, and soon she was afire. Captain Looff did not waste any ammunition by firing back, for the maximum range of his guns was about seven miles and he was more than a mile further inside the delta than *Somali*. *Chatham* continued to fire, aiming at *Königsberg*, and managed to splash the German cruiser heavily with yellow mud, but that was all; she did not score a single hit. Finally the long day ended with *Somali* burned and wrecked and *Königsberg* in mortal danger from her enemies.

That afternoon Captain Looff moved *Königsberg* to a new anchorage several miles upstream. In the course of moving, *Königsberg* went aground as the tide fell, well below the sixteen feet she drew, and for several hours she was a sitting duck, stranded high in the mud of the river, her freeboard extended downward a good ten feet, giving her a silhouette quite unlike that of any warship in the world. The British, however, had no way of knowing what had happened to *Königsberg*, and no way of reaching her with their guns if they had known, so she was safe and got off at high tide.

It was an impasse, of sorts, but the kind of impasse that boded no good for Max Looff; he was alone and under siege, and the British were many.

On 2nd November the *Chatham* was joined by *Dartmouth* and *Weymouth* in the bombardment of all apparent German posts in the delta. *Dartmouth* drew less water than either of the other British cruisers and at high tide in mid-afternoon she tried to go up the Simba-Ouranga branch of the river, and she did go up the river two miles or so, but could find no trace of the *Königsberg* and, becoming nervous about the tide, she came back out to the mouth of the river. The cruisers bombarded both banks and tried to land an armed party ashore, but quickly discovered that the Germans had fortified the entrance to the river with machine guns and rifles. To dig them out of their trenches would be a most difficult job, not one that the task force was prepared to undertake at that time. Captain Drury-Lowe's marine commander estimated that it would take at least a thousand men to make a successful assault on the German positions.

That night *Dartmouth* was sent back to Mombasa to coal, while Captain Drury-Lowe considered his next move of attack. The same night Captain Looff moved his anchorage further upstream and ran a telephone line to the shore, then connected it with the various German positions on the shore, so he could be kept informed of the activities of his enemies. He moored *Königsberg* stoutly to the trees on the river bank with steel chain and settled down for a siege. He did not know quite how he would prevent the British from entering the river, and that was his next problem. As Captain Looff considered the problem on the quiet of his bridge that evening, Radio Officer Niemyer came up the bridge ladder with a message; in the clear the Admiralty in Whitehall had warned Captain Drury-Lowe of London's minimum demands:

Sink or destroy the *Königsberg* at any cost!

7

Blockade

ON 3RD NOVEMBER the *Chatham* made two attempts to carry out Whitehall's orders to destroy the *Königsberg*. First, on the swell of the tide she attempted to move in close to bombard the German cruiser but she could not come close enough; indeed, she could not even find *Königsberg* now because the telltale topmasts had been brought down and tree branches had been laid across the fore and mainmast to camouflage her from the British. Second, *Chatham* bombarded the shore with such intensity that the palm trees fumed with clouds of yellow smoke quite visible from Captain Looff's vantage point, leading him to believe that Korvettenkapitän Schoenfeld, a retired planter who was in charge of the shore defence here, had been wiped out with all his men. Captain Looff was delighted at the end of the bombardment to receive a message from Schoenfeld telling him that all went well and that nothing important had occurred all day long.

In a sense Kapitänleutnant Schoenfeld's statement represented exactly the situation; Captain Drury-Lowe knew by the end of 3rd November that *Königsberg* could be neither destroyed nor captured through the sole efforts of his task-force. He needed reinforcements, and specifically a blockship which could be sunk in the river and prevent the *Königsberg* from coming out, so he began sending messages to Mombasa and Zanzibar. From Mombasa came the 3800-ton collier *Newbridge*, which would be sacrificed as a blockship. More ships were brought into action: the *Goliath*, an old, out-moded cruiser which was good for little at sea, but which carried a motor torpedo boat and whose big guns could help blow the *Königsberg* out of the water, and the coastal steamer *Duplex*, which was to be armed and used as an auxiliary cruiser.

At five o'clock on the morning of 7th November, the motor torpedo boat of the *Goliath*, plus four other armed boats, moved in towards the shore of the Simba-Ouranga branch of the Rufiji, hoping to make a successful attack on the shore defences and wipe them out, but they were greeted by so withering a fire from rifles and machine guns that they withdrew. Kapitänleutnant Schoenfeld was on the job with his rump army, recruited over Governor Schnee's objections from the ranks of firemen, merchant seamen, and stewards of the passenger ships that lay in Dar es Salaam harbour. So well were the German defences planned that the bewildered British seamen could not see a single man firing at them, yet the hail of bullets was impenetrable.

To add to the confusion of the British, during the brief fight a mortar shell from the shore struck the port rail of the *Goliath*'s motor torpedo boat and accidentally launched an armed torpedo, which then ran crazily through the little fleet, threatening every vessel. The British sailors beat a rapid retreat; it was enough to face the fire of the German defenders without being blown up by one of their own torpedoes.

The British were not the only ones thinking of torpedoes; Captain Looff maintained even yet that the best defence was a good offence, and he was considering ways in which the defenders of the Rufiji could attack their attackers. He knew he could not go out and fight against the overwhelming superiority of his enemies without being sunk, but he might be able to torpedo one of them. Under the captain's direction two tree trunks were cut down and fixed together so that between them they could carry a torpedo. All a small crew would have to do would be ride and guide the innocent-looking tree trunks to within about a thousand yards of one of the warships, then launch the torpedo, which ought to run true for the remaining distance.

The torpedo officer and two of his torpedomen worked for two days to perfect their infernal machine, and then they were ready to try it out, without a warhead of course, at eight o'clock in the morning. It was already hot that morning, as the officer and his men stripped down to their shorts and moved gingerly into the river's muddy water, quite recalling that the crocodiles who also inhabited that water had not yet breakfasted. They climbed on to their palm-tree raft, moved out into the middle of the channel well ahead of *Königsberg*, and the torpedo officer released the torpedo, setting it on a course that would carry it into the river bank on the right, so they would not lose it for ever.

It worked marvellously. The torpedo left its improvised tube and ran true and then turned to the right, but the sailor steering the palm-tree torpedo boat apparently had not been let in on the secret of the course, and he steered to the right, too. The torpedo turned, lanced in to the palm trees, tipped them up and threw the whole crew into the river, while the decks of the *Königsberg* rang with laughter.

Suddenly Captain Looff thought of crocodiles, and shouted to First Officer Koch to break out some carbines, but by the time he turned back to the river, the crew of the torpedo-palms had scrambled ashore safely and were making their way ruefully back along the bank to the anchorage.

The infernal machine worked, however, and that was the important point; they would use it on the first dark night that came along.

Unfortunately for the torpedo-palm expedition the British ships in the delta suddenly changed their anchorage. The British, too, had schemes afoot:

On the afternoon of 9th November *Dartmouth* anchored off the east end of Koma Island, to act as a beacon for the blockship *Newbridge*, which was coming that night to try to close up the Simba-Ouranga branch of the Rufiji and bottle up the *Königsberg*. All Commander Raymond Fitzmaurice needed to do then was to set his course for south, thirty-nine degrees west and then to travel eight miles beyond *Dartmouth*, whereupon he would have arrived at his destination. Simple, was it not? Except for a few matters like currents and black night and unknown waters filled with reefs and bars that might cause the most able and experienced captain to blanch a little in the privacy of his bridge.

But Captain Fitzmaurice did the job and did it safely and was on hand next morning for the second stage of the affair.

The British plan of attack was a complex but careful one, making use of the power the Admiralty had put at the disposal of the task force to destroy *Königsberg*. The *Chatham* and the *Weymouth* would move into the entrance to the river and bombard the shore. The *Newbridge* then would move to her anchorage across the mouth of the river, accompanied by the little *Duplex* on the port side and the torpedo boat of the *Goliath* on the starboard, while behind the blockship would come the steam launches of the three cruisers, all heavily laden with armed men whose sole purpose was to establish a field of fire against both banks and protect the *Newbridge* from a surprise attack from shore, and to take off the skeleton crew once *Newbridge* had been anchored and her explosive charges set off.

It all worked just as planned – except that *Newbridge* arrived early and started up the river, to be chased back by the opening of a German fusillade from both banks. But then, when the British got organised and put the plan officially into effect at 5.20 in the morning, it worked like clockwork. *Newbridge* moved to her proper position, running the gauntlet of Korvettenkapitän Schoenfeld's fire, Captain Fitzmaurice anchored her at 5.50 in exactly the proper place, lit the fuses, and at 6 was overboard into the steam launch of *Chatham*, at 6.15 the charges exploded, and five minutes later the *Newbridge* canted over to port and came down by the stern into the mud of the Rufiji.

The British had 'bottled up *Königsberg*,' they reported gleefully to Whitehall that day.

8

Besieged

In London on 10th November 1914, the Lords of the Admiralty needed all the good news they could get, for nine days earlier Vice-Admiral the Graf von Spee, commander of the German East Asia Cruiser Squadron, had inflicted the most serious defeat of the war on the British forces at the Battle of Coronel off the coast of South America. The British had lost the cruiser *Monmouth* and the *Good Hope*, and only the *Glasgow* had escaped, badly damaged, to make her way to Rio de Janeiro for repairs. The British also had lost Admiral Cradock, commander of the cruiser squadron in the Pacific, who had gone down with his flagship.

To be sure, the lords had good news earlier in the week: *Emden* finally was discovered almost by accident, in the Cocos-Keeling Islands, where it had stopped to destroy the British cable station, and after a brief, fierce engagement, the heavy cruiser HMS *Sydney* had wrecked the little German ship that once was known as the Swan of the Pacific.

Still the news from the Rufiji was not good enough for the admirals sitting in London; what they feared most of all was a diabolical plot by the Germans to rescue *Königsberg*, and the most fearful of the admirals envisaged Admiral von Spee already heading across the Atlantic Ocean to cross around the Cape of Good Hope, blow the special *Königsberg* task force out of the water off German East Africa, add *Königsberg* to the German Squadron, and then move into the Indian Ocean to continue the havoc wreaked by *Emden*. These fears took no account of the perennial need for coal by German ships that had no friendly bases to which they might turn, the innocence of the German naval staff of such audacity in planning, and the needs of warships for occasional parts and services. Having so very many bases of their own, the British tended to forget how difficult modern naval warfare had become for nations that did not possess so much. In an earlier day a sailing ship could travel around the world with a handful of canvas, a hold full of salt beef and pork and rum, provided it took on lemon juice or enough other fresh edibles to ward off scurvy; in a few years more modern vessels would be able to travel faster, farther and for far longer periods of time with oil for fuel; and then would come atomic fuels. One might say that the period of the First World War represented an in-between, a transition in which the ships were really worse off, in terms of logistics, than they had been a hundred years earlier or would be half a century later.

So when Captain Drury-Lowe reported triumphantly that he had bottled up *Könisgberg* in the Rufiji, his news was not enough for the admirals, not enough at all. Instead of sitting back to relax, they began to press; they assigned two battleships, ten cruisers, and a dozen lesser ships to destroy the *Könisgberg* and guard against a linkage with von Spee. If Captain Looff and the four hundred men of his command could simply sit in the Rufiji Delta for the remainder of the war playing checkers, they would serve their country well. The *Newbridge* was an Admiralty collier like that which had been anchored behind *Pegasus* in Zanzibar harbour on the glorious morning of 20th September; what difference if such a collier was sunk by *Königsberg* in that harbour or sunk by the British in the Rufiji Delta – she was still sunk and was still a victim of the *Königsberg*.

Then Admiral King-Hall took a hand; the Admiralty robbed him of his heavy cruisers *Minotaur* and *Defence* to send west against Admiral von Spee off South America, and he demanded the return of *Dartmouth* and *Weymouth* if London wanted him to guarantee shipping off the Cape. So *Dartmouth* headed south, and *Weymouth* hung around the Rufiji Delta while *Chatham* ploughed north to Mombasa for her coal, and then *Weymouth* headed towards the Cape as well.

Captain Drury-Lowe had new problems, then. How was he to go after *Königsberg*? He decided that he must have big ships – ships with big guns is what he meant – and he must have airplanes to spot the *Königsberg* and keep track of her.

Airplanes? The Navy did not have any airplanes and was not sure it ever wanted any. But Admiral King-Hall in Cape Town found a Curtiss hydroplane that had been brought down there for exhibition purposes just before the outbreak of war, and he commissioned the pilot, a young man named Cutler, as a temporary officer of the Royal Marines. He requisitioned a steamer named *Kinfauns Castle* to be auxiliary cruiser and airplane tender, and sent the entourage up to Drury-Lowe to make what he could of it.

In the jungle – for one could not be more complimentary than that about the terrain in which *Königsberg* found herself – Captain Looff was busily engaged in the struggle for the survival of his cruiser and crew. When Lieutenant Niemyer had brought him the wireless in the clear from Whitehall demanding the destruction of *Königsberg*, the radio officer had remarked gloomily that the message was '*Königsberg's* death warrant'. Max Looff had turned aside this echo of *Götterdämmerung* with a few jeering words, but he had immediately sensed the propaganda victory achieved over his crew by the British Admiralty in sending the message in the clear and had taken steps to restore the morale of his men.

The first thing to do was to put them to work, and fortunately there was plenty of work for the crew of *Königsberg* in the Rufiji Delta. Lieutenant Hinrichs, the navigator, was given charge of the survey of the channel, and he and half a dozen men took the charts newly made from the *Möwe's* soundings and checked them out, yard by yard, along the Simba-Ouranga channel in which the *Königsberg* lay. In the meantime, in order to confuse the British, the anchorage was changed several times and, in so doing, once again the cruiser was run aground. This second time she had to be lightened; the coal and the ammunition had to be shifted aft to get her off the bar, but this was done and she did get off. Hinrichs and his crew were soon at work and there were no more groundings.

The burning of the *Somali* had created problems for the *Königsberg*, but *Somali* did not burn altogether on the first attack by the British. Unfortunately, on the day of the blockading of the harbour with *Newbridge*, one of the cruisers offshore had plunked a 152-mm shell right into *Somali's* hold, setting fire to her coal, and causing total destruction of the ship and her stores. This lucky stroke was a serious blow in a way, but in another way it gave Captain Looff an excuse to put the men to a new task. There was a fair amount of coal for *Königsberg*, in the lighters in the Rufiji with her, but, of course, Captain Looff did not know how long that would have to last, and where or when he could find a new supply. To husband his coal he used it only for heating the boilers of his ship when he wanted to move her from one anchorage to another. All the subsidiary uses of coal, to vaporise steam and make fresh water, to cook in the galleys, to heat water for shaving and the conveniences of life, were converted from coal to wood heat. The men were sent out to cut and bring back to *Königsberg* three thousand pounds of mangrove roots, knots, and trunks every day, and this kept a good share of the crew busy; and as the crew was busy, the men's morale improved from the low point of the night of that British message.

After 10th November, when *Königsberg's* Lieutenant Niemyer caught another in-the-clear message from Captain Drury-Lowe, the triumphant cry that he had blockaded *Königsberg* in the Rufiji, Captain Looff had a chance to strike another blow for ship's morale. He caused it to be

83

known that day that *Königsberg* was not bottled up at all – that the *Newbridge* lay on the edge of the channel, not in the middle, and that any time *Königsberg* had reason to do so she could simply slip by the blockship. Of course this fact was not to be told to the British – what they did not know might hurt them, it was to be hoped – but the men knew that the British crowing was all for naught, or at least they thought they did. Below the surface, Captain Looff was less ebullient than he appeared, not because of the blockship, but because he knew the lengths the British bulldog would go in order to put him out of action, and he could scarcely see how he could achieve any important help from any German source in the world.

There was both good news and bad news about the war: the bad news came from Europe, where the lightning advance of the Germany army had been stopped in September at the Marne; the good news came from German East Africa itself where Lieutenant Colonel von Lettow-Vorbeck was leading a spirited defence of the colony.

At the outbreak of war, von Lettow-Vorbeck had moved back to Pugu in the mountains behind Dar es Salaam with most of the soldiers and potential soldiers of the colony, but when the British failed to occupy Dar es Salaam even after wringing the surrender from Governor Schnee, some German troops returned there. Von Lettow-Vorbeck then organised a coastal defence force of Askaris led by Germans, and sent them off to the various islands and coastal watching points where they could be of most value to his war effort. He and Korvettenkapitän Zimmer organised the force known as the Delta Force, which had so far protected *Königsberg* with its trenches along the river bank. The coastal force also included soldiers and watchers on Mafia Island to the south of the Delta and Koma Island to the north. The force on Mafia was commanded by Lieutenant Schiller and that on Koma by Lieutenant von Neuenstein, who had two other Europeans to assist him in watching the activities of the British task force.

By the end of September their German coastal defence

force was complete and in place, ready to protec[
berg when she so suddenly and unexpectedly came b[
the delta for help; by 10th November the coastal d[
had fought several engagements with the British[
notably that of the day of the sinking of the blo[
Newbridge, when the fierce hail of fire from shore ....ed
three British sailors and wounded a number of others. The
real value to *Königsberg* of the Delta Force, however, was
not the number of casualties that might be inflicted on the
British, but the restraining effect the presence of these
soldiers and their 37-mm guns and machine guns had on
British activity in the river. Had there been a less effective
military organisation at the mouth of the Rufiji the British
might well have launched a marine invasion in the first
days of the struggle, and then the battle of the *Königsberg*
might well have become a land siege in the jungle.

But the British naval forces off the Rufiji were leery of
coming to grips with the Germans on land, and this was
particularly true after the beginning of November, when
the Germans ashore taught the British a salty lesson.

From the moment that war was declared, Lieutenant
Colonel von Lettow-Vorbeck expected a British attack on
the colony, and his first concern was to secure his lines of
communication. In 1914 two railways crossed German
East Africa, one long new railway running from Dar es
Salaam to Kigoma on Lake Tanganyika, and a shorter line
running from Tanga along the northeast border of the
colony to Moschi, just a few miles from the British East
African frontier. Both lines represented lateral communication with the interior; there was no vertical communication line. Before the war, all travel between Dar es Salaam
and Tanga had been carried by sea, but during the war
this route was obviously untenable as long as the British
held command of the coastal waters, so von Lettow-
Vorbeck set out to build a road from Morogoro on the
southern line to Lorogwe on the northern road. He also
had to build telegraph facilities in the interior, because
previously the coastal wireless stations had carried most

traffic, and with war the wireless stations were destroyed, either by the British, or by the Germans to prevent them from falling into British hands. The building of the telegraph lines was an arduous job in back country; in East Africa the task was worse than might be expected because the white ants (termites) chewed down the wooden telegraph poles. Prewar poles had been made of steel, but there was no steel to spare, so wooden poles were erected, treated, and replaced as the ants got to them.

Telegraph lines and roads were built from Dodoma to Arusha and from Tabora to Mwanza on Lake Victoria, which jutted down into the German colony from British East Africa.

One other line of communication was established immediately: Lieutenant Horn completed the arming of the lake steamer *Hedwig von Wissman* in August and took it out on Lake Tanganyika. There he encountered the Belgian steamer *Alexandre Delcommune*, which he attacked and shot to pieces, thus securing the command of Lake Tangganyika for the Germans.

Von Lettow-Vorbeck expected the British attack to come from the north, and several skirmishes were fought along the border in the early weeks of the war, but the first real British attempt to conquer German East Africa began in October. Then the British assembled in Bombay a battalion of the Loyal North Lancashire Regiment, four battalions of Indian imperial service troops, and one battalion of Indian regular infantry. These troops – eight thousand strong – were embarked on transports and, escorted by the cruiser HMS *Fox* and another heavy warship, they steamed west for Africa.

In these early days of the war, the British were particularly careless in telegraphing their punches. English newspapers spoke openly of the attack to be made on German East Africa, and in the early days of the war von Lettow-Vorbeck captured letters from India to British officers in Africa telling of the embarkation of a force of ten thousand men from Bombay. If the British were coming to East

Africa, von Lettow-Vorbeck mused, they would undoubtedly be coming to attack Tanga, which would give them control of one railway and cut off the northern half of the colony. The German commander was not surprised then, when in the morning of 2nd November he received an emergency message at his headquarters in New Moshi, telling him of the arrival of fourteen British transports and two cruisers off Tanga.

The British ships stood offshore, and a boat went into the harbour to demand that District Commissioner Auracher surrender the town as Governor Schnee had surrendered Dar es Salaam. In defence of the British commander, Captain F W Caulfield, it must be said that Governor Schnee had established a precedent, and there was no reason for the British to believe that the Germans would fight at Tanga any more than they did at Dar es Salaam – they did not know how Lieutenant Colonel von Lettow-Vorbeck felt about that surrender of the capital.

District Commissioner Auracher stalled. He went aboard the British cruiser and began to talk. As to surrender, he said, he would have to consult his with superiors, so he went back ashore and telegraphed von Lettow-Vorbeck, then returned to the cruiser again for more talk.

On receipt of Commissioner Auracher's message, Lieutenant Colonel von Lettow-Vorbeck immediately dispatched two companies of Askaris from the north to Tanga and two companies of Europeans and more Askaris from the west to the railway. For transport he had two trucks, and that was all. The trucks lumbered along the dusty road, carrying troops to the terminus, turning and going back upcountry for more. At New Moshi, the end of the northern rail line, von Lettow-Vorbeck had eight locomotives to carry his troops along the narrow-gauge line one hundred and ninety miles, to reach Tanga and fight off the British before they secured their beachhead.

It was really a miniature railway; the cars were so small that a fully loaded train of a dozen to sixteen coaches could carry only one company of men and their baggage and carriers. Of course this was East Africa, and carriers were an important part of the army, for a soldier – black or white – could not be expected to carry equipment and fight as well, so each company was alloted two hundred and fifty carriers who played the part that trucks and jeeps would play in more modern armies.

Lieutenant Colonel von Lettow-Vorbeck was a master of organisation, and he proved it in his first major engagement with the enemy. The word came to him on the afternoon of 2nd November; that very day a company and a half of troops were dispatched by train, and the next morning two other companies were sent off. There was a simple secret to von Lettow-Vorbeck's success: he called Railway Commissioner Krober to active duty as a second lieutenant and Traffic Director Kuhlwein as well; he was their general and there was no arguing with his orders. He said 'do it', and they did.

From the German point of view, the first call to major action could not have been made under more fortunate circumstances: the blacks loved to ride in the trains, most of them had never had a chance before, and when the Askaris set out for the front they left cheering and waving their hats and smiling; no army ever went into battle with greater morale than these impressed German troops.

At Tanga, Captain Caulfield realised by noon that Commissioner Auracher was stalling, and he ordered the troops ashore to begin the invasion.

The British landing was made at Ras Kasone, the southern point that guards Manza Bay from the sea. Tanga was located inland a mile and three-quarters from the point, on the southern shore of the bay which projected inland, very much like a thumb stuck into the coast of Africa. The European town was on the shore itself, with the native town sprawling south of it, inland. Between them the country was rough – coconut and rubber plantations with cover and brush every few yards. As the British troops began landing, the first force of Germans, called from the north, made its way into the town and east into the thick bush that separated Tanga from Ras Kasone. German patrols went out, met the enemy, and opened fire. The British landing force took cover and made no attempt to move inland that afternoon or night, waiting until the entire force was ashore.

By morning most of the British transports had landed their troops, but the artillery was still aboard the ships. By morning, also, the Germans had been strongly reinforced, until they now had some six hundred European and Askari soldiers to stand off the invasion. Lieutenant Colonel von Lettow-Vorbeck had one thousand troops available at this time in this region, and he was committing his entire force in a do-or-die effort.

On the night of 2nd November the Germans dug in, setting machine guns so they would bring the British under crossfire as they advanced. The next morning, under cover of a barrage laid down by the cruisers, the British troops began to advance. The cruisers began shelling buildings, including the hospital that lay between the town and the landing beach, not knowing that the building was a hospital.

On 3rd November the British continued to land troops; they had been slow in realising that they would be opposed, for they had expected to have the Germans surrender and accept occupation docilely. Instead, Commissioner Auracher had turned his hat around and become Leutnant de Reserve Auracher, and had led the police of Tanga into action as soldiers to join Lieutenant Merensky and the 17th Company, which was first on the field for the Germans.

On the afternoon of 3rd November the first troops had arrived on the railway and had rushed in to the left flank of the British and driven them back. The appearance of these attackers had caused some confusion in the British line, and the retreat was general to the beachhead.

On the evening of 3rd November Lieutenant Colonel von Lettow-Vorbeck arrived at Tanga and went to the hospital, where he found Lieutenant Merensky among the wounded. He asked Merensky how the battle was going, and that officer said they had defeated the British and the action was over. But that same night the commander spoke with Captain Baumstark, who had led the first troops into action on 2nd November, and Baumstark said there was such a strong force of British on the beach that the Germans could not possibly hold Tanga, so he had withdrawn his force four miles west of the town.

Lieutenant Colonel von Lettow-Vorbeck decided to reconnoitre the town himself, to see if the British had advanced on it. He had brought several bicycles down on the headquarters train and he and two officers cycled to Tanga, four miles east, where they found an outpost of the 6th Field Company. The commander of the post could give no accurate information about the enemy, however, so von Lettow-Vorbeck simply rode into town to see for himself on the principle that if someone began shooting at him the town was occupied and if not, then there was a different story.

Von Lettow-Vorbeck bicycled through the silent main street of the town, a street lighted eerily by the rising moon. Not a creature stirred. He could hear no sound but the swish-swish of his tyres. Then he rode down to the harbour, from which he could look out to the east and see the transports lying a quarter of a mile offshore. The ships were as brightly lighted as passenger liners in peacetime and far noisier; the amount of racket going on aboard the ships indicated to him that the landing was being continued even in the night.

The German cyclists rode on to Ras Kasone; they left their bicycles at the big sprawling bungalow that was Dr Ludwig Deppe's government hospital between the point and the town, and they moved quietly on foot to the beach. The two officers stopped sharp as they encountered a detachment of Indian troops, but no one paid any attention to them, save one sentry who challenged them and then immediately lost interest. Lieutenant Colonel von Lettow-Vorbeck and his aides went back to the hospital, mounted their bicycles, and rode back to Tanga, where the commander called up his troops to the west and told them to come and fight the battle.

In his reconnaissance, Lieutenant Colonel von Lettow-Vorbeck had decided how he would fight this battle, and, indeed, that he would make his major stand here at Tanga. To the north the Germans were protected from view by the houses of the town. The town was surrounded by plantations which extended almost to the sea at the point and made a rapid advance by the British impossible (the plantations' rows of trees and bushes were enclosed in hedges that were most effective for defence). Since the only open ground was that leading to the native town on the south, it was apparent that the British would have to attack on the south or right flank of the defence, and so he would place his defence point at the eastern edge of the town, with strong reserves behind the right flank, prepared to launch a counterattack in case of trouble.

The centre of the line was held by the 6th Field Company, the best-trained German force, whose Askaris had learned their business in peacetime at the military centre of Ujiji. The right flank was held by Captain Baumstark and his battalion, which included the 16th and 17th Companies and one other company of irregulars, who had been recruited recently. The commander kept three companies in the rear on the right flank, the 7th and 8th Rifle Companies of Germans with three machine guns, and the 13th Field Company of Askaris with four machine guns. Two other companies, the 4th and 9th Field Companies, were coming down by train but had not arrived, nor had the German field artillery, Captain Hering's battery, which consisted of old guns of the model of 1873, which fired black smoky powder.

Through his field-glasses, Lieutenant Colonel von Lettow-Vorbeck watched the British transports as they continued to unload men on to the beach, and at noon he estimated the number of troops ashore at six thousand. It was growing hot, as it did every day in this climate, and the thirsty German defenders began knocking and pulling the coconut trees to bring down young nuts for their milk. From the town Master Butcher Grabow came to the eastern perimeter of the defences, bringing a barrowload of hot sausages for the troops, and there he found the two German companies under Captain von Prince, who had been sent to this point in the line to hold in case the Askaris fell back with the first British attack.

Lieutenant Colonel von Lettow-Vorbeck was not quite sure that the British would attack on this day, since they seemed to want their war conducted in the most leisurely of fashions, but at three o'clock an Askari scout came to field headquarters, saluted sharply and reported:

'*Adui tayari* (The enemy is ready).'

A few moments later the stillness was rent by the broken popping of rifle fire, emphasised here and there by the staccato pounding of machine guns. The British had begun their advance.

From the command post Lieutenant Colonel von Lettow-Vorbeck could trace the progress of the battle in the ebb and flow of sounds; he heard the firing coming closer from the eastern edge of the town, so he knew that the 6th Company in the centre had been driven back and that the British were driving on the railway station. Captain von Prince rushed forward with his two companies of Europeans and drove back the Loyal North Lancashires and the Kashmir Rifles, who held the British right, coming in along the beach. On the south the 101st Grenadiers came advancing through the bush, suffering heavily from the fire of the hidden Germans, but advancing in that slow, regular British manner, apparently regardless of casualties. Each time a man fell another stepped up from behind to take his place, giving the impression of an irresistible force coming onward.

The impression carried to the Askaris on the right, who had never encountered men so willing to die, and they were mightily impressed. The Askaris broke and began retreating through the palm plantation to the Tanga-Pangani road on the west. Captain Baumstark threw his companies into the breach, but they were being driven back until the officers of the headquarters company rushed forward and began beating and berating the Africans. Captain von Hammarstein, a member of the commander's staff, picked up a wine bottle and hurled it at the head of one fleeing Askari, bringing him to the ground. The lesson, and similar ones, reminded the Askaris that they had the Germans to fear, perhaps more than the enemy, and they rallied.

All this action had used up most of von Lettow-Vorbeck's reserves, and he now had but one company, the 13th Field Company, with which to mount his counterattack on the enemy's flank. He sent out his flankers, with their machine guns, and only when they had come around to the side from the south did they open with the guns. The British 101st Grenadiers had taken a bad beating already, this unexpected fire from four new machine guns broke their morale, and they slowed, then stopped.

At this moment, in the hedgerows of the coconut plantation on the German right, one of the German machine guns began firing through a field in which there were sitting row upon row of beehives. As the machine gun bullets slashed through the hives out came swarms of angry bees to attack any living object near them. They attacked the machine gun company. Men rose, clawing at their faces, dropped rolling over and seeking cover – and this one gun was out of action. The bees also attacked the Indian soldiers on the other side, and these raw soldiers, fighting unknowns in foreign territory, believed the Germans had some new secret weapon – trained bees. The bees frightened the Indian troops far more than the machine guns; they swarmed and stung, and soon soldiers began to bolt to escape the angry insects, running into the trees.

As the troops turned and fled, the three machine guns on the flank and the three others in front opened up, and the British troops were mowed down in crossfire, squad after squad falling, man by man.

At nightfall the British were retreating through the plantation forests in disorder, and in almost equal disorder the Askaris and the Germans were following them. From the dusk in the forest came confused shouts in half a dozen tongues, and then, as the sun went down and darkness set in, the pursuit of the British stopped and they gathered up the bedraggled remnants of their force and moved back to the beach.

Lieutenant Colonel von Lettow-Vorbeck wanted to go to the beach itself, drive the British into the sea or force them to surrender, and under cover of night to shell the British cruisers with his two old-fashioned cannon. But there was too much confusion among the Askaris. One company on his right ended up in the sands of the beach on the north, or left of the line. Askaris moved back west of the town to bivouac in the old camp. So great was the movement back and forth that Captain Hering's battery could not be moved, and so the British cruisers were saved after all from what he might have done to them with those great black-smoking guns.

On the morning of 5th November, Lieutenant Colonel von Lettow-Vorbeck urged his men onward again. Through the night the British had been withdrawing to the transports; the order for withdrawal came when the British troop commander realised that his men were demoralised and would not fight. The first contingents had simply rushed to the beach, thrown themselves into the assault boats, and gone back to the ships without anyone's leave. Most of the officers of the line were killed or wounded in their attempts to keep the Indian troops facing the foe, and there was not enough strength to resume the battle, not enough determination to wipe out a thousand men who were not supposed to have been there or to have fought at all.

Strong German and Askari patrols moved to the beach region and set up machine guns on the morning of 5th November, then began to harry the retreating Indians and even to fire upon HMS *Fox* as she stood close in to shore, driving her to deeper water.

In the afternoon, as the British troops held the beach,

they sent an officer under flag of truce to negotiate for the return of the wounded on both sides; the truce was made, and the wounded were taken back to the ships. As the last British boats returned to their ships, the Germans came down to the shore to begin assessing their victory; they had no idea how many casualties they had inflicted, and von Lettow-Vorbeck placed it tentatively at eight hundred. (After talking to English officers at the war's end he revised the figure to two thousand!) But the action obviously had been a total German victory and a British rout: the Germans captured six hundred thousand rounds of rifle ammunition, the communications facilities of an entire army, and enough clothing, blankets, and equipment to last von Lettow-Vorbeck's little force for an entire year. The Askaris, some of them armed with old black powder rifles, came grinning back from the beach, each carrying two or three modern British Enfields. And as for German losses: Captain von Prince was killed leading an attack, and so were fourteen other Germans, while fifty-four Askaris and carriers had fallen in the fight.

The British armada moved out of Tanga on the night of 5th November, but Lieutenant Colonel von Lettow-Vorbeck was not at all sure they had not simply steamed out of sight to come back again to Tanga or another place and renew the invasion. He mounted his bicycle that night and rode to the north shore of Manza Bay, where he saw the British ships anchoring; but next morning they steamed off north, toward Mombasa, and the German commander knew the invasion attempt was over.

Within a few hours von Lettow-Vorbeck learned at least one of the reasons for the British withdrawal: the attack on Tanga was timed to coincide with a British invasion of German East Africa from the north, and on 3rd November a force had come down on Longido Mountain, northwest of Kilimanjaro, and other troops had attacked along Lake Victoria Nyanza. Both of these attacks had been repelled by German forces, and it seemed apparent that faulty British intelligence had indicated the German strength to be far greater than it was. Lieutenant Colonel von Lettow-Vorbeck's speed in rushing troops to Tanga must have indicated to the enemy that the troops were there already, and consequently the Germans were credited with possession of a force several times the size of the actual Protective Force. Communication between Captain Caulfield's invasion fleet and the field forces in the north indicated considerable German strength; given this information and the broken morale of the Indian troops, the British commanders called off the invasion altogether. All was quiet on the German East African front for the remainder of 1914.

The most marvellous sight of all had come on the evening of 5th November, when Captain Hering's battery finally went into action against the British cruisers. The old guns of 1873 were dragged up to the water's edge and opened fire, scoring several hits on the cruisers. And then two modern British warships, eleven great transports, and the remains of an invasion army of eight thousand men sailed away, leaving one lieutenant colonel, three hundred Germans and eight hundred Askaris in control of Tanga, while two old field guns peppered the water behind the ships, smoking furiously in the bright moonlight.

9

Flugzeug!

THE HYDROPLANE THAT was sent up to the Rufiji Delta from Durban was anything but *le dernier cri* in aviation. It was of the type manufactured by Glenn Curtiss in 1911 to prove to the United States Navy that an airplane could be built which would take off and land from the water on pontoons. The Curtiss plane was a biplane, the two rigid silk-covered wings held together shakily above the big pontoon by a dozen vertical braces and a network of wire struts. Since the Wright brothers held the patent on ailerons or movable surfaces on the wings, Glenn Curtiss had used a different system: his movable surfaces, which controlled the ascent and descent of the craft, were in front of and behind the wings. The pilot sat uneasily on a chair fixed to the lower wing, in front of the engine, on which was mounted a pusher propeller. The whole mechanism was surly, noisy, and given to strange fits during which the engine would not start or would quit because of overheating; pilot Cutler deserved a medal for even taking it up into the air, let alone considering a mission in which his unstable craft would be shot at by the Germans.

Armed with his new commission in the Royal Marines, Lieutenant Cutler made ready to appear on the Rufiji, and Admiral King-Hall wirelessed Captain Drury-Lowe that the airplane would arrive around 15th November. So speedy was the departure that there was not time to put together any spare parts, and when Lieutenant Cutler asked for a mechanic, no one knew what he was talking about. But aboard the *Kinfauns Castle* on the way north from Durban

Lieutenant Cutler learned that a naval cadet named Gallehawk had become fascinated by airplanes, and he enlisted the youth as his mechanic and assistant. Within a week it was possible for Gallehawk to know about all there was to know regarding the maintenance of the hydroplane, or, to put it another way, in that time he was able to learn to do all the things that anyone else could do to keep it running.

Then, on 15th November, *Kinfauns Castle* arrived off Mafia Island in the mouth of the Rufiji and met *Chatham*. The airplane had in truth arrived and Lieutenant Cutler and Cadet Gallehawk were prepared to do their duty.

Captain Drury-Lowe was sure that the hydroplane was the answer to the destruction of the *Königsberg*. The first few days after arrival were spent by the aviator and his mechanic in tuning up the airplane, or the 'cuckoo', the nickname the men of the task force had given the hydroplane. Everyone understood the delay, Captain Drury-Lowe most of all, for it did not take an engineer to see that the craft was old, its hull was fragile, and its radiator heated up like a coffee pot whenever the engine ran. Maximum flying time of the hydroplane was fifty minutes, which was not much to take off from the water in the delta, fly ten miles inland to look over the *Königsberg*, fly ten miles back and land; in fact, it could just about be done in good weather. It was quite enough of a task to fly the airplane at all, but Lieutenant Cutler would have to do much more: there was no room or strength in the airplane to carry an observer, so Cutler was to fly the machine and observe at the same time.

At seven o'clock on the morning of 19th November, Lieutenant Cutler climbed up on to the wing of the hydroplane just off little Niororo Island in the mouth of the Rufiji, sat down in the chair on the lower wing, and started up the engine. Soon he was in the air, and flying at three thousand feet. The men of *Chatham* saw the airplane fly over, disappear into the clouds and then they did not see the airplane again. An hour went by, two hours, three, and no airplane. Four hours went by . . . five . . . and six . . . and still no airplane returned. After the first hour it was apparent that the hydroplane was down somewhere, but it was not until the sixth hour that pilot Cutler was discovered, along with his airplane, on the island of Okousa, thirty-four miles south of Niororo, eighteen miles south of the southern tip of Mafia Island. He had simply got lost, he said nonchalantly, so he had tried to retrace his course and had landed on the first island he saw.

Of course the frightful racket of the old hydroplane's engine was enough to wake the dead, let alone the Germans of the Delta Force on the banks of the Rufiji, and so early on the morning of 19th November Korvettenkapitän Schoenfeld picked up the field telephone and announced to Captain Looff that they had an aerial visitor. Captain Looff had not yet seen the airplane but the news of its coming disturbed him seriously. He knew absolutely nothing about airplanes, and he had never seen more than one or two of them in his life. If the British were bringing up an airplane, it must have some dreadful possibilities, and it behoved him to consider them and the line of defence he was to take against this new device; in fact he sat down to reconsider his entire situation.

Although she was scarcely 'bottled up', no matter what Captain Drury-Lowe had to say on the subject, the *Königsberg* most certainly was in an uncomfortable position in the Rufiji. Looff could go out, but he could not afford to go out because he had nowhere to go and not enough coal with which to get there. As for getting out, it was relatively a simple matter: the Rufiji consisted of a half-dozen branches, but only two of them were worth considering: the Simba-Ouranga in which he lay, and the Kikunja branch, three and a half miles north of him. He knew – and the British did not – that these branches connected in several places and that it was possible to navigate the Rufiji to come in one branch and out the other, or to perform a large number of circles in the inland waterways of the delta. There was plenty of water in here for him, and perhaps plenty for one of the British cruisers – if they ever found out the secrets uncovered by the *Möwe* in her soundings of the river bottom. What troubled Captain Looff at this moment was the fear that the airplane might uncover his secrets. He realised that the airplane would soon be flying over him, looking down on *Königsberg*, spying, and he was now more inclined to accede to Korvettenkapitän Schoenfeld's request that some of the lighter guns of the ship be taken ashore and used for the defence of the *Königsberg*. Until now he had resisted such an idea, because taking the guns ashore meant an admission that *Königsberg* was besieged in the river, and was not likely to come out again. Captain Looff now rationalised his decision to remove some of the guns because of the airplane and because it would be simply a matter of hours to re-embark them once help came, in the form of a coal supply or another warship.

Lieutenant Cutler had one bit of bad news to give Captain Drury-Lowe when he was finally found on the wrong island after that first flight: the radiator of the 'cuckoo' had passed the line of impossibility and just would not do any more at all. Could the British navy do something about a radiator?

Airplanes were nonexistent and cars were not exactly old hat in Africa in 1914, but someone aboard *Chatham* recalled having seen a Model T Ford meandering up and down the streets of Mombasa, and a wireless message was sent off immediately to the naval command there; within a matter of hours the unhappy Ford owner was deprived of his radiator, and this piece of machinery was brought aboard HMS *Fox*, which immediately got up steam and set off for the mouth of the Rufiji. Here was a bit of history: the first time a man-of-war was ever used to deliver a car radiator, some four hundred miles away; quite a tribute to man, the machine, and the *Königsberg*.

HMS *Fox* arrived at the mouth of the Rufiji, bearing its precious cargo, and Lieutenant Cutler and mechanic Gallehawk derisively threw out the old Curtiss radiator and hooked up their new Ford radiator to the airplane. The engine was started, it ran, and for the first time in months the plane's engine did not begin to overheat after five minutes of operation.

At about the time that *Fox* came on her missionary errand, the armed tugs *Adjutant* and *Helmuth* arrived also, bearing sweeping devices, and busied themselves by sweeping the channel around the sunken *Newbridge* for imaginary mines. (*Helmuth* had been refloated and repaired.) From the shore Commander Schoenfeld and his Delta Force regarded these proceedings with more concern than amusement, and the commander reported daily to Captain Looff. It appeared that the coming of the airplane had triggered an entirely new strategy: perhaps the British were making ready to send a warship up the river. So much the better; *Königsberg* was ready for a fight.

Of course it was not to be so simple; Captain Looff was itching for action but the British had no plans to send one of their light cruisers alone up that river, and although the captain was afraid that his secrets had been discovered, they had not, and Captain Drury-Lowe regarded the Rufiji still as all but impassable.

On 22nd November, Lieutenant Cutler made his second flight, a very successful one: he flew over the *Königsberg* and observed the fact that it had moved two miles upriver from the position which the fleet believed her to occupy. That much was success; then came failure. On landing Lieutenant Cutler crashed and although he was not hurt, the nacelle of the airplane was completely destroyed.

Fortunately for the British another airplane was available, another Curtiss hydroplane in Durban, and the *Kinfauns Castle* was dispatched to pick it up and bring it back to the Rufiji. The cargo ship went and was back in a few days. The new airplane was tested and found to be capable of carrying two persons, so Lieutenant Cutler took up a series of naval officers on flights over the *Königsberg*. Captain Denis Crampton was the first and he was followed by Commander Fitzmaurice of the *Chatham*. Captain Looff began to be quite disturbed by the constant flow of unwanted visitors who came and went above him. He moved further up the river, but the next day the airplane was back and his new position was known. Captain Looff now saw one of the dangers to the *Königsberg* – his power of secret movement was lost. The British saw it too, and realised that the airplane was their eyes and that they must have their airplane to fight the *Königsberg* and prevent her escape from them.

After a few days, the *new* airplane (which was not new at all) was so worn with its efforts that it could carry only the pilot, as had Cuckoo No. 1, and so on 10th December Lieutenant Cutler went up alone to observe the *Königsberg*. It was a bright, sunny day so all concerned, Germans and Englishmen, could see as the airplane seemed to flutter over the *Königsberg* and its engine began missing just as it reached the area of the cruiser. Lieutenant Cutler turned around and began making for the delta, but he could not fly the distance back to the Simba-Ouranga entrance, so he flew the shorter path to the Kikouya entrance. Cadet Gallehawk boarded the armed tug *Helmuth* and sped for the spot where the plane was seen to go down behind the trees, and in an hour he was there, and found the airplane, deep in the water but not sunk. He supervised the rescue of the airplane, but of the pilot there was no trace.

What had happened, of course, was that when Captain Looff put his small guns ashore, he created a tiny anti-aircraft battery along the banks of the river, and one of the guns firing at the airplane as it came over had been lucky enough to hit the craft, disabling it. Lieutenant Cutler had managed to crash land in the mouth of the river, and had swum ashore, straight into the arms of Commander Schœnfeld's Delta Force. He was made a prisoner and taken back to the Delta camp. So that was the end of the airplane – or, one might say, the first one and a half airplanes.

10
The Tale of the *Hilfschiff* – I

THE DEFEAT OF the British landing force at Tanga and the continued survival of *Königsberg* in the jungled delta of the Rufiji were sources of considerable embarrassment to the British in the autumn of 1914 and pressure was brought on Admiral King-Hall to tidy up matters by securing the surrender of the colony and the destruction of the cruiser. The British really believed they had already secured the surrender of the colony anyhow, because of the agreements made with Governor Schnee; they could not understand that Lieutenant Colonel von Lettow-Vorbeck simply had repudiated the whole idea of surrender and seized supreme military power to carry on the fight against the British.

To put an end to the resistance, on 28th November, Admiral King-Hall in the old battleship *Goliath* and the cruiser *Fox* arrived off Dar es Salaam harbour, accompanied by the armed tugs *Helmuth* and *Adjutant*, both of which had been German ships before they were seized by the British at the beginning of the war. Under the agreement signed with Governor Schnee, the British were to have the right to send a boat into harbour from time to time to check on the activities of the German ships there. The object, of course, was to be sure that the German merchant ships were not being used to harbour enemies of Britain, and specifically that nothing was being done to bring supplies to the *Königsberg*. But an agreement to bring in one boat occasionally, and a descent by an admiral in his flagship and three other naval vessels were two different matters, and von Lettow-Vorbeck took this occasion to declare that the British had violated the agreement. Of course von Lettow-Vorbeck had no use for the agreement anyhow and had been busily engaged in ignoring it and doing whatever possible to fight the British all the while.

Instead of sending one armed pinnace into Dar es Salaam harbour that day, as the agreement stipulated, the British sent in three armed pinnaces, and they approached the German East Africa Line steamers *Feldmarschall* and *König* under their flag of truce. The British were certain that these ships had been giving aid and comfort to the *Königsberg*, and they blew up the engines and took off a number of members of the ship's crews – while other crewmen fled ashore to avoid capture. On their way back through the narrow mouth of the harbour, the British pinnaces passed under German defence installations, and Captain von Kornatzky and the defenders were so angered by the kidnapping of their friends that they opened fire on the pinnaces. Seeing this, the two cruisers in the harbour began firing on Dar es Salaam, and the defenders on shore redoubled their efforts to destroy the armed pinnaces.

The shooting began at 1.30 in the afternoon and lasted until five o'clock, with the *Goliath* throwing some two hundred of her huge 305-mm shells into the town and on to the ships anchored in the harbour. The *Feldmarschall* and the *König* both were badly damaged, although neither ship was sunk, and the town was very badly hit.

Dar es Salaam had not seen the end of the British; they returned two days later, again apparently to talk under a flag of truce, but the Germans were no longer having any and did not send boats out to the warships, which lay again just outside the harbour. So the British again bombarded the town, throwing in three hundred big shells, and at the end of the day one might say that for the first time Dar es Salaam joined the rest of German East Africa in the war. One had only to look at the gutted casino, the ruined bank, the smashed brewery, blasted soda water works and the shell-riddled governor's palace to realise that the British had done exactly what Lieutenant Colonel von Lettow-

Vorbeck might have wanted them to do: they had united German East Africa in the war effort, and even Governor Schnee no longer talked about peace.

In the Rufiji, where Admiral King-Hall repaired next, the British operations had become stalled with the destruction of the Curtiss hydroplanes and the capture of Lieutenant Cutler by the Germans. On his arrival at the delta this time, the Admiral made certain representations to London, and soon Whitehall decided to send out a squadron of hydroplanes, two officers of the royal marines, and eighteen men, but only two airplanes made by the Sopwith aviation manufacturing company. These planes were more modern craft than the Curtiss hydroplanes. The new aircraft boasted 100-horsepower Gnome engines, and the Admiralty had expressed great hopes for their immediate success. But, of course, it would take time for the planes to be shipped to the Rufiji, and so the final battle with *Königsberg* must wait a little longer.

In the absence of his airplanes – any airplanes – Captain Drury-Lowe began to grow worried about the *Königsberg*. Was she, at the moment he thought of her, getting up steam and planning a breakthrough to the sea? There was no direct way for the British commander to discover Captain Looff's plans, but he could gain an idea of them by a simple stratagem, and he decided to attempt it: two days before Christmas Captain Drury-Lowe sent the shallow-draught vessels *Duplex* and *Adjutant* into the Simba-Ouranga branch of the Rufiji, with orders to move upstream as far as they could go and spy on the *Königsberg* if possible. The moment the British ships entered the channel and passed the wreck of *Newbridge* at the bar, the two craft came under a hail of fire from both shores, and as they moved upstream the fire did not diminish. The rain of shells came from 36-mm and 47-mm guns, of the type that the *Königsberg* was known to possess. The British turned after a few minutes and came out again; they had discovered what Captain Drury-Lowe wanted to know: the small field pieces were still in position on the river bank, which indicated that in all likelihood *Königsberg* was not preparing to depart, for it was expected she would gather up her armament and restore it to the ship before trying to break the blockade.

Two days after the reconnaissance mission it was Christmas, 1914 – a day just about like any other day in the Rufiji Delta. On the *Königsberg* there were schnapps and beer for the men and wine with dinner for the officers and a football game on the playing field the men had constructed on the bank near the ship; yet it was a sad holiday by and large, for a good percentage of the *Königsberg* crew was in sick bay, mostly down with malaria. The long embattlement was wearing on the crew of *Königsberg* – the doctors were running short of quinine and other medicines; probably every man on the ship had been infected by the anopheles mosquito and, as the men's resistance lowered with continued poor food and debilitation from jungle life, more and more men fell actually ill with ague and fever.

The British, standing offshore in the sea breeze, had a much better time of it all around. On Christmas their spirits were unusually high, and the officers of *Fox* sent a message to *Konny*, as they called her:

'We wish you a Happy Christmas and a Happy New Year; we hope to see you soon.'

Aboard *Königsberg*, Captain Looff's sense of humour was touched by this gay greeting and he sent back a reply in kind:

'*Danke, das gleiche wunche ich Ihnen; wenn Sie mich zum sehen wunschen, ich bin stets zu Hause.* (Thanks, same to you; if you wish to see me, I am always at home.)'

Ashore, at New Moshi on the Northern Railway, the spirits of the Germans of East Africa were much higher, and with good reason, than those of the men of *Königsberg*. The military men had been winning victories in the Kilimanjaro area while the naval arm was stalemated, there was no problem about food ashore, there were plenty of vegetables, the army bought cattle from the Masai, and on

Sundays Lieutenant Colonel von Lettow-Vorbeck and his officers went out game-hunting from the headquarters at New Moshi. So far as central operations were concerned, it was a very quiet period, with the British scarcely stirring, except on the fringes of the colony, and Christmas at von Lettow-Vorbeck's headquarters was a solemn affair, celebrated at the mission church at New Moshi, and then a very gay affair, celebrated at the officers' mess in the railway station. Captain Zimmer of the *Möwe* spent Christmas in his mess at Kigoma on Lake Tanganyika, where he had established headquarters to supervise operations, since they would conduct largely naval operations on the lake. The Belgians had some two thousand troops on their side of the Belgian Congo border, and activity there had to be watched until the Germans were strong enough to deal with it, but of course, not at Christmas. Among other things, Captain Zimmer was supervising the construction of a big lake steamer, the *Graf Götzen*, which would augment his naval force (*Hewig von Wissman*) on the lake. Christmas over, the war began once again. Lake Victoria Nyanza was firmly in the hands of the British, as everyone expected, for the lake was largely in British territory, and the British maintained seven armed lake steamers on the water, but the Germans had their own armed steamer, *Muansa*, and at this holiday time she had freedom of movement, and was helping to guard the southern shores of the lake, in German territory, from British attack. In October, the Germans had tried to send an expeditionary force by water from Muansa to Bukoba on the western shore, and *Muansa* led two armed tugs and ten dhows, but the force was quickly scattered by enemy steamers and the attempt failed.

North of Lake Tanganyika lay little Lake Kivu on the border with the Congo, and here Lieutenant Wunderlich of the *Möwe* had gone to take charge of defence, his flagship a motor boat requisitioned from the civilians. Lieutenant Wunderlich and his men fought several skirmishes at Kissenyi with Belgian and British troops, and drove them back each time. Between the two lakes was the region called the Russissi country, after the river that connected the lakes, and here, too, the Germans fought skirmishes; four field companies, part of the crew of the *Möwe*, successfully engaged superior forces of Belgians and Askaris over several weeks.

But it was Captain Zimmer on Lake Tanganyika whose defence force was the key to German stability in the west, Captain Zimmer, with about one hundred men from the *Möwe*, a handful of civilians, and about three hundred Askaris to defend the long coastline of the lake. Soon, although he was still only a Korvettenkapitän or lieutenant commander, Zimmer was actually an admiral of an inland fleet: there was the *Hedwig von Wissman*, the big *Graf Götzen* being built, and the small steamer *Kingani* brought up by rail from Dar es Salaam, armed and joined to the flotilla. Admiral Zimmer also built at Kigoma a large sturdy raft, mounted a 3.5-inch naval gun on it (because none of his ships could stand the recoil of so large a gun), and used the floating artillery to harry the Belgians across the lake with bombardment all during the autumn of 1914. Compared to the war raging in Europe these operations in Africa were infinitesimal, and yet some of these battles involved two or three thousand men, each side fighting for king and country. Some skirmishes were won by British and Belgian troops, but more by the Germans, and by the end of the year the German boundaries were largely intact, and they had pushed a small invasion force into the southern portion of British East Africa.

At the end of 1914 the British high command examined affairs in East Africa and the admirals and generals were not pleased with what was found to be happening there. They sent orders to Admiral King-Hall to step up his blockade of the Rufiji and extend it to the entire coast of German East Africa. To the English one of the troublesome points on the coast was the big island of Mafia, held by Lieutenant Schiller, two German sailors, and twenty Askaris. On 10th January, 1915, the British landed six companies of Indian and African troops on Mafia, under a barrage laid down by

Chatham, Fox, Kinfauns Castle, and *Adjutant.* Lieutenant Schiller fought back with his twenty-two men; finally reduced to a sniping operation from a grove of palm trees in the centre of the island, he was forced to surrender when he was severely wounded. The British took over Mafia, destroyed the communications tower there by which Lieutenant Schiller had kept *Königsberg* informed of comings and goings south of the delta, and occupied a little harbour on the northwest side of the island for the anchorage of the new air fleet and its mother ship.

Constantly, the British now were changing the guard outside the Rufiji, eager to make use of their newer warships elsewhere, and after the beginning of 1915 Captain Drury-Lowe and *Chatham* were released from responsibility for the destruction of the *Königsberg* and sent to India. Spurred by pressure from London, the Admiral took charge himself; those messages from London were growing stronger every week.

On the bright, sunny morning of 6th February, *Adjutant* was sent up river on an exploration trip to see what she could discover as to the whereabouts and condition of *Königsberg* once again. She steamed up the Simba-Ouranga branch, past *Newbridge,* and into the expected hail of fire from the Germans on the two sides of the river, Germans led by Oberleutnant Herm of the Delta Force. A lucky shot from either the 60-mm gun or one of the two 37-mm guns struck *Adjutant* below the water line, breaking her steering connection, and she went aground, where she was at the mercy of the Germans firing from both sides with field guns and machine guns and rifles. The Germans redoubled their fire, the English return was slight, and in an hour down came the British flag and up went a white flag – *Adjutant* was surrendering!

One officer, twenty-one British seamen, and two Africans – not a soul wounded – put up their hands as the party from shore came aboard and took possession of the little ship. The *Adjutant*'s three 47-mm guns and two machine guns, along with a large quantity of ammunition, were quickly dismounted and taken ashore to add to the coastal defences of the Delta Force. Then the damage wrought by several hundred shells fired at the tug was repaired, the hole below the water line was stuffed up, and *Adjutant* was taken triumphantly up river to anchor alongside *Königsberg*. Lieutenant Price, the commander of the *Adjutant*, railed bitterly against his crew. He told the Germans his men had lain down on the deck at the first shot from shore, and had shown utter cowardice throughout the engagement; they had run up the white flag without really fighting.

This small victory in the Rufiji did more than a carload of cigarettes to raise the morale of the German forces fighting the boring, debilitating war of the delta; particularly the abject surrender of the cowardly crew indicated to the Germans the unwillingness of the average British seaman to fight for his country, and they translated that hope into belief that Germany soon would win the war. Captain Looff made much of the cowardice and took steps to see that every man of *Königsberg*'s crew knew of it.

The British retaliated petulantly to the capture of *Adjutant* (or so it seemed) by declaring a blockade of the entire German East African coast. Of course the blockade had nothing to do with petulance or the capture of the *Adjutant*: it was very much a part of overall British strategy in these waters. The Admiralty had begun to realise that *Königsberg*'s problem was a shortage of supplies and London was determined that the German ship should not have any supplies; yet the admirals in Whitehall realised that every day that went by increased the danger that somehow German supply vessels would reach the little cruiser and then she might somehow slip past their blocking force and out to sea, to wreak havoc on the shipping in Africa, Asia, or even Atlantic waters.

By 1st March off the Rufiji, then, came new British forces. On that day at anchor lay the cruisers *Weymouth* and *Hyacinth*, the New Zealand cruiser *Pyramus*, the Australian cruiser *Pioneer*, the auxiliary *Kinfauns Castle*, four converted whaling craft of 160 to 180 tons, armed with two three-pounders each, and the auxiliary ship *Duplex*, plus the promised new squadron of hydroplanes brought from Bombay by the *Kinfauns Castle*. On 7th March, Vice Admiral King-Hall came up to the delta in his flagship *Goliath* to supervise what he hoped would be the destruction of *Königsberg*. Perhaps she could be bombed to death by the new airplanes. Perhaps the British could direct fire from the 155-mm guns of *Goliath* and these could sink the German ship. Admiral King-Hall rather had the idea that Captain Looff would choose to come out on the high tide of the equinox and he wanted to be ready to intercept her.

This year the demands of the war elsewhere were felt by the British for the first time since Admiral King-Hall's squadron had been stripped to catch the *Graf Spee* at the Falklands. Captain Looff did not know it, but his lot in the spring of 1915 was made somewhat easier by the demands of the Turkish war in the Middle East; a plan had been afoot to land two thousand marines in the delta and move against the *Königsberg* by land, but this plan was abandoned in the need for British troops in the Dardanelles, and, further, Admiral King-Hall was asked to shift his flag back to *Hyacinth* so *Goliath* could be sent for duty in Turkish waters as well.

Early in March Radio Officer Niemyer had been pleased to report to Captain Looff that *Königsberg* was being called up by the Admiralty for the first time in many months. The word came from Radio Station Windhuk on the western coast of Africa, the first official word to reach the cruiser since 1st August, and it was news that a *Hilfschiff*, a help-ship, or supply ship, was being sent out directly from the homeland for the succour of *Königsberg*. The *Hilfschiff* would be arriving off the East African coast around 1st April, and Captain Looff was to set up a rendezvous with her.

Captain Looff was concerned: the German radio stations on the east coast of Africa had been silenced, and so it would be a ticklish job to be in touch with the *Hilfschiff* without arousing the suspicions of his enemies, yet it must

111

be done. How? The answer was to send out a confusing group of messages, apparently aimed at ships all over the map, and within the barrage to have a very slight traffic with the ship that was actually coming to East Africa.

This ship was known in Admiralty parlance as *Sperrbrecher A* – Blockade Runner A – but she had two names as well. She was actually the British merchantman *Rubens*, a 6000-ton freighter in the channel trade between Germany and England, which had been unfortunate enough to be caught by the Germans in harbour at Hamburg by the outbreak of war. But for the purposes of this trip she was known as the Danish freighter *Kronborg*.

Captain of this ship was tall, fair-faced Leutnant zur See de Reserve Carl Christiansen, a daring and able seaman who had been chosen by the Admiralty to follow in the footsteps of such successful captains as the Graf Nicholas zu Dohna-Schlodien, the eminently successful commander of the raider named *Möwe* for the gallant ship destroyed in Dar es Salaam harbour. The Germans had proved they could run the blockade of the German coast, and they now had further decided that it would be possible to send supplies to the beleaguered Captain Looff by following the same pattern.

Sperrbrecher A was loaded with sixteen hundred tons of Westphalian coal for *Königsberg* and twelve hundred tons of coal for her own use. She was fitted with special tanks to carry seven hundred tons of fresh water for *Königsberg*, she had a thousand rounds of ammunition for the 105-mm guns, and many thousands of rounds for the 37-mm guns, machine guns, and rifles; she carried machine tools and parts, fresh and canned provisions, canteen supplies, two new 60-mm guns with a supply of ammunition for them, an oxy-acetylene cutting torch and its equipment, and clothing for the sailors. She also carried eighteen hundred rifles of the new Model 98, six machine guns, and about three million rounds of ammunition, provisions, clothing, and medical supplies for the land forces of German East Africa.

On 17th February, Captain Christiansen was called to

Berlin for last-minute instructions and, as much as anything else, a pep talk to leave no doubt in his mind about the importance of his mission. He took the fast train down to Wilhelmshaven that night and the next morning set out to sea in the usual sticky weather of the North Sea in winter – wet and choppy with a dark grey sky and a strong wind blowing from the west. He headed north and for the Sognefjord, and when out of German waters he stopped and the name *Kronborg* was painted on the bare stern. The christening had been delayed until they were out of sight of land so that British spies could not note her name and inform the enemy that *Kronborg* had sailed from a German harbour. Her documentation was pristine; she was a neutral, sailing between Denmark and the La Plata. Only if a boarding officer began poking around in her holds and her deck load would anything suspicious be seen – and as long as the searchers stayed away from the bundles of German military clothing and the actual guns and ammunition the ship still might get by.

Once the ship had her name and jaunty Danish character, Captain Christiansen (a very Danish type himself) set a course for the northwest and followed it into heavy, sloppy weather that became more evil every day, so foul that he lost a part of his deckload and had to turn south before he wished to do so; in order to save his ship he was running in far closer to British waters than he wished. On the night of 23rd–24th February he ran the blockade line of the Shetland Islands, the very evil of the weather working for him that night. Heavy seas broke completely over the decks, and visibility was reduced to a few feet ahead of the ship, which worked as much against the blockaders as it did for Captain Christiansen. In the North Atlantic the weather was worse if anything, much wetter, but at least he soon had a following sea, *Kronborg* was making thirteen knots, and there were no British in sight. On 6th March the blockade runner reached the Cape Verde Islands and, one might say, the blockade was then well run. *Kronborg* stayed a hundred miles off the normal Cape Verde-Cape of Good

Hope sea-lane, and no one bothered her, although a steamer from Mombasa addressed her and accepted the word that she was what she said she was.

So all went well until the blockade runner passed the Cape of Good Hope and came up north in the gradually warming waters of the Indian Ocean. Her passage north through the Mozambique Channel was uninterrupted, although she did not come within less than half a mile of a 10,000-ton ship one night. Captain Christiansen was certain the ship was a British auxiliary cruiser; fortunately the blockade runner was travelling without lights and slowly enough that the bow wave and wake were unobserved by the other. Yet although the captain and crew of the German ship were unaware, the enemy was beginning to close a ring around them; whether or not they would be able to escape the ring would depend on the speed with which they acted. Coming from so far to Africa, the blockade runner now needed specific instructions from higher authority, and this could only mean the *Königsberg*, since all German land radio stations on the coast were out of service. *Kronborg* had two tasks: to deliver her supplies to the land forces fighting on the German West African hinterland and to deliver to *Königsberg* the coal and munitions and then become its supply ship.

As he came north through the Mozambique Channel, Captain Christiansen ordered his radio man to break silence and make contact with *Königsberg*. It was risky, even using code, for coded or not, the transmissions could be recognised as German, and they were recognised by a French radio station on Madagascar. The information was quickly transmitted to Admiral King-Hall in the Rufiji region. The intelligence problem here was absurdly simple: *Königsberg* was still in the Rufiji River, and here came German transmissions from somewhere in the Mozambique Channel; it did not take much deduction for the British to realise that someone was coming to make contact with *Königsberg*, and the precautions of the blockaders were increased and in the next few days increased again as the transmissions

114

moved northward and gained in intensity. Admiral King-Hall was an intelligent man, and he came to the conclusion that a supply ship coming to East Africa soon would discover that it could not move into the Rufiji. Where would it head then? That was to be determined.

In the course of the communications between *Königsberg* and the *Hilfschiff,* Captain Looff made it clear that the cruiser was still in the Rufiji River. The news disturbed Captain Christiansen for he had hoped that by the time he arrived in African waters *Königsberg* would have broken out and made her way into the high seas. If Christiansen must wait in this dangerous area, his chances of ever getting home again or of completing his mission were very slim indeed. Already he had problems: the blockade runner's bunkers were nearly empty and she must stop somewhere and shift her coal supply so she could make use of her reserves. Also, it was clear that the supplies for *Königsberg* and those for the land forces of Lieutenant Colonel von Lettow-Vorbeck must be carefully separated, and the blockade runner must be able to deliver to either party on short notice.

Kronborg passed the Cormoran Islands on the night of 7th April and Captain Christiansen began looking for a deserted atoll where he might put in, where his engineering officers might prepare for the sudden dash into the blockade region by cleaning their boilers and making all possible adjustments to the engines to guard against failure. The Admiralty had prepared well. On board the blockade runner was an experienced pilot named Abels, an old hand in East African waters who until war came had been an officer on the *Somali.* Abels suggested that most deserted of island groups, the Aldabra Islands where *Königsberg* had coaled from *Somali,* and Captain Christiansen headed for this group. On the night of 9th April the ship moved up next to the shore of the southernmost island of the group, with the intention of sounding the channel that broke the coral reef around the islands and going inside. As the ship anchored near the shore, outside the breaker line, Captain

115

Christiansen saw a small boat put out from shore, and soon alongside came a man in a shirt, trousers, and a straw hat – obviously the 'king of the island'. The civilian came on board and Captain Christiansen gave him the prepared information about the nature and business of the ship, which the straw-hatted one accepted without question. The man was a mulatto in charge of tortoise hunting for a French company; he employed a hundred native divers and turned his shell in to the French representatives who came visiting by sailboat twice a year. The boat had just left the island two weeks before, Captain Christiansen was pleased to learn, and there would be no other for six months. Captain and crew christened the man Robinson, because his style of life was so much like that of Robinson Crusoe (and so was his hat), and they asked him to guide the ship into the channel. Robinson was aghast: so big a ship could not possibly go through the channel into the lagoon, he said, and he refused to become a party to their destruction. But pilot Abels said the ship could go through, and so a boat was put over the side, the channel was sounded carefully, and at high water the *Kronborg* steamed into the lagoon to anchor in fifteen fathoms of water so clear and blue that the anchor could be seen next morning on the bottom.

For two days Captain Christiansen and his men worked to shift cargo and bring enough coal into the ship's bunkers so that she would be protected against a sudden stoppage even if she must travel for several days at top speed.

Aboard the *Königsberg*, the simple fact that a *Hilfschiff* was on its way spread through the messes, and morale took a sudden spurt upward. On the one hand Captain Looff would have liked to make a sudden dash for freedom and join the supply ship, but before he could move or jeopardise the ship and its precious cargo, another mission must be performed: the supplies must be delivered to the land forces of Lieutenant Colonel von Lettow-Vorbeck. The supplies of the land force were running dangerously low; they had only one hundred and fifty cartridges per man and fewer than ten thousand for the machine guns.

116

Captain Looff held a council of war with his senior officers and developed a plan of action. All during March Radio Officer Niemyer had been sending out, for several hours each day, long messages which contained imaginary news and facts and figures. The British receivers in the area picked up these messages and sent them to London for decoding, with the hope that the Admiralty would be able to make sense of them. Only a few times, then, in April, did Captain Looff include messages for the *Kronborg*, and so far as he knew they were not detected by the enemy for what they were. Now, on 11th April, Captain Looff revealed his plan, and a final message was sent to *Kronborg*, to be picked up where she lay in the lagoon among the Aldabra Islands.

Kronborg was to steam to Tanga in the northeast part of the colony, where the railway connected with Lieutenant Colonel von Lettow-Vorbeck's headquarters at New Moshi. The supply ship was to unload all she had brought for the land forces, and then prepare to sail again. In the meantime, *Königsberg* would try to break through into the Indian Ocean, steam south along the African coast, and join the supply ship at a rendezvous to be indicated later.

The supply ship received the message, concealed as usual in a long string of statistics sent out from *Königsberg*, and Captain Christiansen's engineer made his final preparations. The water cooling system was inspected for flaws; every bearing was oiled and the firemen were ordered to stand by with oil cans to watch each moving part; the safety valves on the boilers were tied down, so that in case of need the ship could have all the extra speed her system would take; and *Kronborg* raised her anchor and set out on the evening tide for sea, leaving behind a Mr Robinson who knew no more about the ship than he had known when she anchored and who thus could say nothing of importance to the British auxiliary cruiser that stopped in the next day to investigate radio transmissions from that area.

According to her orders, *Kronborg* steamed north to pass by Britain's Pemba Island and then turned south to enter the Pemba Channel that carried ships safely through the treacherous reefs off the East African coast. On the night of 13th April, *Kronborg* was fifty miles off the north point of Pemba; she turned south and entered the Kilulu Channel, a very narrow waterway known only to the coastal pilots, but she had a coastal pilot aboard in Abels, so all was well. That night she passed very near *Duplex*, which was out hunting, but apparently the British ship did not see the blockade runner.

By dawn on the morning of 14th April, the blockade runner was in sight of her goal; she stood off Manza Bay in which Tanga lay, just two miles north of the entrance, and was waiting for a pilot boat to come out. Suddenly her masthead lookout shouted a warning that coming up fast from the south was a column of smoke; at first Captain Christiansen thought it might be a British auxiliary, but then the lookout reported three smokestacks and a heavy bow wave and the captain knew he faced a British cruiser.

11
The Tale of the *Hilfschiff* – II

THERE WAS NO time early on that morning of 14th April 1915 for Captain Carl Christiansen to muse over reasons as the British cruiser came rushing down on his ship, but the fact was that he was the victim of technology and British ingenuity, for Admiral King-Hall in the *Hyacinth* knew exactly what Christiansen was doing, where he was going, and when he would get there; the British in London had broken the *Königsberg's* naval code and had been a party to the intership conversations between the German cruiser and the *Hilfschiff* all the while.

On the night of 13th April the Admiral had brought *Hyacinth* very close to the entrance to Manza Bay, knowing that *Krongborg* would try to slip into the bay just after dawn, and when dawn blinked, the British were ready to speed in and snatch their victim before the supply ship could escape to the protection of the harbour.

Captain Christiansen looked inshore, and there could see the pilot boat heading out towards his ship, carrying the pilot and harbourmaster to bring him in to Tanga through the narrow channel to the southwest. To the northwest, separated by a point of land from Tanga harbour and by a long spit from the sea, lay Manza Bay proper, a narrow inlet that led to a small anchorage bounded by a sandy beach on the south and a mangrove swamp on the north. With the warship bearing down on him the captain saw that he had only two choices: he could stop, pick up the pilot and go into Tanga harbour, hoping that the harbour was protected by mines and that the British would not follow him in, or he could go into Manza Bay with the assurance that the British ship could not follow him all the way because the warship drew too much water. A look at the smoke cloud coming towards him convinced the captain that the first choice would leave him open to destruction from the warship's guns before he could make the harbour, so he called for full speed ahead and dashed northward, away from the pilot boat, into the bay.

Up came *Hyacinth*, boiling along, and then suddenly, she slowed: her starboard engine seized up, and she could proceed at no better than half speed to chase the German blockade runner. (Had Captain Christiansen known this just before he turned into Manza Bay he might have sped away from land and escaped the cruiser altogether.) At the entrance to the bay, then, the cruiser hesitated, then moved north, on the outside of the spit, where she could be seen by the men of the blockade runner, her masts projecting above the trees.

Captain Christiansen moved inshore as rapidly as possible. From the beach came an outrigger canoe with a white man paddled by several blacks, a man in the khaki of the German Protective Force.

Obviously the man in the canoe could not see the cruiser and did not know what all the excitement was about. He gestured repeatedly for the ship to stop and take him aboard, but *Kronborg* swept past, her bow wave nearly swamping the canoe, and all the captain could hear of the man's words were a few words of warning about 'machine guns overlooking the channel'.

In a few minutes the *Kronborg* approached the north end of the bay, and the anchorage where Captain Christiansen knew that at low water he would have one yard of water under the keel. The engines were stopped, the anchor was heaved and the chain was running out, as Captain Christiansen stepped down from his bridge to go to the radio room and send a message to *Königsberg*. Just then the first shells from *Hyacinth* whined overhead. The first salvo missed *Kronborg* by seventy-five yards, but the second salvo was nearly on target, and the captain was sure *Hyacinth* would soon begin scoring hits.

Captain Christiansen's first thought was that here they were, having come thirteen thousand miles from Germany, having reached the haven of German East African waters, and now they were to be blown out of the harbour at the end of the journey before delivering their goods – for he could hardly see how the shells could fail to explode the hundred tons of high explosives lodged on the afterdeck as part of the deck cargo.

The first shells to strike the ship came with the second salvo, a smashing blow in the bow, and one that struck the starboard plating, plunged through the hull and started a fire in the coal bunkers, threatening the munitions which were stored aft in the deck just above the coal. The smoke began to rise above the ship, and it was apparent to all the world that *Kronborg* was burning.

Captain Christiansen's thought now was to save the munitions from explosion. To do this he must put out the fires below, so he ordered the bottom ventilators and the sea cocks opened and all the black gang to come on deck.

With cocks and ventilators open the water came pouring into the engine room and in a few minutes the fire was cut off so that it could not rise to the munitions storage area; they would have to take the chance that the high explosives could be salvaged, but there was at least hope that the ship would not blow sky-high. But the coal still burned, the engine room had been turned into a great furnace by the explosion of another 150-mm high-explosive shell there and smoke was pouring upwards from the centre hatch; shells were exploding on deck, too, and many men were wounded, although none seriously.

'*Alle mann aus dem Schiff*,' ordered Captain Christiansen – 'All men off the ship' – and two boats were swung over the side. Captain Christiansen stepped down from his bridge to his cabin for a moment to pick up some papers and his revolver, since he was going ashore into unknown territory; a shell hit the cabin and destroyed everything,

every paper, every belonging, yet left him completely un-
scathed. He went back on deck, where the first movement
that caught his eye was the wagging of his hound's tail.
The dog was whining quietly, waiting for his master to
appear. Crew, dog, and captain soon were in the boats,
heading for the shore, when the shelling suddenly stopped.
The captain ordered his boat turned back towards the ship,
hoping that *Hyacinth*, which he had recognised, had gone
away and that he could put out the fires and save the cargo
he had come so far to deliver.

Then, as the boat turned, one crewman hailed out:
'*Feindlicher Kreuzer erscheint in der Buchteinfahrt.*'

The enemy cruiser had appeared in the entrance to the
bay.

She came steaming in slowly, guns spitting from both
sides. Her starboard guns were brought to bear on the ship,
firing high-explosive shells into the poor old *Kronborg*; her
port guns fired high explosive and shrapnel at the two boats
and the landing beach, so that the German boats bore away
and headed for the safety of the mangrove swamp, which
was farther from the enemy. The first boat landed, the men
tumbled ashore, and luckily too, for a second later a shell
landed squarely in the boat and blew it to pieces so small
they could not even be recognised. The second boat came in
five minutes later, and the men also rushed ashore, into
the slippery mixture of mangroves, mud, and cutting marsh
grass. It was good that they ran so quickly, because the
Hyacinth set up a heavy bombardment of the shore from
their landing place to the beach on the other side of the
bay.

Soon the crew had far outrun the captain, and he and
four men were left behind; he could hear the shelling, it
seemed to be heavier ahead of him, and he worried lest his
crew had gone into the open to be decimated. The shelling
of the ship continued. From time to time he could hear
explosions, which indicated that some of the high explosives
on the rear deck was going up. He could not see the bay as
he stumbled along inland and did not know how the poor

ship was faring, except that he could hear the constant booming of shells from the cruiser as they flew on their missions of death.

Suddenly, just ahead of him in the swamp, there was a sharp explosion, and he felt a pain in his right leg. He looked down, and saw his leg bleeding, then he collapsed, unconscious.

When Captain Christiansen regained consciousness, he was propped up against a palm tree on a little knoll overlooking the bay, but sheltered in a grove, and his four men were sitting and squatting awkwardly around him, waiting for him to awaken. They had bound up his wound, they said, but he must be quiet because he had lost a great deal of blood. His men made a litter of palm fronds and belts for him and began carrying him towards the beach area, for behind the beach as the ship came in they had seen a cluster of thatched huts that indicated some people must live there. As they went along, however, the men soon were overtaken by a detachment of the Protective Force, huge Askaris in khaki shirts, shorts, and great red tarbooshes on which were affixed the arms of the German Empire. The Askaris and their officer, Lieutenant Kempner, former secretary of state of the colony, were part of Captain Baumstark's Tanga defence force, stationed here to prevent British landings in the bay.

It was nearly eleven o'clock, the sun was high in the sky, and the temperature was rising. The men from the ship, unused to the African heat, were feeling it and soon they were wrapping rags and shirts around their heads to keep the sun away. Captain Christiansen had kept his boat whistle with him, and from time to time he sounded it as a signal to his crew, hoping thus to round them up. Finally when he reached another knoll above the bay, he saw the crew – all the rest of them – waiting there for him. Not a man was lost!

At noon the British still were shelling the *Kronborg*; from their vantage point behind the bay the survivors could see the ship's upper works rising above a cloud of black and grey smoke which indicated she still was burning. Captain Christiansen could also see that half her funnel had been shot away, she was low in the water because she had been scuttled, and she looked every bit a wreck. The British apparently thought so too because suddenly they stopped shelling the ship. Two boats were put out from the *Hyacinth* – the British were going to board, investigate, and probably destroy the cargo of the *Kronborg*.

Captain Christiansen watched in anguish as the boats moved toward his battered ship, but suddenly his mood changed, for from the shore on both sides of the bay the boats were raked by machine gun fire. *Hyacinth* could not stand in closer, but she unlimbered her guns against the machine gun installations, trying to knock them out. The Germans were too well protected, or at least the ship's guns could not find them, and after the boats had suffered a number of casualties from the machine gun fire, they were recalled and the effort to board *Kronborg* was abandoned. The cruiser shipped her boats, turned, and steamed out of the harbour and away.

12

The War of Nerves

EVEN WHILE *Hyacinth* was away from station on the Rufiji
River Delta bombarding *Kronborg* in Manza Bay, and the
Germans on the *Königsberg* had no direct knowledge of
these events, Captain Looff knew that something was afoot,
for while the British outside could not see what *Königsberg*
was doing unless they had an airplane to aid their vision,
Max Looff's eyes were the coast watchers and defenders on
every finger of the delta, who crept high in the palm trees
and swept the waters outside with their high-powered
glasses, then reported back by telegraph, signal flag, and
runner to the German captain on the movements of his
enemies. On 13th and 14th April as Captain Looff made
preparations to go to sea, he knew that something was
amiss because more British ships than ever were concentrated outside his delta, and their nervousness indicated
that they were expecting some movement on his part.

So instead of moving, Captain Looff sat and waited for
word from his supply ship.

No word came.

Hyacinth returned, however, and again began prowling
back and forth outside the delta, and soon Captain Looff
knew that his *Hilfschiff* had fallen into evil. He suspected
the truth – that the British had broken the naval code and
that they were reading his messages in London – but he
did not know, so he determined to find out. On 15th April,
Captain Looff prepared a special message in code for an
imaginary second *Hilfschiff*, reporting that the *Kronborg* had
been sunk, that its cargo was completely destroyed, and

that the Germans had sowed mines in Manza Bay, so the second ship was to avoid that harbour and come in at a point much farther south. He set a Sunday evening for the landing. Sure enough, on Sunday evening, his shore watchers reported, Admiral King-Hall and *Hyacinth* showed up at the appointed spot, and waited, and waited, and waited. . . .

Captain Looff then sent runners to Tanga, with orders that the troops were to spot a number of petrol drums in Manza Bay. Admiral King-Hall soon learned of the presence of the 'mines' in the bay, and made no attempt to return and investigate the condition of the *Kronborg* for several weeks.

Meanwhile, then, the Germans on the mainland had been at work.

On the day after the disaster, Captain Christiansen was taken to Dr Deppe's government hospital outside Tanga for treatment of his wounds and recuperation. He did not give up his duty, however, but made arrangements for work to begin immediately to salvage what might be saved of the cargo of *Kronborg* before the water destroyed it all. That very next day members of the crew returned to the ship. The fires were out, they found, although the deck was still hot, where deck could be said to exist at all. The bridgework was twisted, the plating was torn and broken by some of the eighty shells that had struck the ship, and one shell had so wrecked the smokestack that it could not be repaired; but that was the least of it. The mainmast had taken a crazy angle, falling back on deck, below-decks there were holes beneath the water line, the compartment bulkheads were broken and twisted, and the engine room had been burned out; the *Kronborg* was absolutely wrecked.

Yet surprisingly enough a good deal of the cargo could be salvaged. It was true that the munitions had received a good wetting from the sea water – that was the only measure to stop their explosion in the intense heat from the burning coal – but the rifles and machine guns were packed in tight cases, and inside were heavily coated with grease that kept the sea water out. So the boats began moving back and forth from the hulk to the shore, carrying crew-men of the *Kronborg*, German officers and German soldiers from the Protective Force, native carriers, and, above all, native divers, for they would have to go down into the water of the hold and prepare boxes, crates, and drums for hoisting to the deck – or what had been a deck.

Day after day the work went on: there were uniforms and wines and liquor for the *Königsberg*. (Half of that supply somehow disappeared en route to the warship, but the other half arrived: spirits for the spirit!) There were rifles, pistols, machine guns, and a thousand items for making war and for the warriors' comfort.

Captain Schade, Tanga's port officer, and pilot Abels undertook the management of the unloading, and they kept men, ships' boats, and Arab dhows working all day long, every day. In one day, for example, they brought off 293 rifles, 375,000 cartridges, one field gun, four machine guns, 40 officers' tents, 100 cases of 105-mm ammunition for the *Königsberg*'s guns, 150 cases of 88-mm shells, more than a hundred boxes of cartridge cases, and a boat repair kit for the *Königsberg*. There was damage, of course; the field forces discovered that the rifle cartridges were affected most by their immersion and that fully twenty per cent of the bullets misfired; but a great deal of war material had been salvaged, and it was virtually certain that had not Captain Christiansen ordered the sea cocks opened, the ship would have blown sky high, with nearly every bit of its cargo.

It seems unbelievable, but the material that was *Königs-berg*'s, except for the coal, of course, was to be shipped to *Königsberg*, even though there were no ships or lighters available. The route? By rail and the heads of native carriers from Tanga to Amboni to Pangani, Bagamoyo, Dar es Salaam, to the Rufiji Delta and to the ship. It was to be done, just as the material destined for Lieutenant Colonel von Lettow-Vorbeck and his men was shipped to them. And so, several weeks later when Admiral King-Hall came into Manza Bay with a pair of mine-sweepers and swept up the fifty-gallon gasoline drums in the middle of the bay, he found the *Kronborg* a battered hulk with nothing worth while aboard her that might be salvaged. He had to admit to London that the cargo had been taken off; London was very unhappy about the delay in returning to wreck the German ship, but there was nothing to be done.

A few weeks after the unloading of the *Kronborg*, Captain Christiansen was well enough to obey a summons from Lieutenant Colonel von Lettow-Vorbeck to come to New Moshi for a meeting. He went, met the commander, and rejected the idea of staying on in East Africa to fight the war. He was a sea-fighter, he said, and his place was back in Germany, taking out a raider, or whatever other vessel the Admiralty wanted him to command. So he started the long and dangerous voyage back to the homeland to report on the activities of the defenders of German East Africa and to give the people at home a true picture for the very first time. First, however, he spent two days aboard *Königsberg*, to discover the state of affairs there and then report on it. But by this time, the news to be taken from *Königsberg* was sad news. Captain Looff had seen the writing on the wall, he had ordered the officers ashore to cease and desist in bringing such materials as the guns and ammunition for his biggest guns. Without coal, without a supply ship that brought all kinds of replenishments to him, his chances of escape from the Rufiji were growing slimmer every day. Imagine: by the spring of 1915, *Königsberg* had been without a refit for an entire year, and she had subsisted for months on the sea supplies with a few replacements – supplies obtained in July 1914. Here was a little cruiser, never designed to go for more than a month or so without the kind attentions of a dockyard, going on a year in battle quite alone.

Captain Looff was not giving up, but he was determined not to run the chance of wasting supplies that could mean the difference between defeat and victory in Africa. He was ready to go out, just as soon as he saw any possibility of emerging free from the delta and some chance of survival once he was outside. Were another *Hilfschiff* to come to Africa and be available to him in the south, with coal and parts and ammunition, he was ready. The question in the spring of 1915 was whether there would be another supply ship.

13

Two Plans

CAPTAIN LOOFF'S PLAN for escape from the Rufiji was known to every man on the ship, and yet outside the ship no one knew at all – that ability to keep a secret was a sign of the high morale that existed on the *Königsberg* seven months after she had been blocked up in the river. The plan depended on several factors, one of which was the superior knowledge of the Germans about the nature of the Rufiji Delta, and most of the rest of which were dependent on the whims of fortune. For two months Lieutenant Hinrichs secretly had been constructing an anchorage near the mouth of the Kikunja branch of the river; since the *Königsberg* was moored in the Simba-Ouranga branch, the British really did not expect that she would emerge farther north. On the night that they had waited for news from the *Kronborg*, captain and crew were ready for the attempt, steam had been raised, all men on detached duty had been recalled, and even the little guns over which the British had shown so much concern had been brought back aboard. And then had come disappointment.

But far worse than the disappointment of Captain Looff and his men over the failure of the *Kronborg* to accomplish her impossible task was the next step of the Reichsmarinant in Berlin. The admirals abandoned *Königsberg* – she never gave up and she would never give up – but the admirals quit her all the same. Lieutenant Colonel von Lettow-Vorbeck, having won the battle of Tanga, had also secured considerable respect at home, and his word now carried more weight than that of Governor Schnee or Fregattenkapitän Max

Looff. Of course it was always the German way – the Kaiser's generals had it all over the admirals and the army all over the navy in this war. Von Lettow-Vorbeck asked Berlin to let him have the crew of the *Königsberg*. She would never escape from the delta, he assured the generals, and so the generals went to the admirals and repeated the story and Berlin ordered Max Looff to make part of his crew available for the military defence of the colony. Captain Looff asked Lieutenant Colonel von Lettow-Vorbeck what he wanted, and the commander of troops said he wanted all the sailors possible, so Captain Looff sent off one hundred men of his crew under Oberleutnant T Angel, leaving him only two hundred and twenty men to man the ship.

What difference it would have made had the Admiralty sensed the need to send two ships to East Africa, one to meet the needs of the army and another to meet the needs of *Königsberg*! Captain Christiansen had realised the impossibility of his task as soon as he learned that the *Königsberg* was still beleaguered and that he was supposed to run into the blockaded coast, deliver half his merchandise, and then run out, unarmed and unhelped, and hide under the nose of enemies searching frantically for him until *Königsberg* came out, then meet the cruiser, transfer supplies, and flee with her under the noses of half the British navy – which would by that time be assembled off the East African coast.

From the beginning Captain Looff realised the difficulties attendant in the manner in which *Kronborg* had been dispatched, but he was a good officer to his Kaiser and he did not complain about the stupidities of higher authority. When *Kronborg* met the fate he had feared, and when the Admiralty lost faith, he did not complain. He simply set out to restore the morale of his men and to await events, hoping for that one chance in twenty he gave himself to run the gauntlet of his enemies and emerge from the delta.

In the many months since he had taken refuge among the crocodiles and the hippos, Captain Looff had moved within the delta a number of times. At first he had sought refuge at Salale on the Ssuninga branch of the river, which joined with the Simba-Ouranga branch just behind the northern tip of the Kiomboni peninsula; he had remained there until 11th November 1915, and then had moved upriver. He had anchored *Königsberg* at the joining of the Simba-Ouranga and Ssuninga branches on 5th November and had remained there until 14th December, when he came down the Simba-Ouranga across one of the branches and up the Kikunja branch to Batja, a point so far up the river that the British could not believe a seagoing vessel could navigate the water. On this day, 14th April, waiting for *Kronberg* Captain Looff had moved back down the Kikunja to a point near Kikale, quite sure the British did not know that he could flee out the mouth of the Kikunja; and even in the failure of the *Kronberg* to make wireless contact he was tempted to make the attempt, but was discouraged by the obvious alertness of the blockaders on that day. Two days earlier there is little doubt but that he could have slipped by the blockade, headed north between Koma Island and the Dira Reef, cut southeast around Niororo, giving Mafia a wide berth, and made his way southward.

With a minimum crew all was changed; Captain Looff could not really hope to give battle to *Hyacinth* or any other strong cruiser without enough men to man the guns and the fire parties, the dozens of jobs essential to survival of a warship in action. He was now reduced to playing the waiting game, without hope that anything would happen to change his situation.

As for the British, they were still trying the aerial method of disposing of the *Königsberg*, with Lieutenant J T Cull and Lieutenant H E Watkins of the Royal Marines, eighteen enlisted men as specialists, and their two airplanes. After the arrival of the hydroplanes in February, the British had experienced nothing but trouble. On the first flight from the air station at Niororo Lieutenant Cull had loaded his Sopwith hydroplane with an observer, extra petrol, two fifteen-pound bombs and two forty-eight-pound bombs, and himself. He had revved up the engine and moved into a take-off pattern, and the hydroplane had stubbornly stuck to the water as though glued down. Then came four days of trying every combination, and Lieutenant Cull finally got into the air, by himself, with one hour's fuel, no observer, and no bombs. It was no better a performance than that of the old-fashioned Curtiss planes – worse, because Cull could fly no higher than five hundred yards, which made him a floundering duck for the batteries of defenders over whom he must fly to reach *Königsberg*.

The shore defenders were not to be trifled with in this spring of 1915; they maintained no less than thirteen posts and each post had a 47-mm or a 37-mm gun and perhaps two of them, plus a machine gun or two, and men armed with high-powered rifles. These defenders guarded every channel, every point, every landing place, and they had an enviable score; one plane shot down, one British ship captured, at least two water attacks repelled. Little by little the British had occupied all the islands in and around the delta, but they had not been willing to risk the man-power necessary to seize land control of the delta itself.

The coming of the *Kronborg* aroused the British blockade force to new heights of activity, stimulated no doubt by the angry reaction of Whitehall to Admiral King-Hall's report that the supply ship had delivered its supplies to the main-land, even though in unorthodox fashion. The British did not know that the Reichsmarinant had abandoned *Königs-berg*, or that Lieutenant Colonel von Lettow-Vorbeck had triumphed in his demands for a concentration on the land defence; what they did know was that *Königsberg* was constantly calling up *Hilfschiffe* on the radio in code, and one of these supply ships might break through to her somehow – God only knew how, but it might be done – and then if *Königsberg* broke out there would be the butcher to pay and no question about it.

Lieutenant Cull and Lieutenant Watkins spent every waking moment trying to make their airplanes fly well enough to bomb *Königsberg*. They experimented with

133

various octane concentrations of petrol, they adjusted the carburettors until the threads of the screws were worn, they trimmed and retrimmed the aircraft for weight variations, they built new exhaust systems. Finally, the Air Department of the Navy decided that hydroplanes were not the right type of aircraft for the job and sent on three new land planes. Just after the débâcle of the *Kronberg* the planes arrived at Durban aboard the armed steamer, *Laconia*, along with an armoured boat which could be used for plucking downed airmen out of the sea in the face of German rifle fire. The new airplanes were far from perfect, but by the end of April they had been brought north to the Rufiji; still, it was Lieutenant Cull in his limping hydroplane who made the next flight in Captain Looff's direction, on 25th April. He and his observer (for they had made the plane fly that well) flew south and then circled until they found the *Königsberg* in her new position, apparently ready to dash for the sea. They scurried home to the safety of the waters outside the delta, followed all the way by shrapnel from the German guns, which hit the plane in several places but did not bring it down. They reported then that *Königsberg* had steam up, was pointing north and not far from the entrance to the delta, appeared to have been painted recently, and seemed likely to rush at full speed out of the mouth of the river at any moment. A few days later Lieutenant Cull took a camera along with him and succeeded in taking a picture of the *Königsberg* at bay.

Nearly every day Lieutenant Cull took the hydroplane aloft, even though he could not attain enough altitude to be really safe. Along with him on most days came Commander Richard Bridgeman of the *Hyacinth* as observer, and on every flight they nearly met with disaster, either from air currents, enemy fire, or the nature of the airplane itself. Lieutenant Watkins took up the hydroplane one day, received a disabling shell from a German gun, and crash-landed it – a total wreck. This turn of events was troublesome and delaying, because the highly touted land planes were not flying at all; in fact the only value from that shipment seemed to be the armed motor launch, and Lieutenant Cull, Commander Bridgeman, and the others suggested with straight faces that they be allowed to make a torpedo boat of it and attack the *Königsberg* at night. They aroused themselves to a fever of enthusiasm for the project – and then Whitehall vetoed the idea.

The admirals sitting in lordly session in the spring of 1915 sat down and reconsidered the problem of the *Königsberg*. She was tying up valuable cruisers that were needed in the North Sea, in home waters, in the English Channel, at the Dardanelles, and along the trade routes, for although most of the German cruisers had been sunk or put out of action, the auxiliary cruisers or raiders were effective and a growing threat to British sea power: *Prinz Eitel Friedrich* and *Kronprinz Wilhelm* had made great names for themselves; and a new menace was becoming an important part of the war at sea, the submarine, whose capabilities in commerce raiding were only just being discovered in 1915.

The admirals needed those vessels off the Rufiji, and they were being made to look more than slightly ridiculous by the amount of time, effort, and money that one German cruiser was costing the British government. They had tried the fire of big guns, to no avail; they had considered and abandoned landing after the Tanga disaster showed them the cost of a landing in East African terrain; they had tried aerial attack, with no success; now they would try something new, but really a tactic that was very, very old.

14

The *Severn* and the *Mersey*

IN THE SPRING of 1862 when the odd raftlike USS *Monitor* drove the Confederate ironclad *Virginia* from the ocean waters around Norfolk, the major navies of the world took note, and for the next twenty years there occurred in Europe a spate of building of small, heavily armoured craft with low freeboards, known by the generic name monitor. These were defensive weapons, small, heavy and very slow in passage, but making up for their lack of speed with heavy guns that could sink a much larger attacker.

Yet simultaneously another development was observed in naval warfare, particularly in the Russo-Japanese War, and it turned out that the torpedo-boat destroyer, or destroyer as it was to be known in modern navies, was the wave of the future; the admirals soon realised that their *raison d'être* was to attack, not to defend, and the monitors lost ground with the major navies of the world. By the beginning of the war of 1914 Britain did not have a single monitor and did not want any; nor would the Admiralty have considered wasting money on monitors if anyone had asked them. But war changed everything. The Brazilian government had ordered three monitors from the Vickers Manufacturing Company, and they were nearly finished in August 1914, when the Admiralty requisitioned them. Two of these monitors were the *Severn* and the *Mersey*. They were small ships, ninety-six yards long and displacing 1260 tons, only fourteen yards wide, and they drew only about five feet of water, which meant they could go anywhere in the Rufiji Delta without trouble at high tide. The odd ships could make a top speed of only twelve knots and that for a very short time. They carried less than three hundred tons of fuel, but they were strong enough to withstand great recoil, and they each mounted two 152-mm guns and a 128-mm howitzer. They were not handsome craft. They resembled nothing so much as the boats a child makes with a piece of two-by-four nailed to a flat board and a spool for a smokestack, but the guns were what counted, not the beauty, and here were small craft, capable of moving up the Rufiji, which could outgun the *Königsberg.*

So the monitors were the Admiralty's new weapon, and they were sent through the English Channel, through the Strait of Gibraltar, to Malta, Suez, Aden, and down to the Rufiji Delta, accompanied by the auxiliary cruiser *Kent,* which carried the crews of the little ships, and four ocean-going tugs which pulled them. It was a slow voyage, for the monitors were scarcely seaworthy craft, but on 2nd June the new force arrived to join the assemblage of cruisers, auxiliaries, gunboats, armed whaleboats, and airplanes that blockaded the river against the *Königsberg's* emergence. Just after the arrival of the monitors came a new set of airplanes: the Admiralty was determined to put an end to the *Königsberg* without further delay; the new auxiliary, the *Laurentic,* carried two Henry Farman and two Caudron airplanes, battle-tested planes that ought to be able to do the job. Mafia Island was the point selected for the air base, and an airfield was built there by native labour.

The news of the coming of the monitors was known almost immediately aboard the *Königsberg,* and the coming of the airplanes was announced by the planes themselves within thirty-six hours of their arrival, when the two Henry Farman planes were put in the air for reconnaissance.

Since April, a kind of fatalism had set in among the members of the *Königsberg's* crew, from the captain down to the youngest seaman. Captain Looff thought perhaps it was brought aboard by the blacks who came each day to bring their three cubic metres of wood for the furnaces of the ship; with the departure of a third of his crew Captain Looff must make use of the Negroes whether he liked it or not. No matter what their tribulations, the blacks had a philosophical answer – *Haizourou* (It makes no difference); or *Amri ya mououngou* (It is the will of God) – and it was not long before the men of the *Königsberg* began to believe that whatever was going to happen to them was the will of God as well.

The Negroes informally enlisted in the crew of *Königsberg* served under a leader from the Seychelles named Hans who was quite familiar with Germans and German ways, having made the voyage to Germany with *Seeadler*, one of *Königsberg*'s predecessors on the East African station. First Officer Koch had known Hans in those days, and in these times of trial Hans became a favourite of his and of the captain's; he was given the official title of Negro quartermaster. He watched how the other quartermasters worked their men, and he adopted German naval ways as his pattern.

In these long months Captain Looff had some opportunity to use his 9-mm rifle, for he and the other officers went hunting nearly every day for the tables of the ship. This freedom was no breach of discipline. Captain Looff knew that the British could attack only at high water, which meant that half the waking hours of the day were free from concern and the ship's company could relax. As for himself, he seldom went out. Weighed down by the responsibility for the ship, he was three months in the delta before he made his first foray, and that after hippos. It was a matter of considerable wagering among the crew whether 'the old man' would get anything. He did – he brought back a live hippo baby, about the size of a yearling pig, but that was not all. He had shot the mother, not knowing she had a young one with her, and his conscience bothered him so much that he saved the baby as a mascot for the ship.

The crew turned out immediately to help. The ship's carpenter built a wooden hut for the baby on the deck and the ship's chief cook assumed the responsibility for preparing the food, and the chief medical corpsman fed him every day. But alas, the baby lived only two weeks and then died for reasons neither captain nor crew could ever discover.

Haizourou.
Amri ya mououngou.

15
The Attack

AT THE END of June, as the officers and crew of *Königsberg* hunted and fished and watched for the coming of the enemy with the growing belief that they would never leave the Rufiji River, the British outside were preparing feverishly for the assault on their quarry. They were still having airplane trouble. Within two weeks half the planes were grounded for one reason or another, one Caudron had a broken wing and a disabled engine and one Henry Farman had crashed with a bang that destroyed the body completely. This attrition created problems and worries, because Admiral King-Hall was planning a combined aerial-naval attack to finish off the *Königsberg*, and he needed airplanes that would fly, not crash.

Captain Fullerton of the *Severn* and Captain R A Wilson of the *Mersey* met every day with the aviators, and every day the two usable planes flew and the monitors practised their gunnery, waiting for the day of days when they would launch the attack.

Tuesday, 6th July, was the chosen day for the assault on the *Königsberg*; and of course long before that day Captain Looff knew the fight was coming because his coast watchers had observed the British practice sessions. On Monday the captains of the monitors took their secret documents to the flagship for security in case of disaster; the steel shields for the guns were shored up with hammocks to prevent fragments from flying in the faces of the gunners, and every possible preparation was made.

On Tuesday afternoon a fleet of fifteen of the twenty-one

British ships in the task force set out for the Kikunja branch of the river, choosing this branch with especial daring because they did not know that it was deep enough for a ship as big as *Königsberg*. The British expected to find shallows, but they were confident that at high water the monitors could risk the shallows, and they did not want to take chances on the long roundabout trip up the Simba-Ouranga branch, for who knew what might happen if the ships were once enmeshed deep within the delta?

The plan called for the monitors to enter the mouth of the Kikunja but only as far as Gengini Island that stood a short way upstream. They would stop downstream of Gengini Island, and protected by it they would begin firing on the cruiser on the other side. The airplanes would be the eyes of the British ships, telling them where their shots were going and making it quite unnecessary to see the enemy. Captain Looff would have somewhat the same advantage through communication with his shore watchers, but the timing could not be as good and the usefulness of the airplanes in this regard was obvious.

At 6.45 pm, the monitors began their trip, hoping to reach the firing point under the cover of darkness, so as to be unobserved by the *Königsberg*. At the same time the auxiliary cruiser *Laurentic* opened fire on Dar es Salaam – a purely nuisance demonstration conducted from outside the harbour to prevent the land force from sending field guns or troops towards the delta. At four o'clock in the morning the monitors began the ascent of the river, the *Severn* leading. At 5.20 in the gathering light the German defence posts found the fleet and began firing as the monitors entered the mouth of the river. The monitors fired back with small guns, 47-mm, which had been added to their armament; they would not waste their big shells on outposts.

As Captain Looff heard the first shells fired from the mouth of the river, and learned by telephone what was happening, he was relieved: at last the confrontation had come. He was in touch with Unterleutnant Schlawe on the river bank near the island. Schlawe would serve as the *Königsberg's* eyes in the coming fight.

As the light grew brighter, from the mouths of the Simba-Ouranga and the other branches of the Rufiji other ships of the task force began shooting in the general direction of *Königsberg*, not with any hope of hitting her, but to warn of their presence so she would not attempt to turn and escape through another branch of the river. The cruisers *Weymouth, Hyacinth, Pyramus* and *Pioneer* were all firing their big guns; the auxiliaries and the whaleboats made as much racket as possible, and up the Kikunja came the monitors through the crocodiles.

At 6.23 the monitors had reached the shelter of Gengini Island; here they opened fire from about eleven hundred yards, and a few minutes later *Königsberg* began to return the fire. The German ship's first two salvos struck the island in front of the monitors, but then Lieutenant Schlawe began talking the guns into position and they bracketed the *Severn*.

As the firing began the British planes moved into position to direct the monitors, but their aerial observation was much distracted by the constant zigzag pattern the pilots had to fly to avoid the black clots of smoke that represented shrapnel fired at the planes from the ground and from the decks of the *Königsberg* by the smaller guns. By 7.25 the firing into the air was so accurate and the firing from the monitors was so inaccurate that the aerial observers had difficulty in giving any sensible directions at all.

At 7.40 *Mersey* took her first hit from the *Königsberg*; a 105-mm shell smashed into her forward 152-mm gun, killing the four men at the gun and wounding four others. The flames set fire to the shell ready to go into the gun, and only by the heroism of crew members who threw the shell into the sea was the *Mersey* saved from more death and destruction.

Another shell landing alongside destroyed a small boat. Captain Wilson of the *Mersey* sent up a signal, telling the *Severn* that he was all right, and set about putting his ship into fighting stance again, even though the Germans had the range and a constant stream of shells fell around her; she made a half turn and then she signalled that she needed the assistance of a tug. She had ceased fire.

All this information was returned to the *Königsberg* by telephone, in a play-by-play description by Lieutenant Schlawe, who had a ringside seat in a tree atop the bank on the island.

At 7.55, *Severn* scored her first hit on the *Königsberg*, knocking out the forward 105-mm gun, and killing Seamen Helfferich and Appel at their posts. In the next quarter hour the monitor scored three more hits, demolishing the cruiser's main galley, smashing the bridge, wounding Captain Looff, navigation officer Hinrichs, and a signalman, smashing through to the lower deck and wounding Lieutenant Wenig in both legs. At 8.10 the *Mersey* was turned around and was firing again with her after gun. The firing slowed and grew less accurate because the airplanes were having trouble again, either with fuel or engines. At about nine o'clock the *Severn* retired to try to escape the accurate firing of the *Königsberg*, and as she retired Captain Fullerton discovered the observation point on the island, and peppered it with 47-mm cannon shells. The captain of *Severn* was a very lucky man that day; he had no sooner quit the anchorage behind the island than *Königsberg* sent a salvo of five shells, perfectly grouped, which would have put *Severn* out of action or sunk her had she not moved at precisely the right time.

The battle reached virtual impasse; the monitors moved out of range, for all practical purposes, and Captain Looff reduced his firing to one or two guns, in order to save ammunition. Although the monitors could see the tips of the *Königsberg*'s masts from their new position, they had no way of knowing how they were firing. Lieutenant Cull tried to come back with his airplane, but it was hit by machine gun fire and the oil line was broken, so he barely made it safely back to the base at Mafia Island. *Severn* was firing over *Königsberg* and *Mersey* was firing short, and that is the way it continued all during the rest of the morning.

Aboard the *Königsberg*, the hits on *Mersey* were greeted with noisy hurrahs, and the morale of the two hundred and twenty men was as high as it had been since the day they steamed into the Rufiji Delta after sinking *Pegasus*.

As the sun reached its zenith, the day grew very hot and the men serving the pieces began to sweat and some grew dizzy with the heat and had to retire to the sick bay. Lunch was served, in a hasty fashion: a piece of bread and meat and a mug of hot tea to refresh parched throats.

The torpedo-tree that the men of the *Königsberg* had prepared was ready to go down the river after the two monitors, but the enemy moved out at three o'clock on the outgoing tide, and the torpedo was left far behind. Actually the officers and men of *Königsberg* had prepared another torpedo in case the first torpedo-tree failed, but neither was this to be used this day.

As the British retired, they counted the fruits of battle. They had expended no fewer than 635 projectiles, and they had 78 different observations from the airplanes, but they had done practically no damage to *Königsberg*. One monitor, *Mersey*, had lost a gun and sustained another hit aft. *Severn* had missed being blown out of the water by what her captain called sheer luck, for time after time salvos of shells from the *Königsberg* had struck either ten yards ahead or ten yards behind her – the tiniest fraction of an adjustment of the guns and she would have gone up in smoke.

Yet the British were not downhearted; they realised among other things that Captain Looff's rate of fire had slowed, and they knew that since they had not scored any important hits on his guns, he was cutting down on ammunition. So they also came to the conclusion that there would be little danger that *Königsberg* would attempt to run the blockade in the very near future.

On the way downriver, the monitors were undisturbed until they reached the mouth of the Kikunja branch, which was covered on both sides by German installations. Two field guns on the north bank opened up on them, *Mersey* took one shell and three others narrowly missed the two monitors. Then, at 4.45 in the afternoon, they were out of the river and the battle was over.

On balance, the Germans had all the best of it, as Captain Looff knew; he had sustained four hits on the ship and no part of it was out of action. His casualties were minimal. The *Mersey* had one less 152-mm gun than she had boasted in the morning – one-fourth of the total gunpower – and besides the dead and wounded on that ship, there were dead and wounded Britons from the three small boats the Germans had sunk that day. Yet such victory was bitter in Max Looff's mouth, for it was not victory at all, but simply delay of the day when *Königsberg* would be shot from under him. There was no question in his mind, none at all, that that was to be the end of his ship. All that remained for Captain Looff and the crew was to act out the play to the end, knowing the end, as one would know the culmination of a Greek tragedy of ethics, only unsure as to the details.

16

The Last Fight of the *Königsberg*

WEDNESDAY FOUND BRITON and German engaged in the
selfsame occupation – the mournful task of burying the
dead of the day before. On *Königsberg* the dead were few:
Bootsmann Bantelmann and the young sailors Appel and
Helfferich, both of them assigned to the forward gun which
had been squarely hit by the first shells that struck the
Königsberg. That same shell had struck the bridge and had
seriously wounded young Lieutenant Wenig, the baby of
the officers, nearly tearing off his left foot. Fortunately
Wenig was taken to the lazaret and his wounds bound up
before he could bleed to death. Captain Looff was wounded
slightly in the lower arm, Lieutenant Hinrichs was wounded
in the upper right arm, and Paymaster Christiansen was
also wounded slightly, by a splinter.

For the next four days all was quiet, but Captain Looff
knew that his enemies were simply trying to work out a
better plan of attack than the one they had used on 6th
July with so little effect despite all their superiority in
everything but marksmanship and courage.

Early on Sunday morning, 11th July, the two remaining
airplanes began flying circles around *Königsberg*: except for
perhaps one survey mission a day this was the first concentration of air interest, and Captain Looff knew what was
coming. Soon his shore watchers confirmed it; the enemy
was returning with his monitors. The plan was the same,
except that Admiral King-Hall took personal charge of the
attack, moving his flag to *Weymouth*.

The monitors were taken in tow by tugs at eight o'clock

in the morning, by 10.40 they were in the entrance to the river, and at 11.35 they crossed the bar into the mouth of the Rufiji. Soon they came into range, and *Königsberg*, with its eyes ashore, in the person of its watchers, began firing on the two ships. Her gunners hit *Mersey* with two shells, and one smashed through the captain's cabin, wounding two men and putting the rear gun out of action. The other struck the sandbags on the deck and did relatively little damage. *Mersey* then retired from the action and *Severn* moved up to the place she had occupied five days earlier; *Mersey* was supposed to draw the German fire while *Severn* did the shooting.

Things did not work out that way; Captain Looff refused to be drawn into shooting only at the *Mersey* and placed the *Severn* under fire as well, concentrating on the latter, after he learned that *Mersey* was out of the action. *Königsberg*'s guns were firing well, and shells were bursting all around the *Severn*, so that the decks were littered with pieces of shrapnel. *Severn* was quiet, waiting for the first airplane to come back and direct her fire. When the plane arrived at 12.30 *Severn* began firing, and this day the system worked well, as would be seen when *Severn* fired her first salvo:

Four hundred yards long and twenty-two yards to the left, said Lieutenant Cull, and the observer in his plane tapped out the message on the wireless for the monitor.

One hundred yards long, twenty-two yards to the left, came another signal, and the gunners corrected their aim.

On the eighth salvo the monitor found its target, and after that point the battle consisted simply of trading fire, with the heavier guns of the monitor having much the best of it.

Captain Looff's men were firing with only four guns, not as the British supposed because they had put half the guns out of action, but because the *Königsberg* was very short of ammunition.

Because of the high trajectory the shells fell heavily on the decks of the *Königsberg*, each 152-mm shell doing tremendous damage as it hit; the first shells destroyed the forecastle and the foredeck, and several smashed through the main deck.

From his station on the bridge, Captain Looff watched in pain as the ship began to take punishment. The bridge was not protected and several times Looff's officers asked him to seek the protection of the blockhouse where Lieutenant Apel stood directing the fire of *Königsberg*; but the captain felt that this was *Königsberg*'s last fight, that he was asking two hundred and sixteen men to take enemy fire and perhaps to die for him, and that it was far better that he show himself on the bridge than seek protection when there was so little else that he could do.

Then came one lucky shot, or a pair of them, which struck hard aft, smashed down into the after munitions room, and burst, causing a huge multiple explosion, destroying much of the remaining 105-mm ammunition. The fore guns were put out of action by the first shells, which made a holocaust of the deck; one shell burst on the bridge, totally wrecking it and tearing Captain Looff's clothes and wounding him slightly. Most of the men in the blockhouse were wounded, but Lieutenant Apel was untouched. A few minutes later a shell put the ship's telephone system out of action. The fire aft sent a huge tower of smoke into the air, and the popping of small arms ammunition began to accompany the sound of *Königsberg*'s firing and the crashing sounds caused by the hits of the British.

By 1.30 the ship was a wreck; the British had salvoed in on her and kept hitting simply by keeping their guns aimed at the same spot – there was none of the artistry and science of shooting at sea, moving target against moving target; it was like sitting in the middle of the river, shooting fish in a barrel. The contest would not have been so one-sided, but *Königsberg* had little ammunition for her guns to begin with, and the lucky shot that struck her after 105-mm magazine destroyed the reserve. By 1.30 the ship was down to two guns, each with two rounds left. One of those last rounds was shrapnel, and it was saved for the airplane; Oberleutnant Niemyer and Oberleutnant Kohtz and Fireman Kaiser manned that gun – not a professional gunner among them – and with their one shot they hit the plane and forced it to crash in the river between *Königsberg* and her attacker. The fires belowdecks threatened to spread into the amidships magazine and blow the ship out of the water, and Captain Looff ordered the magazines flooded, which ended any chance of continuing the fight; but it was that or take the chance of losing the crew.

One more shell came in to do its terrible damage. It sliced through the cabin, smashed into the poop where Captain Looff was standing, and wounded him in a dozen places, so badly that his men thought he was dead and First Officer Koch moved to take command until the captain signified that he was still able to hold the ship. This shell killed the brave amateur gunner Radio Officer Niemyer, Fireman Kaiser, and seriously injured Lieutenant Kohtz. The last gun was out of action; *Königsberg* was silent, except for the shocks and sounds of disaster on her decks. Captain Looff spoke swiftly, lying where his men had placed him in a litter on the deck, telling First Officer Koch what he must do. The wounded, including the captain, were removed from the ship in the boats, and the rest of the crew came along after them, all but a handful of men led by First Officer Koch. The first officer went down below-decks, where he rigged a pair of torpedo heads with fuses so they would blow the bottom out of the ship. He lighted the fuses, the guns of *Königsberg* were stripped of their firing mechanisms, and guns were thrown over the side – just in case the enemy thought they might make use of these fine German naval guns. One last quick look around, and Georg Koch was over the side and swimming, last man off the ship, because his captain had been carried off, more dead than alive.

As the captain left his ship he saw that his flag and the battle flag were still flying, and that is exactly how he wanted it; he looked back from shore and saw First Officer Koch swimming in without a single thought for the crocodiles; and then, just after two o'clock, as the British shells continued to fall around her and her flags waved on the crooked mast, *Königsberg* gave a little grunt, as the torpedo warheads exploded in her belly, then the grunt became a roar, she turned slightly to port as she settled on the bottom, and soon nothing could be seen but the tops of her masts, flags still flying.

17
Ashore

Captain Looff raised himself painfully on the rude hospital cot in his room in the hospital on the plantation at Neustieten, five miles inland on the Mbuni River, and flexed his sore right arm for a moment, then began to write.

'The *Königsberg* is destroyed but not beaten,' he wrote, beginning his official report to the German Admiralty.

It was true; of her crew of three hundred and twenty men three were killed in the first attack and nineteen in the second; twenty-four were badly wounded in both attacks and twenty-four were lightly wounded; a hundred men had been detached and were already serving elsewhere; and the unwounded would soon be able to carry on the war against the British.

There was a good deal for the naval men to do in East Africa, for the war was to be prosecuted briskly on the inland seas: Lakes Tanganyika, Victoria Nyanza, Nyasa, and Kivu. Control of Lake Tanganyika, in particular, was essential to Lieutenant Colonel von Lettow-Vorbeck's war plans, because in the absence of a north-south railway he must use the lake to transport troops rapidly from one front to another. The Germans could not expect to gain control of Lake Victoria Nyanza, but they must retain freedom of movement.

For this task now there were 24 naval officers and 559 non-commissioned officers and men, 332 from *Königsberg*, 97 from *Möwe*, 94 from the South Seas ship *Planet*, men who had first gone to Mozambique but had come up to German East Africa instead of trying to make their way home, 31 from the *Kronborg*, and five from another German ship. In addition 30 reserve naval officers were found in the colony along with 325 reserve officers and men, many of them seamen employed by the German East Africa line. Some of these men would serve with the various naval units on the lakes and some would serve with the army of 'General' von Lettow-Voberck – yes, General (the soldiers called him that even though he was not actually appointed general until later) – for although his promotion was not immediately forthcoming, von Lettow-Vorbeck had seized military power from Governor Schnee, and so effectively was he manipulating the small forces in the colony that Berlin had no choice but to accept his action gracefully; and, indeed, Berlin was grateful for such vigorous leadership in German East Africa.

As of July 1915, the military situation in East Africa was relatively quiet; the British had launched a few half-hearted attacks since the Tanga débâcle, but that was all. The Germans were committed to fighting a defensive battle, not through any will on von Lettow-Vorbeck's part, but because they had neither the men nor the equipment to push farther than a few miles into British or Belgian territory.

The British quite comfortably controlled Lake Nyasa to the south, the Germans controlled Lake Kivu to the northwest with a single motorboat under Lieutenant Wunderlich of the *Möwe* crew, and the British were superior on Lake Victoria Nyanza, although the Germans could use the lake's southern end for their purposes, too.

On Lake Victoria the Germans had been fighting defensively, no more than that, because the British so heavily outgunned them. By war's beginning there were five good-sized British steamers available for battle and troop transport, the *Sybil, Winifred, Clement Hill, Nyanza,* and *Kavirondo*, ranging from six hundred to nine hundred tons; the biggest vessel the Germans could boast on the lake was the thirty-four-ton *Muansa*. In the beginning days of the war the Germans had sent an expeditionary force north to

Karoungou on the British side of the border, using the little steamer *Muansa*, only to have the force driven back by superior British strength. Since the *Muansa* was the only German steamer on the lake, the British undertook very early in the game to put her out of action – a task that did not seem very difficult, given the odds of six British steamers to one German. The *Winifred* and the *Kavirondo* were chosen to do the job and in the early hours of 6th March 1915 they moved into the Speke Gulf at the extreme southeast end of Lake Victoria Nyanza, to lie in wait for the German vessel. The *Winifred* hid herself behind the island of Nafouba, which was separated from the larger island of Oukenoueoue by a narrow channel with steep banks on either side, called the Rougesi passage. It was the practice of the *Muansa* to use this passage because the water was too shallow for the larger British steamers and she often had escaped her enemies previously by darting in here when under pursuit. This time the British were determined that she should not escape.

While *Winifred* lurked hidden at the southern end of the passage, *Kavirondo* set up its ambush at the northern end. The British then settled down to wait, knowing their opportunity would not be long in coming because *Muansa* was the only German ship in these waters and part of her wartime task was the supplying of the various small German posts that guarded the lakefront from British landings. Sooner or later she would come through the narrow strait, the British knew.

They did not have long to wait. That very night the shore watchers from *Winifred*, stationed in the trees on Nafouba Island, reported that *Muansa* had entered the strait from the south, heading north and towing a barge filled with what must be provisions for the outposts up the lake. Early in the morning, *Kavirondo* showed herself at the exit to the channel, and *Muansa* turned swiftly, returning as she had come, but heading for Speke Gulf, hoping, obviously, to land her provisions at Gouta, where they could be taken north overland. But as *Muansa* came out of the shallow water, *Winifred* emerged from her hiding place and began to chase the little German ship. *Muansa* put on steam and sped for the safety of shallow water along the coast; she came into water nine feet deep – and went aground. *Winifred* was armed with an old 37-mm gun and a Maxim, and both of these were firing on *Muansa* all the while. Soon the crew was driven from the stricken German ship, and from the British position in deeper water *Winifred's* captain could see that his enemy had suffered such serious damage that she was apparently a total wreck. So that day *Winifred* sailed away, her captain confident that he had destroyed *Muansa* and secured undisputed control of Lake Victoria Nyanza for the British.

Muansa was not destroyed; some salvagers might not have been willing to take a chance on her, but the Germans were stubborn and tenacious. They would not give up their slender claim to the use of the lake's waters so easily; they began to rebuild their little ship. They rebuilt her completely, and she was again seaworthy. This time, however, Captain Zimmer was cautious: he saw the odds and decided that *Muansa* should be used only as a supply ship; her guns were dismounted and although she was used for nearly two years to transport supplies along the lake the enemy never saw her again until she was captured in 1916. She had travelled only under cover of darkness and only along the coastal waters.

Early in the war the British steamer *Sybil* had gone aground in Mayita Channel, just north of Rougesi Passage, on the German side of the lake, and had been abandoned there. The Germans had some hope of salvaging her and brought in guards to be sure that the British did not try to take her off the rocks, but in April 1915, since she was in enemy hands, the British decided to destroy her and *Winifred* came up nearby and put so many holes into the poor ship's hull that the Germans gave up the attempt at salvage. Then, suddenly, the British reversed their plan and decided to recapture the ship and save her themselves. At the end of April 1915, they sent a force of four hundred men in *Winifred, Kavirondo,* and *Nyanza* to Mayita Bay, and when the Germans retired before so superior a party, the British occupied the area and the ship without a battle. With pontoons and pumps the British floated *Sybil* off the rocks in four days and towed her back to Kisoumou, the British port on the northeast corner of the lake; there *Sybil* was rebuilt and put back into service, no longer a ship of war but a simple transport like *Muansa.*

Lake Tanganyika was the centre of German naval activity. Here Korvettenkapitän Zimmer had his head-quarters at Kigoma. Here Oberleutnant Horn in *Hedwig von Wissman* ruled the lake after damaging the *Alexandre Delcommune* of the Belgians in the first days of the war. The 600-ton *Graf Götzen* started before the war was about to be completed, which should give the Germans undis-puted control of the lake. It was for this ship, in particular, that men of the *Königsberg* had been commandeered by 'General' von Lettow-Vorbeck. Oberleutnant zur See Freund, Lieutenant Rosenthal and Engineer Bockmann, two young deck officers, and sixty-five men from *Königsberg* had been sent to Kigoma to man the *Graf Götzen*, at the same time that *Königsberg*'s Lieutenant Angel and sixteen others had gone off to join the land forces in the north, taking two 60-mm field guns with them.

Lake Tanganyika is the longest lake in the world, over four hundred miles from end to end; it comprised nearly the total western border of German East Africa, so its strategic value to Lieutenant Colonel von Lettow-Vorbeck was easy enough to understand. Since the lake at no point is wider than thirty-five miles, and since in 1914 and 1915 it could be called almost a strictly Belgian-German property, it was here that the Germans faced the Belgians and almost no other enemies in the war of East Africa.

In the original battle between the 100-ton *Hedwig von Wissmann* and the 90-ton *Alexandre Delcommune* on 25th August 1914, Lieutenant Horn had put the *Alexandre Delcommune* out of commission, but he had not destroyed her, and destruction was what was wanted. She had been run aground at Albertville, about midway along the Belgian side of the lake, and Captain Zimmer had undertaken a few months later to destroy her in a daring action. *Alexandre Delcommune* was lying aground near the mouth of the Lukuyu River, and it was to this point that Captain Zimmer and two of his lieutenants, Horn and Odebrecht, directed themselves in *Hedwig von Wissmann* and one of her steam launches – really a steam launch that had belonged to the *Möwe* before she was scuttled in Dar es Salaam harbour. One night in October 1914, Lieutenant Horn set out with a handful of men to reach the Belgian ship and to blow her out of the water within the earshot of her protectors. Silently the lieutenant and his men approached the Belgian ship, sneaking through the line of picket boats that patrolled the Belgian side of the lake; they clambered aboard the deck of the *Alexandre Delcommune* without being noticed by the sentries ashore; no alarm was given, no sound was heard save the lapping of the waves against the side of the ship in the darkness. But then their small boat was seen alongside the larger shadow of the Belgian craft, and they just had time to throw the dynamite into the ship's firebox, light the fuse, scramble overboard and beat a hasty retreat towards *Hedwig von Wissmann* before the Belgians raised the alarm and began firing, only to have their shots drowned out in the greater explosion.

The next night Lieutenant Odebrecht and seven men went ashore a mile north of the wreckage of the *Alexandre Delcommune*, and sneaked back to the vessel to make sure, in the light of their torches, that the job really had been done this time. They were not sure that it had been done, and Captain Zimmer decided the task was worth pursuing even another time.

On this third expedition, Captain Zimmer launched a combined attack, involving the *Hedwig von Wissmann* and a steam launch, plus a number of men from the *Möwe* and a group of Askaris on land. Besides, he brought into play two 100-mm guns, taken from the old *Möwe*, by putting them aboard his specially built raft, which was towed by *Hedwig von Wissmann* as a sort of shooting platform.

It took a considerable amount of courage to launch any kind of attack under these conditions: towing the raft, *Hedwig von Wissmann* could scarcely make two knots in an absolute calm, and Lake Tanganyika was not likely to be absolutely calm at any given moment. Nonetheless Captain Zimmer decided on the attempt, and set out with his impromptu fleet – Lieutenant Horn in command of the steamer, Lieutenant Odebrecht in command of the steam launch, and himself in charge of the raft and guns.

The plan was to wipe out the *Alexandre Delcommune* forever and do whatever damage might be done to the Belgians in Albertville.

Very soon Captain Zimmer discovered that the Belgian position was impregnable, or very nearly so from land, since the entrances to the town were surrounded by barbed wire entanglements and guarded by many soldiers well entrenched behind revetments. And as for attack by water, as soon as the Germans came within four thousand yards of the port on this third attempt, they were sighted and fired upon by a pair of 75-mm guns ashore. One of these guns was almost immediately silenced by what must be described as a lucky shot from the gun platform behind *Hedwig von Wissmann*, and the other was kept busy along with the Belgian defenders by the smaller guns of the lake steamer. When the distance was cut to 1750 yards the 100-mm guns of the raft opened up on the *Alexandre Delcommune* and began smashing her; then Captain Zimmer ordered Lieutenant Odebrecht to move into the harbour of Albertville with his steam launch. Just as Zimmer had suspected, the Belgians had repaired the ship and were ready to put her into the lake once again. The steam launch never made the *Alexandre Delcommune* – the Belgian fire was so fierce she turned tail and ran, her rudder broken and her hull riddled with shell fragments. Yet the mission was a success nonetheless; the shells from the raft's guns put the *Alexandre Delcommune* out of action for good.

Captain Zimmer was a busy man in those first few months of war: after destroying the *Alexandre Delcommune* he turned his attention to a pair of old British hulks at the southern point of Tanganyika, when British territory bordered on the lake. The fact that these two old ships had neither engines nor boilers did not destroy the German fear that they might be installed and the ships put upon the lake to threaten German movement there. So in November Captain Zimmer sent *Hedwig von Wissmann* and the *Kingani* to destroy the ships. *Kingani*, sister ship to the *Wami* that still rode the channels of the Rufiji, was fifty-six feet long and made seven knots – quite enough for this mission, and soon the hulks were destroyed and Captain Zimmer ruled Lake Tanganyika, its supreme Admiral, commanding two small steamers, two steam launches, and two motorboats.

On the face of it, the lake war might appear to be the joke of 1914, but to the men who fought and died on these lakes it was no joke, and even as the British bottled up *Königsberg* in the Rufiji, the Germans had the Belgians bottled up on their side of Lake Tanganyika and had turned the lake into a German sea. Nor was Captain Zimmer ever content to fight a passive war on his miniature ocean; he was constantly in motion, harrying the Belgians with surprise raids. His boats and ships continued to bombard Belgian outposts, and the men of *Möwe* often went ashore in landing parties to attack land installations.

Then, on 9th June 1915, just before the end of *Königsberg*, came the launching of *Graf Götzen*, which could carry nine hundred soldiers and their equipment. The Germans were very much in control of the waters of the west.

Until the end of 1915 they continued in control of the lake, with no serious effort made by Belgians or British to dispute them. Men of *Königsberg* joined the men of *Möwe* and the reservists from the German East Africa steamship line.

The Lake Tanganyika force was growing, thanks to the presence of the railway that ran from Dar es Salaam. As the 30-ton coastal steamer *Kingabi* had been brought west to the lake by train, so was a steam pinnace from the sunken *Möwe*. The *Kingani* and the *Hedwig von Wissmann* had joined forces just before the first of January to support an attack on a Belgian company near Bismarcksburg on the southern end of the lake and had captured four machine guns and something much more important to the beleaguered Germans of East Africa – ninety miles of telegraph line which had been destined for the Cape-to-Cairo transcontinental telegraph line.

Most recently, the *Adjutant* had been brought up to Lake Tanganyika, armed with an 88-mm gun, a 47-mm gun, and two machine guns. Reserve Lieutenant Herm was put in charge of her.

Ashore, the crew of *Königsberg* needed some time for rest and recuperation – even those who were not wounded in the last actions against the monitors. Forty per cent of the officers and men were down with malaria, or should have been in bed, had they not been fighting for their lives. But even more important than rest and recuperation was one problem that presented itself on the day after Captain Looff scuttled the ship.

On the afternoon of 11th July, after the crew had left *Königsberg*, the British monitor *Severn* continued to fire on the cruiser; her airplane had been shot down and Captain Fullerton did not know the ship had been scuttled and deserted. So he threw another forty-two salvos – eighty-four 152-mm shells – towards the ship and was immensely pleased when he heard at least eight explosions that sounded as though he had struck home.

At about the time that the crew of *Königsberg* was going into the boats, *Mersey* had decided to get back into the fight with her one operational howitzer and had come up to a point about four miles from the cruiser, then began shooting. The last remaining airplane showed up at this time, with Lieutenant Watkins in the pilot's seat, and, directed by the plane's observer, *Mersey* began firing salvos at the stricken ship as well, twenty-eight of them, with hits beginning on the third salvo.

At 2.20 the British finally decided they had fired enough shells, and *Severn* decided to make a reconnaissance of the enemy position. But ten minutes later the order to return to base came from the admiral's flagship, and the two monitors began their trip back down the river on the outgoing tide. The airplane reported *Königsberg* sunk in the water to the bridge and smoking heavily as though fires were still going aboard her. The mission to sink or destroy the *Königsberg* was accomplished, Lieutenant Watkins said.

Yet the end of *Königsberg* had not come yet, as Captain Looff said in the official report written from his hospital bed. On 12th July, Korvettenkapitän Schoenfeld of the Delta Force suggested that it would be valuable to salvage the guns of the cruiser, and within a matter of hours a salvage detail of thirty men under Kapitänleutnant Hinrichs returned to the ship and began to work. Parts of the guns had been thrown overboard, but divers went down and recovered them. The guns and the one unbroken searchlight of the ship were found. Lieutenant Hinrichs employed a hundred natives, and with rafts and small boats they began to bring up the guns. While this salvage was in process, Admiral King-Hall began to wonder if the *Königsberg* really had been completely destroyed or if just such salvage could be carried out, and Major Cull (for he had been promoted) flew over the battered hulk. Just as the admiral had suspected, the major saw boats and rafts drawn up alongside the ship, and surmised that the Germans were salvaging the guns.

The unwounded of the crew assembled near the wreck and gave three cheers for the Kaiser and for Germany; the battle flags were retrieved from the mast of *Königsberg* where they still fluttered, and were taken to the hospital to be presented to Captain Looff. Surgeon Eyerich had all the work he could manage tending to the wounded; but there was little to be done for most of them except bind up their wounds and give them morphine for the pain.

As for the unwounded, they passed their first nights

ashore huddled together in little groups around campfires with no protection from the mosquitos, contracting dozens of cases of malaria.

In the hospital, Captain Looff and Ensign Wenig shared a veranda – as close an approach to privacy as might be attained in the awkward quarters offered Eyerich for his work. Two sisters of the Red Cross of Dar es Salaam magically appeared at the plantation and undertook the hard work of nursing the wounded and the sick.

Badly wounded as he was, Captain Looff finished his report to the Admiralty in the next few days for the very good reason that Captain Christiansen was still in German East Africa, itching to start on his long journey home to Berlin. He took with him the completed report, travelled to Portuguese Mozambique, and found a neutral ship that took him back to Europe. Three months later Captain Christiansen delivered the report in Berlin.

18
Ready for Battle

CAPTAIN LOOFF'S MAJOR worry when he was brought to the hospital was that his intestinal wall had been penetrated by the fragments that had wounded him in the body, and when Surgeon Eyerich assured him that the wall was intact, he set confidently about the task of recovery from his wounds. Lieutenant Wenig's wounds were more painful: his left foot had been slit from ball to ankle by a fragment and had to be amputated, and the other was nearly as badly hurt. Wenig also did not have the advantage of the captain, who had already suffered from malaria and was no longer prey to most strains of the fever; the younger man was delirious for several days.

Among the officers there were many wounded, and loyal red-haired Radio Officer Niemyer was dead, killed at his gun as he fired the last shots of the *Königsberg* against her enemies. As the days went by, other wounded men died, and finally they were buried and a cairn was built near the site of the wreck, listing the names of the dead and reminding the world of the ship's old motto:

> To be strong before the enemy, to be the upholder of your country, and to remain faithful until death and through battle and all trials; that will always be the supreme rule of your crew.

And so they had been, firm before the enemy for nearly a year, the supporter of the Fatherland, and faithful until death through all the combat and trials, the worst of the trials being the long months of waiting without knowing, and then finally knowing they had been deserted by the Fatherland itself.

As the officers and men recuperated in the tiny makeshift hospital it was decided that the remainder of *Königsberg*'s crew would be kept as a fighting unit. Lieutenant Colonel von Lettow-Vorbeck wanted to break up the crew and assign the men to his various units around the colony, but Captain Looff appealed to Governor Schnee; it is an indication of the relationship between Schnee and von Lettow-Vorbeck that the governor was able to have his way in such a matter, and Captain Looff kept his command.

Actually, when the news of the gallant defence of the *Königsberg* reached Germany, it was not long before the Kaiser awarded Captain Looff the Iron Cross, first class, and bestowed enough Iron Crosses, second class, on the *Königsberg* to equal one for every other man of the ship. (Captain Looff was to pick out the recipients.) Further, Fregattenkapitän Looff was promoted to Kapitän zur See, which meant that technically he outranked Lieutenant Colonel von Lettow-Vorbeck, even if everyone in the colony, and most of all Captain Looff, recognised that von Lettow-Vorbeck was the commander of the forces in East Africa, and properly so. The naval people and the reservists did not have sufficient experience in tropical field operations to undertake command of such a force. Captain Looff and his men knew that they had a lot to learn from the colonial soldiers, and they undertook the task.

The steam lighter *Hedwig* had been lying secreted in a creek nearby and was brought alongside the wreck of the *Königsberg* two days after the sinking. Then her crew worked with the rafts and natives to bring aboard the guns. In two more days six of the guns were aboard, and a few days later the rest came on. They were loaded on wagons and dragged the one hundred and twenty-four miles to Dar es Salaam, over river fords, rough bridges, and across a log road much of the way. Each of the sixteen-foot guns was a heavy load – it took four hundred Negroes to pull the wagons into the colony's capital.

There the battered guns were taken to the naval repair yard and the railway yards which had the machine tools necessary for repairing and replacing the steel parts. In a few weeks all the guns were made serviceable again, giving the defenders of German East Africa ten invaluable pieces of 105-mm artillery, or four-inch guns, with which to fight off the British. Five of the guns were mounted for the defence of Dar es Salaam, two were taken to Tanga, two to the port of Ouidjidji on Lake Tanganyika, and one to Mwanza on Lake Victoria Nyanza. Mounting them was a real problem, for these guns, unlike field pieces, were meant to fire from a fixed pedestal. Lieutenant Carl Hauser and Lieutenant Apel, the *Königsberg*'s gunnery officer, worked out the problem mathematically and then physically with the chief naval engineer of the port, and several gun carriages were built at the shops of the naval port facility.

For the crew of the *Königsberg*, there was little time to be wasted after they had gained their second wind. Lieutenant Colonel von Lettow-Vorbeck was agitating for their immediate removal to Dar es Salaam, and Governor Schnee concurred for once; he feared an attack on the capital city, for now that *Königsberg* was destroyed the British naval forces in the area were left with very little to do but carry out nuisance raids. But the crew could not be moved quickly; in the last fight they had lost nearly everything they possessed. The supply officer managed to find enough clothing to outfit fifty men in the khaki of the Defence Force, and they marched off through the bush towards Dar es Salaam. For the hundred and eighty men left, including the wounded, there was much work to be done. The ship's tailor and the ship's cobbler managed to salvage enough leather and canvas to begin making clothing and shoes, and volunteers were put to work to help them. The biggest problem – or at least one of the first – was creating a dye from tree roots and mangrove bark which turned the white cloth just the right colour. The tailors worked day

164

and night to cut and sew the clothes for the men.

By the end of July the divers who had been working on the sunken *Kronborg* in Manza Bay were finished; among other things they had brought up one thousand rounds of ammunition for the guns of *Königsberg*. They came to the Rufiji Delta to see what could be salvaged from the interior of the warship, and in the magazine flooded by the order of the captain to avoid explosion they found four hundred and fifty more shells. They worked to salvage everything savable, but soon the salvage was turned over to the Delta detachment, and they supervised the work for many weeks. The divers brought up one hundred and fifty ammunition boxes and other invaluable material but found some of it already destroyed by the river water. This work continued for a long time, and when all was done that could be done the remainder was blown up with dynamite so the British might not find any value in the ship in case they came to capture her.

As Captain Looff made ready to assume the responsibility of defence of Dar es Salaam, he considered the plight of his men: they were totally unfamiliar with bush warfare or bush life; the experience of the naval contingents which had gone to the north and west was proof of the difficulties of conversion from one service to another; of Korvetten-kapitän Zimmer's men from *Möwe* and the first detachment from *Königsberg*, some eighty per cent came down in the first few weeks with malaria.

But as it turned out, there was time for the navy men to learn something about the country and bush warfare, because the real battle for German East Africa was not to begin until the spring of 1916.

Captain Looff brought his men to Dar es Salaam, and established his headquarters in the customs house there. Then the training began. The navy men had learned to shoot and to march, but now they were to spend many hours in the field on long and short marches, to harden them and accustom them to the hardships of soldiering in a tropical climate. Furthermore, if they were to be effective

165

fighting men they must learn to talk with the blacks, so every German seaman undertook the study of Swahili, the lingua franca of the East African coast. The language study was easier than it might seem, since each German was assigned a black as an orderly. Even white privates had black servants in these times; the men of *Königsberg* had a very good reputation among the blacks because they actually did physical labour on ship and ashore, and the blacks had never before seen a white man lift his finger thus. There was method in this madness of Captain Looff's of giving each man a servant; in order to lord it over the blacks the whites must learn the language, and that is what he wanted.

The men of *Königsberg* marched and worked and marched some more. After a few months they began playing war games, and on one occasion Captain Looff was captured by 'the enemy', the part of his force that was simulating an attack on Dar es Salaam, and managed to free himself only by pleading that he was the arbiter of the war game.

Not so many of the men of the *Königsberg* were to be left to Captain Looff as he had hoped, however. Lieutenant Colonel von Lettow-Vorbeck was to have his way, crying out his need for troops to go into the field, although Captain Looff had his way, too; the troops culled from the *Königsberg* on this second go-around were kept together, in what was called the *Königsberg* Company, and they were commanded by Kapitänleutnant Georg Koch, Looff's first officer. They were one hundred and twenty men, with fifteen Askaris to guard their baggage and four hundred and fifty porters to carry it in the bush. They trained with the Dar es Salaam defence force for many weeks, but it was understood that they were a fighting force that would be sent out into the field at the first opportunity.

Kapitänleutnant Koch was a good soldier, just as he had been a good seaman. He trained his men to be able to march twelve or fourteen hours a day in the broiling heat.

The training began in the autumn and continued through the winter months, although winter is a relative word in East Africa. Then came the month of March, 1916.

19

The War on Land

GOVERNOR SCHNEE AND Lieutenant Colonel von Lettow-Vorbeck were faced with the difficulty of policing and protecting an area twice the size of Germany with a force that numbered no more than three thousand whites and eleven thousand Askaris. During the first phase of the war the numbers did not make much difference, for the action was desultory and confined to little more than skirmishes; the Germans could not mount a major offensive against the British and the British were not ready to mount an offensive for the first year and a half of the war.

The geography of East Africa controlled the placement and movement of von Lettow-Vorbeck's troops and those of the naval force. Much of the naval contingent was concentrated in the west, in the lake country, but the rest of the force, Captain Looff's defence command and Lieutenant Koch's *Königsberg* Company, were to fight their war in the southern and southeastern parts of the colony. Lieutenant Colonel von Lettow-Vorbeck was pleased enough to have them take responsibility for defence of this long line because his hands were quite full enough in the north. In the early fighting he had lost many of his trained officers. Major Kepler was killed, as were Lieutenants Spalding, Gerlich, Kaufmann, and Erdmann, and Captain von Hammerstein died of a wound – altogether one-seventh of the professional officers knocked out of the fighting in the first six months.

The worry of the Germans was that the immense resources of South Africa would be turned against them, but in the early months of the war the intervention of South Africa did not seem to materialise. Instead General Christian DeWet and other old Boer leaders staged an abortive rebellion, keeping the South African government occupied at home. Lieutenant Colonel von Lettow-Vorbeck concentrated his Germans and Askaris in the Kilimanjaro country, where the British and their Masai allies threatened. In July 1914 the British attacked in the area, without much success, but there came ominous news from the Germans' intelligence units: the British were building a railway in the area, from Voi to Makatan, which meant the war would soon be stepped up.

Some commanders might have regarded the increase in British attention to this theatre with dismay, but part of the greatness of von Lettow-Vorbeck as a soldier lay in his attitude: he welcomed the coming of more British troops to his front. 'It was important,' he said, 'to encourage the enemy in this intention, in order that the South Africans should really come and that in the greatest strength possible, and thus be diverted from other and more important theatres of war.'

At the end of 1915 the British were moving stronger forces into the Kilimanjaro country, and the Germans were attacking the Uganda railway with patrols and larger units, harrying the British. A typical operation was that against Kasigao Mountain, some twenty miles from the Uganda railway. In the summer of 1915 the Germans sent a force of several hundred Askaris and Europeans against a small British outpost there and captured the place. One position after another was taken until the Germans held the mountain.

Lieutenant Colonel von Lettow-Vorbeck supervised this operation himself, for he intended to push to such positions, hoping the British would come in vastly superior force to try to drive his men out of the redoubts. Kasigao thus was an admirable base for patrols against the British inside their own territory.

By the end of 1915 the British had become quite annoyed

with the incursions of the Germans into British East Africa, and General Sir H Smith-Dorrien was detailed from London to Africa to put an end to German resistance. General Smith-Dorrien sailed to South Africa, but at Cape Town he fell ill and could not carry out his assignment. Then the British General Staff made the historic decision to use General Jan Christian Smuts, one of their old enemies from the days of the Boer War, but now a loyal British citizen. General Smuts's appointment was immensely popular in South Africa and made it possible for the British to recruit thousands of South Africans to the colours. On 12th February 1916 General Smuts sailed from South Africa for East Africa, in command of an army raised in South Africa itself, and on his arrival in East Africa he immediately moved into action, for there were only five weeks remaining before the rainy season would start in the Kilimanjaro district.

As early as the summer of 1915 von Lettow-Vorbeck had begun planning for his eventual retreat into German territory, and it was apparent to him that the country through which the northern railway passed would fall to the enemy as soon as a sufficient concentration of British troops was brought into the area, so a new German railway – a short north-south line – was built that year from Mombo to Handeni, and the majority of the German stores were moved south. Obviously, Lieutenant Colonel von Lettow-Vorbeck was planning a defensive war. The German positions in the mountains could be held only briefly; they depended on carriers by the thousand to bring in everything including water.

As the concentration of troops began to build, the Germans made a strong defensive position at Oldorobo Mountain, held by three companies with two light field guns under Major Kraut. The mountain arose from the flat thorn desert near the main road that ran to Taveta, and the position was located seven and a half miles from that town. It was a strong position, for the mountain dominated all the plain around; its great deficiency was the absolute lack of water, and although von Lettow-Vorbeck brought in Lieutenant Matuschka, a celebrated water witch, even this expert could locate no moisture on the barren mountain, and all water had to be carried by donkey cart from Taveta to the entrenchments the Germans and Askaris were cutting into the rock.

Later in the winter the British pushed to within three miles of the mountain and established a base camp, supplied by their railway, and even brought in their own piped water supply from the springs in the Bura Mountains behind them. A daring raid by Lieutenant von S'Antenecai destroyed the British reservoir, but it was soon restored and the British troops were only temporarily discomfited. By the time General Smuts was appointed, the British troops in the area had moved to within three hundred yards of the German position at Oldorobo in an abortive attack and had been driven off with heavy losses, retreating to their camps three miles away. This situation existed when General Smuts arrived to take command of the British effort in East Africa.

General Smuts had no intention of losing men in attacks on the strong Oldorobo position; he decided to outflank it and go around, simply leaving the Germans there to survive as best they could, while he fought von Lettow-Vorbeck elsewhere. On 8th March the British began the real land war, which was to continue unabated for the next two and a half years.

On 8th March the British began their move, as far as the Germans were concerned; on that day the outposts on Oldorobo saw columns of troops first sweeping round to the north from their camps on the east, then moving west, to reach a point an hour's march north of Taveta. The British idea was to march through the gap between Kilimanjaro and the Pare Hills, to strike the main force of the Germans in the neighbourhood of Taveta and Salita. Meanwhile another unit, the First Division, was to cross the waterless desert between Longido and Engare Nanjuke, to cut the German communications on the northern railway

and outflank von Lettow-Vorbeck. The British estimated
the German strength in the area at six thousand rifles – a
term they used because of the difficulty of semantics in
describing Askari troops and European troops separately.
(A rifle was still a rifle, no matter who used it.) The British
strength was nearly four times as great.

By afternoon the British were well along in their march,
accomplishing their aim, and Lieutenant Colonel von
Lettow-Vorbeck saw that his position at Oldorobo had
been rendered untenable; all those months of preparation
had been wasted and he must withdraw his men for a
fresh stand on the mountains that overlooked the gap
between Kilimanjaro and the Pares. That night Major
Kraut was ordered to move out to a position on the Resta-
Letema Mountains on the road from Taveta to New
Steglitz, and, on the northwest, Lieutenant Schulz's
detachment was detailed to cover the withdrawal and
occupy the mountains of North Kitovo.

So on the morning of 9th March, the Germans were
deployed for battle, yet the mountain position they had
taken was not very advantageous to them because they had
so few troops to cover a front that was now twelve miles
long. Lieutenant Colonel von Lettow-Vorbeck fought in
the only manner he could: he covered the main trails and
roads and breakthrough points with troops, but kept the
bulk of this force in reserve at Himo, to be used as the trend
of British movement indicated.

Meanwhile, as von Lettow-Vorbeck knew very well, the
British were also advancing to the south from Londigo in
another column; but although he knew, there was nothing
he could do immediately to stop this advance. In the months
past he had quite expected it. He had prepared trails and
roads north and south, east and west, so that he could move
troops rapidly from Kilimanjaro to the rear, but now he
first must fight the British in this area, then dash back and
fight them again, if he was lucky enough to turn them at
the passes.

From Tanga one of the *Königsberg*'s guns was brought

up by rail to be fixed in position on the passes. It was carried to Kahe, on the south bank of the Pangani River, and placed, ready for action.

On 10th March the British reconnoitred the front line in the mountain area and sent airplanes into the area to bomb and to observe the German positions as well as they could. The next day the airplanes reappeared over New Moshi, the German headquarters, and dropped bombs, and a few hours later the British attacked from Taveta on the mountain positions, a feinting action to keep the Germans occupied in this area while the major movement was made to the British right and the German left, along the south-eastern slopes of Kilimanjaro.

For two days the battle was in the balance in the Latema Mountain area, where Major Kraut was defending, and when the superiority of British power was felt the Germans moved back in a night march, but not all of them moved. The fighting was so severe that the troops were soon out of contact with headquarters, and it was not until 12th March, that Lieutenant Colonel von Lettow-Vorbeck learned the British had returned to Taveta. His men were still in control of their original positions, but not having known this, the commander had evacuated their flank, making their position untenable and forcing their with-drawal from the mountain gap. The British threatened New Moshi momentarily, so von Lettow-Vorbeck moved his headquarters back to New Steglitz plantation in the rear, halfway between Kahe and Resta. Here the commander took over the main building of the plantation.

In a few days the two British columns had moved in to control the Taveta-New Moshi-Aruscha area, and on 21st March they occupied Kahe Station and Kahe Hill. The next day the South Africans moved on to the Ruvu River in a dawn attack and crossed. Here was the point at which the four-inch gun from *Königsberg* had been placed by Captain Schoenfeld. During the battle the gun had worked nobly, driving the British back several times and putting their pompoms out of action. But on the afternoon of 21st

March, Lieutenant Colonel von Lettow-Vorbeck received an urgent message that strong British forces were advancing in the rear of the German positions towards the railway, and he issued orders for an immediate withdrawal towards Kissangire. The position on the south bank of the river was abandoned, and the gun, which had no carriage, was blown up rather than left to fall into the hands of the British. Thus perished the first of *Königsberg*'s ten big guns.

How unnecessary it had been – Lieutenant Colonel von Lettow-Vorbeck arrived at the Kissangire Station to discover that the British were not there at all, that they had not even come near, and that he had abandoned his position without reason. But what was done was done, and what remained was to fight a delaying action, waiting for a chance to outmanœuvre the superior enemy forces and to keep his own lines of communication intact and his force from being surrounded.

So, by 22nd March, the German defenders had been driven out of the country along the Ruvu River and the Kilimanjaro region was in British hands. It was a matter of triumph for the British; for Lieutenant Colonel von Lettow-Vorbeck it was the expected, and he lost neither heart nor sleep over a situation he could not avoid. Bedded down at night on the couch in the living room of the old plantation house, he slept like a baby and plotted deeply in his dreams against his enemies.

The Germans moved southwest in the Pare Mountains, and brought up more of their precious horde of artillery, including another of the guns of *Königsberg* – this one mounted on wheels. But the British kept advancing, almost south, along the road to Kondoa-Irangi in the interior, and there was nothing von Lettow-Vorbeck could do to stop them. The German commander brought troops down from the northwest, where he had three companies in the Lake Kivu area, and brought other troops up from Dar es Salaam. He left the northern railway in the hands of Major Kraut and headed south to defend the central section of the colony. He went by train to Korogwe, then along the new line south to Handeni, then set out by car for the new front deep in the interior.

The rainy season had set in, and the going was difficult. The road was little more than a track, and it was washed out here and there by the flooding of normally dry stream beds, impassable in parts because of the rutting caused by the wooden wheels of army carts that had preceded his car. Telephone and telegraphic communications were broken down by the torrential rain and by giraffes, who moved across the country without concern, breaking the lines and knocking down the poles.

As the commander moved inland the rain came down harder and harder and the roads became less passable. Before they reached Tuliana they had been forced to stop a half-dozen times, and it took twenty or more carriers to haul the car out of the mud each time it mired. Just beyond Tuliana it appeared that they were stopped for good – the torrential stream had washed away the wagon bridge. The car was abandoned, but even the men were not sure of getting across the swiftly flowing muddy river. Lending a hand himself, von Lettow-Vorbeck had a tree felled across the river. The tree was three feet thick, but as it fell into the river it was carried away like a matchstick.

The commander's adjutant, Lieutenant Müller, tried to swim across the current, but was cast back upon the bank and was lucky to get out alive. Captain Tafel tried, and he managed to reach the other side, but he could not carry a line. So there they were, the captain on one side, naked as a baby, and the officers on the other, with a torrent of muddy water between. Finally the day was saved by a native who told the party of a ford some miles downstream, and down they went, to find a ford so deep they had to struggle across in shoulder-deep water holding on to one another, and even then the crossing took three-quarters of an hour.

The journey continued all night long in the pouring rain, on foot and on horseback, wading in water up to their necks or up to the horses' withers. Finally they reached the temporary rail line that had been built between the Wami

174

River and Kimamba Station, and there they boarded a handcar which would take them to Kimamba on the central railway line – a point from which they could reach Dodoma and be within striking distance of the enemy threat to the north. What a journey: the trackage of the little line was improperly laid and the handcar kept going off the rails as the crew took the curves too fast, dumping Lieutenant Colonel von Lettow-Vorbeck and his aides alongside the railway time and again. But finally, early in the morning, they arrived at Kimamba, and the commander found dry clothes and made himself presentable for a meeting with Governor Schnee, who had come to the town especially for this conference. The governor was convinced – and there was no question about it – that the colony must be defended in the interest of the homeland. For almost the first time, governor and military commander saw eye to eye.

From Kimamba, Lieutenant Colonel von Lettow-Vorbeck made a four-day trek north to the Burungi Mountains, south of Kondoa-Irangi, where Captain Klinghardt was leading the defence force, and soon brought up two field guns, one of the *Königsberg* guns and a 3·5-inch gun, which were used to shell the British positions just south of the town.

He arrived there early in May. Skirmishes and patrol action were all to be reported in the next few weeks. Early in June the British brought up field guns to reply to the four-inch gun of *Königsberg* but they did not find or damage the gun.

So, in the middle of June 1916, the guns of *Königsberg*, like the crew of the cruiser, were scattered all about East Africa. Nine guns were left, one here in the Burungi Mountains, under Lieutenant Frankenberg, two in the west on the borders of Lake Tanganyika, one at Mwanza on Lake Victoria, and five guarding the waterfront at Dar es Salaam.

20

The *Marie*

THE *KRONBORG* HAD been sent to German East Africa by the German Admiralty, but the Admiralty was not the only government agency of the empire concerned with events in the colony; quite independently, Governor Schnee had appealed for help from the Ministry of Colonies in the days after Captain Looff arrived at Dar es Salaam. Governor Schnee had called to the palace a German of Baltic descent who, although he carried a Russian passport, was a loyal subject of the Kaiser. The governor had entrusted this courier with vital messages for Berlin and, protected by his Allied passport, the Balt had set off by way of Portuguese East Africa for Europe.

In his pocket the messenger carried a letter from the governor detailing the cargo most needed for the continued defence of the colony, a letter composed after many long sessions with Captain Looff and representatives of Lieutenant Colonel von Lettow-Vorbeck. So the needs were ticked off one by one, among· them such items as gun carriages to be built by Messrs Krupp for the naval guns of *Königsberg*, and a hundred other items.

But no matter what was to come, it was almost as important in these days how it came; one of the first requirements was that the load of the second blockade runner be prepared in parcels weighing sixty-six pounds apiece, the weight of a proper load for an African bearer.

The Balt's was a difficult journey, but not nearly so dangerous as the outward journey of the second blockade runner was to be. The messenger arrived in Germany before the end of 1915; his message received immediate and forceful attention in high places, and within a month Lieutenant Sorenson of the German navy was on the high seas with the innocent-looking merchant ship *Marie* that was actually a navy auxiliary, loaded to capacity with what the men of East Africa needed most. Captain Sorenson ran the British blockade much as *Kronborg* had done, yet from the beginning his mind was at rest on one point: he knew exactly where he was going, because in the absence of direct wireless communication with the homeland it was necessary for Governor Schnee to specify the place of landing for the cargo. The place was to be Lindi, in the southwestern corner of the colony, dangerously close to Mozambique, yet comfortably far from the blockading British who still lurked off the Rufiji Delta.

Marie was two months at sea, making her way carefully around Scotland, down the South Atlantic well away from the steamer lanes, skirting the Cape of Good Hope in darkness, as far out from land as she could comfortably travel in the foul weather.

This time there was no tell-tale wireless to give away the movements of the *Hilfschiff*; this time she avoided notice at Madagascar and steamed directly, if cautiously, into Ssudi Bay, the harbour for the port of Lindi. Early on the morning of 17th March, Captain Sorenson conned his ship between the headlands, and again he was assisted by a loyal German merchant mariner, another of those old captains of the German East Africa line who had chosen to risk his neck by shipping as pilot on a blockade runner.

Having learned so disastrously from the fate of the *Kronborg* what could happen to a blockade runner, the Admiralty had equipped *Marie* with a supply of mines and technicians who knew how to sow them. As she came in to harbour that March morning, the blockade runner laid eggs behind her, a mine field which would effectively prevent pursuit or the interference of any enemy ships before she had accomplished her important task.

Knowing she was coming, Captain Looff had detached

Lieutenant Hinrichs to become commander of the Coastal Defence force in the Lindi-Ssudi Bay region, and for days the Lieutenant had kept a lookout for the coming of the relief ship. A small army of bearers was on hand, waiting, and the unloading of the ship began within a matter of minutes after she was safely anchored in the harbour.

Everything had been planned at Hamburg and Wilhelmshaven. The *Marie* brought her own double pontoon bridge; it was thrown out and carried ashore, and the porters began moving to the ship, taking off their sixty-six-pound loads Indian file in a never-ending circular movement that quickly emptied the hatches. In four days fifty thousand of these loads were taken from the ship, carried to hastily erected storehouses, and arranged in orderly piles. The cargo, fifteen hundred tons of it, would soon be carried deep into the interior of Africa on the shoulders of thousands of porters. Meanwhile it was hidden safely in camouflaged godowns, far from the shore.

The reason for this care became apparent within a matter of hours after the last porter had taken the final load across the bobbing pontoon bridge; the British fleet arrived outside Ssudi Bay, armed with the information from spies in Mozambique that a German ship had arrived at Lindi. The force consisted of patrol boats, cruisers, and airplanes, and soon the ships were firing on the *Marie* while the planes rushed in to bomb her. She was hit some twenty times, above and below the water line, and developed a strong list, while her superstructure appeared quite badly hurt. From a distance it might well seem that she would never move outside Lindi port again, and the British were apparently so confident of their marksmanship that they took her appearance at face value and went away.

But the appearance was deceptive. By mid-April Captain Sorenson had made repairs and was satisfied that his ship was seaworthy enough to attempt an escape through the double blockade he now faced: on the African coast and in the North Sea, should he get so far, chased as he was sure to be by every British ship afloat in the region between.

On the dark night of 22nd April, assisted by Mother Nature in the guise of a cloudy moonless sky, Captain Sorenson started his engines and crept out of Ssudi Bay beneath the very eyes of two patrol boats on guard duty. By dawn he was well away from the coast and speeding as fast as the *Marie*'s engines would carry him, south towards blue water and safety. That next morning, Admiral King-Hall arrived off the bay in his flagship, carrying a captive balloon. The balloon was launched and raised a thousand feet in the air. Through field-glasses, Lieutenant Hinrichs and his men watched the fun as it developed. Hinrichs swore that he could see the expressions on the observer's face as he went up confidently, looked around him with complaisance as the balloon reached its peak, getting his bearings, then began sweeping the shore with glasses, first slowly, in one clean sweep, expecting to see *Marie* in her accustomed place, canted to starboard – then doing a double take, sweeping back and forth, and finally signalling frantically to be cranked down again to deck level to make his doleful report.

Hinrichs also swore that he knew, a few moments later, that the observer had been assailed by someone in authority, for up again came the balloon, and up again came the observer, sweeping the port again with his glasses, and again demanding to be taken down to repeat his negative statements.

And then – hell broke loose along the coast. Cheated of their quarry, the British ships began shelling everything in sight, and in the course of the shelling all Germans ducked for cover.

An hour later the British were gone, carrying their chagrin away in swirling wakes behind the ships, and the Germans emerged from blockhouse and slit trench to count the toll taken. Not a man was hurt, but a stray shell or two had found its way into the secret hiding place of the cargo of the *Marie*, it was reported. Lieutenant Hinrichs went to investigate. Sure enough, there was damage from explosives in one camouflaged godown where part of the supplies were stored. Strangely enough, the only destruction came in the midst of the cases of wine and liquor which had been sent for the officers' mess at Dar es Salaam. Several cases were missing altogether, blown to smithereens undoubtedly, said the *matrossen* who had been guarding the godown so carefully all these days. There were a few fragments of broken glass to prove it.

Undoubtedly, agreed Lieutenant Hinrichs.

21

The Battle of the Lakes

THE GERMAN SEAMEN of the *Königsberg* who left their ship
under orders to proceed to Lake Tanganyika and join
Captain Zimmer's flotilla in the summer of 1915 found
themselves in an entirely different position from the days in
the Rufiji Delta. Here on the lake the Germans were
supreme; it was almost boring: so superior was the lake
force that opposition melted away when the *Hedwig von
Wissmann* or the *Kingani* moved inshore along the Belgian
Congo coast, and it was only if they attempted to come too
close to Albertville or another fortified town that they saw
any action at all.

Yet the Belgians were not as quiescent as their apparent
diffidence would make them seem; before the end of 1915
the rumour filtered along the Belgian coast and crossed the
lake: the *Alexandre Delcommune* was to have a fitting
successor, a 1500-ton steamer named the *Baron Dhanis*
which would be launched very soon.

Receiving this news, Captain Zimmer was not slow to act.
Immediately he sent the *Hedwig von Wissmann* and the
Kingani on a reconnaissance mission: they were to move
along the entire Congo coast of the lake, to spy out the
shipyard, bay, or hidden creek where the new ship was
building; she must be found and destroyed before she could
be launched to threaten German superiority on the lake.
Captain Zimmer pored over his maps and interrogated his
spies and finally came to the conclusion that the most likely
spot for the construction of this vessel was the Lukuyu
River, which emptied into the lake a few miles below

Albertville. The German searchers stood outside the river mouth (they dared not go inside for fear of enfilading fire from the banks or a mined harbour) and they saw absolutely no indication of shipbuilding. They returned to Kigoma to report to Captain Zimmer. Yet the activity was going on apace, and soon the Germans were aware of it. The Belgians were so unwise as to report progress in uncoded radio transmissions between the Congo and Brussels, and these messages were picked up by the German radio station at Bukoba and quickly transmitted to Captain Zimmer.

Captain Zimmer saw an urgent need for further information, so he dispatched Lieutenant Oedbrecht on a desperate mission to secure the intelligence; Odebrecht crossed the lake one dark night, moved in to shore in a boat with muffled oars and crew warned to absolute silence, and landed just south of the river bank on the sloping shore. Alone he crept forward to a point where he had a clear view of the inner mouth of the Lukuyu, and there he discovered a miniature shipyard, capable of building a single ship. Lieutenant Odebrecht's practised eyes measured the length; she could be eighty-three yards long – but at this moment there was nothing, not even a framework of ribs fastened together on a keel. It was a happy discovery that the *Baron Dhanis* was not finished, but if she ever was launched she might be a good seventeen yards longer than *Graf Götzen*, and that was most definitely bad news. Or was she finished, and in hiding farther up the river?

From this moment on Lieutenant Odebrecht and Lieutenant Rosenthal (of the South Seas survey ship *Planet*) decided to keep the Belgian secret shipyard under surveillance. They did so by taking the most outrageous chances with their own lives, disguising themselves with cork and blankets as natives and stealing ashore night after night, together or alone, to report almost daily on the Belgian shipbuilders in the river. It meant slipping through lines of sentries, approaching the ways at close distance, almost feeling the timbers, and then slipping out again, not once, but a dozen times. One night Rosenthal captured a picket boat loaded with Africans, who confirmed all the reports made by the officers. A ship was to be built. Had it been built? The natives said it had.

On 1st December 1915, Lieutenant Rosenthal embarked on his most daring exploit; before dawn he moved the *Hedwig von Wissmann* to a point only two hundred and twenty yards off the mouth of the Lukuyu, at an angle so that as dawn came up he was able to take a photograph of the ship works inside the mouth. The light was so dim that he had to take a time exposure, and as he kept the ship there, the Belgians discovered him in the growing light of dawn and began peppering the water around the steamer. Only when he was sure that his exposure was correct did he move out into the lake away from the enemy fire.

The next night he was back again, in a small boat, quite aware that the Belgians had redoubled their vigilance. He was rowed to within three hundred and thirty yards of shore, not daring to go in closer with a boat because so much fuss had been kicked up in recent days; then he slipped into the water, swam the rest of the way to shore, made his way through the lines of sentries, and again to the shipyard, where he checked on the supplies laid aside for the building of the ship. Some movement, some prescience of the enemy must have alerted the sentinels that all was not well, because as Lieutenant Rosenthal examined the shipways, suddenly lanterns began flickering all around him, and he could hear voices muttering in Swahili and in French. He escaped by plunging into the river and swimming out to his boat.

The next night he was back, this time with a life belt in case he must swim for it again, his shoes slung around his neck, wearing only a shirt and trousers. He actually entered the ways and there found two powerful motorboats of a new design – the craft the natives reported to be finished – but no steamer nor any sight of one upriver.

That night, before dawn began to break, Lieutenant Rosenthal swam back out from the shore to the point where he was to meet the landing boat, but he could not find it this time, and although he swam around in circles he did not find the boat. Dawn came, finding him still in the water, stiff and cold, and to the north he could see the *Hedwig von Wissmann*, steaming back to the German side of the lake, his friends having given him up for lost.

It was a desperate moment; in the growing light he might expect to be discovered any moment from the shore, and his escape route was destroyed. Yet Lieutenant Rosenthal did not give up. He swam two miles south of the entrance to the river, and then, nearly exhausted, struggled to the beach and hid himself in the forest beyond.

By the time he arrived at a place he considered safe it was broad daylight – 8.30 in the morning – and then, after hours and days of the most unusual kind of luck, fortune deserted him, and he walked straight into the arms of a patrol of Belgian Askaris.

Yet even captured, Lieutenant Rosenthal did not give up; he still had a job to finish, to tell Captain Zimmer about the presence of the two motorboats in the mouth of the river. He obtained permission to write a letter to Kigoma, on the pretext of asking for clothing to comfort him in his captivity. (These were still the days of the gentleman's war, at least in the colonies.) On the back of this innocent letter, in urine, he inscribed a secret message of quite another variety. Lieutenant Rosenthal's job was done.

The same bad luck that dogged the lieutenant that dark night seemed to have transferred itself to all the German fortunes on the lake; the message was two months delayed.

Another officer, Lieutenant Schoenfeld, was given Rosenthal's job when the *Hedwig von Wissmann* came back to report the doleful news of Rosenthal's disappearance, and this time Captain Zimmer was so nervous about the activity in the Lukuyu river that he gave Schoenfeld *carte blanche* to take any action that seemed necessary to preserve German superiority on the lake. The *Kingani*, commanded by Lieutenant Jung, was also assigned to assist Lieutenant Schoenfeld.

Captain Zimmer was nervous. He did not quite know why, but he had the definite feeling that something was afoot – the lake was far too quiet and the British were doing nothing apparent to reduce German control; such action, particularly in anything relating to naval authority, was quite unlike his British cousins.

Captain Zimmer's intuitive suspicion was precisely correct: the British were well along in their plans to bring disaster to the Germans by December 1915. The *cadeau noir* they proposed to offer their enemies was bound up in the two motorboats that sat so tinily in the ways behind the mouth of the Lukuyu; they represented the highest-level planning of the Admiralty in Whitehall.

In Whitehall the admirals had sat for many hours around long conference tables, poring over the facts of the war in the lake country of Africa. How best could they challenge the German superiority of Lake Tanganyika, with fast boats lightly armed or with slower craft capable of outgunning the *Hedwig von Wissmann* and the *Kingani*? In the Rufiji Delta they had chosen to use their monitors, little more than floating platforms for 155-mm guns, but the lake war was of an entirely different nature. In the Rufiji they were facing a stationary enemy who was not expected to move; in the lakes they faced an enemy with command of water four hundred miles long and thirty miles wide, who could move back and forth to any point in that lake, almost with impunity. So while the big-gun, slow-speed plan was adopted for use against *Königsberg*, the small-gun, fast-craft idea won in the discussions of means to defeat the Germans on the lakes – and the two motorboats were the result. The boats secured were thirty-nine feet long, seven feet wide, and they displaced four and a half tons each; they were like the big party boats that one often saw on the lakes of Switzerland and Scotland, carrying perhaps a dozen or so sightseeing tourists; they were capable of fifteen knots – the important factor, for that meant they were considerably faster than either *Hedwig von Wissmann* or *Kingani*. Each motorboat carried a 47-mm gun and a

Maxim rapid-firing anti-personnel gun. The little boats were aptly named, *Mimi* and *Toutou*, as dainty a pair of creatures as ever existed on Lake Tanganyika. They had come from the docks of England to Cape Town in the summer of 1915 and had been brought as far as Livingstone, Rhodesia, on the railway. The railway ended there, and the remainder of the thirty-four-hundred-mile trek was made overland, under nearly impossible conditions.

The key word was *nearly*: the British and Belgians combined a huge party of bearers, soldiers, and engineers to bring the two motorboats overland to the lake. The engineers went ahead, guarded by soldiers, cutting down trees, and building bridges (more than two hundred of them), blazing a trail across the desert. Behind came two steam tractors, pulling the boats on their carriages, the tractors pushed and pulled by human hands almost as often as pushing and pulling on their own power; so slow was the progress that it averaged less than six miles per day. The route went through jungle and desert and across mountains six thousand feet high, until they reached the rail terminus in the Belgian Congo and the boats were carried by train to the banks of the lake at the mouth of the Lukuyu.

Unknown to the Belgians and the British – although certainly suspected by anyone with a grain of common sense – was the fact that Captain Zimmer had been tracing on his map the daily progress of the expedition until the time it reached the lake. The trouble was that Captain Zimmer did not know exactly what the expedition carried; the jungle telegraph was capable of telling him of the coming of tractors and men cutting their way through the jungle carrying boats, but he did not realise the exact nature of the threat. Thus, as it turned out, the critical moment in the British-Belgian plan was the night of 2nd December 1915, when Lieutenant Rosenthal saw the two motorboats at their moorings in the river but was abandoned and captured before he could transmit the information to Captain Zimmer. Just that close did the British effort come to disaster before it was launched – for Captain

Zimmer would have correlated this information to all his other intelligence, and the result would have been a do-or-die raid on the budding shipyard which certainly would have destroyed the *Mimi* and the *Toutou*.

Christmas Day came and went, the next day was Sunday, and that morning Lieutenant Commander B Spicer Simpson and the twenty-eight officers and men who would man the two motorboats were ready for action.

The crews were attending church service, actually, when Lieutenant Schoenfeld arrived in the *Kingani* to undertake the destruction of the little shipyard – for that was the course he had chosen, deciding to take no chances on what was happening at this strange river scene. The *Kingani* did not come straight in, however; Lieutenant Schoenfeld was combining a normal reconnaissance mission with his attack on the shipyard. Indeed the decision to destroy the shipyard was a casual one, taken without thought of any emergency but simply as a precaution which could be carried out at leisure. Consequently, the *Kingani* turned south seven miles offshore and headed in for the Bay of Tamboua, where the Germans often began their reconnaissance missions, sweeping up the coast north from that point.

On this Sunday morning the British finished their prayers and manned their boats. The weather was worsening rapidly; it had been sunny at 9.30 but by 11, when they were ready for action, it was raining and the wind had risen to Force 7 on the Beaufort scale, a half a gale, one might say. At 11.40 the motorboats were under way; at 11.47 they were in sight of the *Kingani*, lying, engines stopped, in the bay.

When the two little dots appeared from around the corner of the Belgian coast, Lieutenant Jung ordered his engineer to make ready to steam away, for these boats came where no boats ought to be, and at this moment the motorboats opened fire with their 47-mm guns.

Kingani carried only one gun, a pompom mounted on the foredeck; in the past this piece had been more than adequate for the tasks she was singled out to accomplish, but today it was no more than a popgun. Lieutenant Jung began firing back, and he did hit the *Toutou* once; but once was all, because the superior speed of the British ships, as calculated by the admirals in their chairs in Whitehall, enabled Lieutenant Commander Simpson to run around behind *Kingani*, thus masking the motorboats from the fire of the steamer, while they fired at will.

The motorboats moved in to a point fifteen hundred yards off *Kingani*'s bow, the gunners aiming at her high white silhouette and their shots – high explosive – striking true almost every time. One shell came in over the shield of the pompom, wrecking the gun, cutting Lieutenant Jung in two, and killing an underofficer. A moment later another shell killed the first mate, and a third smashed three natives overboard. In a few moments only two Europeans were left alive on the steamer: the helmsman and the engineer. The helmsman was stunned by shellfire, but he automatically kept the ship headed northeast for *Kigoma* and safety. The engineer was unhurt and he tried to get every bit of speed out of the engines to flee from the enemy; coming above deck he discovered how much fleeter were his adversaries, and seeing the uselessness of further flight and the impossibility of fight with a burst gun, he moved aft to the mast and hauled down the German battle flag. He stopped the engines, and the fight was over. It was 11.58 – the battle had been joined and lost in eleven minutes, so quickly that poor dead Lieutenant Jung had not really had time to understand that he was in a battle to the death.

By this time the lake was raging like a sea in a storm and it took an hour to bring *Kingani* in to shore. No men could be shipped from the motorboats to the steamer in the sea; three times it was tried and on the third time *Mimi* struck the steamer so hard the motorboat began to take water through her seams. There was nothing to be done but to order the steamer steered into the river by the Germans, and this was done. She was beached gently on the sand there, and the affair was ended. The British, who had not lost a man in the battle, had nearly lost their motorboats. *Toutou* would go from bad to worse and would soon become quite useless, but she had done her job; the *Kingani* was now British property, to be renamed *Fifi*.

Captain Zimmer waited in vain for the return of the Schoenfeld detachment, and it was not for two months that he learned definitely that the *Kingani* was beached inside the mouth of the river, even then he was led to believe that she had fallen victim to shore batteries. The message of Lieutenant Rosenthal had not yet arrived at his headquarters, and so he was unaware of the presence of a force strong enough to offer him a threat.

Fifi was some time in being repaired and was not seen abroad on the lake until 20th January 1916, when she went out south on her 'maiden' voyage as a British man-of-war. Seeking the wood she burned as fuel, she moved in towards shore on the Belgian side – and so well kept had been the secret of her capture that the Belgians ashore opened fire on her, in the mistaken belief that she was still a German ship – fortunately for her, without scoring a hit.

Poor *Toutou* sank in a storm that struck the lake at the end of January and had to be raised for repairs. Also, with the British on the job and looking for ships, the *Alexandre Delcommune* was recovered, and although pierced by forty German shells, she, too, was restored, although she needed a new engine.

On 8th February, Captain Zimmer decided to recapture the *Kingani* and to destroy whatever installation and whatever vessels existed unseen inside the mouth of the river. To undertake the assignment he choose the *Hedwig von Wissmann* and the newly launched *Graf Götsen*, manned by the men of *Königsberg*. These ships would be accompanied by the steam launch from the *Möwe*. The plan called for the *Hedwig von Wissmann*, under Lieutenant Odebrecht, to run down the east coast to a point opposite the river, then head south as if going off on a long reconnaissance, sweep around forty miles and come up to the mouth of the river before dawn, drop native spies, and then rejoin the steam launch on the other side of the lake. The *Graf Götzen*, with Captain Zimmer in command, would join them there and at midnight on the night of 9th February they would make a combined attack on the river mouth, destroying or taking everything there.

So it was that on the morning of 9th February, having dropped the spies, Lieutenant Odebrecht saw coming towards him a strange procession. In the lead he recognised the *Kingani*, but she was flying a British flag. Following her came a strange narrow motorboat (the *Mimi*), and in the wake came two other, slower motorboats, the *Vedette* and the *Dix Tonnes*, actually petrol tankers for the motor launch *Mimi*, which burned a tremendous amount of fuel at top speed.

Seeing this force coming against him when there was supposed to be no such force on the lake, Lieutenant Odebrecht ordered full steam, and turned to retreat to the safety of the company of *Graf Götzen* on the other side of the lake. But his speed was only six knots, and even by adding oil to his fires he could manage only two knots more, while the *Kingani-Fifi* made eight knots, keeping the British up with *Hedwig von Wissmann*.

The *Hedwig von Wissmann* carried two 25-mm guns, one fore and one aft – no match for the shooting power of *Fifi* and *Mimi* combined. That was the story: speed and gun-power. *Mimi* circled out around *Hedwig von Wissmann* and on her second shot from eleven thousand feet smashed the port wing of the bridge. Both *Mimi* and *Fifi* could stand out of range of *Hedwig von Wissmann* and pound her – and so they did, *Fifi* sending some sixty shells at her old companion in arms.

Lieutenant Odebrecht had little chance, but what chance he had would be augmented by the appearance of the *Graf Götzen*. She was new and shining, the pride of the German lake fleet, her paint scarcely dry. On her deck was mounted one of the *Königsberg*'s great 105-mm guns, and if she came in sight, the odds suddenly would be reversed – the little motorboat could be blown out of the water with a single shell, and treacherous *Kingani-Fifi*, fallen on such evil days, could be rendered *hors de combat* with another.

But *Graf Götzen* was nowhere to be seen, and the one-sided battle raged on.

A shell penetrated the engine room of the *Hedwig von Wissmann* and the end was in sight. The engineer was killed and the oil, ignited by the high explosive, began blazing high; another shell pierced the boiler, smashed through the hull and opened a huge breach through which water came pouring in, and the *Hedwig von Wissmann* began to list even as she blazed. Lieutenant Odebrecht ordered his men to abandon ship. One lifeboat was put over and the rest of the crew, black and white, jumped into the water clutching life vests. The ship sank in ten minutes. The lifeboat crew was captured and so were many of the swimmers; all but seven were saved, to be captured and taken to the wrong side of the lake.

The British flotilla had scarcely disappeared from the scene when the *Graf Götzen* appeared at the rendezvous. Where was the *Hedwig von Wissmann*? The steam launch had seen nothing so there was no answer to the question. The only clue that the crew of the steam launch could give was that between nine and ten o'clock in the morning they had heard the sounds of guns in the direction of the Lukuyu.

Captain Zimmer was mystified. Two of his three major vessels had disappeared and he did not have a clue as to their fate save the note that guns had been heard. He intercepted boasting messages from the Belgian radio, announcing the sinking of *Hedwig von Wissmann*, but the Belgians were sworn to secrecy as to the means by which this had been done, and Captain Zimmer could only believe that the ship had ventured too closely, too carelessly beneath the shore guns on the west.

But he was not sure, and not being sure, he took *Graf Götzen* back to Kigoma.

There the 105-mm gun from *Königsberg* soon was dismounted, because Lieutenant Colonel von Lettow-Vorbeck

191

called for all the heavy artillery to be given to the land forces. Captain Zimmer was deprived of the one weapon that assured him superiority – that kept the British safely at bay.

Graf Götzen, the pride of the lake navy, sat in port with a pompom on her stern – suitable only for defence against aircraft – and a *false gun* on her bow, representing the *Königsberg*'s gun which had been taken away from her. Here was Captain Zimmer's major problem: Lieutenant Colonel von Lettow-Vorbeck was beginning to fight a guerrilla action, really, and he was concerned with the land forces. Almost as soon as the British had begun movement against the northern railroad at Tanga, von Lettow-Vorbeck had realised that the lake country was lost, that he would be forced southwards along the east coast, and that his survival depended on his ability to group and regroup his forces in a small area. He had, in fact, already given up the west as lost and in his mind had sacrificed the brave men of the navy who were fighting a battle without arms.

The disarmament of the *Graf Götzen* was a case in point – other cases were those of the *Adjutant* and the *Wami*. The *Adjutant*, once a German tugboat, then a British armed tug, and then a German boat again, courtesy of capture and recapture, ran the blockade to Dar es Salaam. So did the little *Wami* after helping raise the guns of *Königsberg*. These two vessels were placed aboard flatcars and brought to Lake Tanganyika to augment the German fleet – but of what good was it to bring in new vessels when all Captain Zimmer had for armament were popguns? He secured a pompom for *Wami* and that was all. *Adjutant* was actually taken apart for shipment to the lake and was put down on the shore at Kigoma for reassembly.

Then in the summer of 1916 the British secured air power in the region and began bombing Kigoma. With the Belgians ready to cross the lake and now having the means to do so, obviously the end was in sight. In July, Captain Zimmer sadly supervised the filling of his great ship *Graf*

Götzen with cement and then scuttled his pride and joy, the ship that should have ruled the lake and could have, with the guns of the *Königsberg* – if even only for a little while. The *Adjutant* – which had served under two flags, as ocean steamer and river steamer, and for which Captain Zimmer had such hopes on the lake – was destroyed so that she could not be reassembled. Captain Zimmer and his naval detachment boarded the *Wami*, and headed south for the mouth of the River Malagarassi. There, having done her job, the *Wami* was scuttled, and the navy men were sailors without ships, reduced to the status of soldiers in the bush. Their task now was to stay alive and continue to fight Germany's enemies in any way they might, and to do so they moved westward. As for the guns of the *Königsberg*, it had been small use for Lieutenant Colonel von Lettow-Vorbeck to commandeer them from Captain Zimmer, thus stripping the Kigoma harbour defence and the *Graf Götzen* as he did – for when the Belgians advanced across the lake they quickly captured those same two guns. They were too heavy and could not be moved quickly enough to escape. Another gun, which Lieutenant Vogel had used with good effect to protect Mwanza, was necessarily left in place at that port because no carriage had been made for it, and this, too, was captured by the enemy. So four of the guns of *Königsberg* were gone, taken by forces of overwhelming superiority. Yet six guns remained, guns built without concern for portability, whose very conversion to field use indicated the determination of the Germans of East Africa that they would never lose this war.

22

The Battle for Dar es Salaam

IN THE BEGINNING of the war in East Africa the British and German troops were fairly matched, with only a few thousand whites on each side, plus a normal police force of perhaps eight or ten thousand Askaris, but within a matter of months the ratios changed radically. By the beginning of 1916 some thirty thousand new British troops were brought in from South Africa, and by the time the offensives were well under way British and Belgians together mounted a force of nearly a hundred and fifty thousand men against some three thousand Germans and eleven thousand Askaris in the entire colony of East Africa.

Lieutenant Colonel von Lettow-Vorbeck could never win the war in East Africa under these conditions; all he could do was avoid *losing* it. By maintaining his freedom, no matter where he had to move, he could tie up a considerable portion of the physical and financial resources of the British empire. In the case of East Africa, anything short of defeat must be considered a victory – for just as *Königsberg* had been eminently successful as a weapon of war during her long siege in the Rufiji Delta, so the German East Africa force was successful as long as it could fight. This strategic consideration was far beyond the ken of most of the defenders of East Africa, of course, and it was a tribute to von Lettow-Vorbeck and Captain Looff that they maintained the morale of their troops at a high level when the Germans were being squeezed day after day from west and north, down upon Dar es Salaam and the east coast.

The British held Kondoa-Irangi on the plain between the two German railways, but the taking and holding of it cost them dear in the first six months of 1916; von Lettow-Vorbeck estimated that through disease, patrol actions, battles, and ambushes the British lost one thousand Europeans in and around Kondoa.

By the end of June, 1916, the Belgians had pushed in from Lake Kivu and the Russissi River country, the English had come in from the Kagera west of Lake Victoria Nyanza. July marked the end of Mwanza as a German holding, and all the allied forces moved east. From the south, Belgians and British moved east from Lake Tanganyika and from Bismarcksburg, the southernmost town of German East Africa. In the battle for the territory between the railways, the single gun from *Königsberg* remaining under Lieutenant Commander Schoenfeld's command was gradually moved east and south with troops. The gun was his most formidable weapon but not enough to stop the inexorable surge of the British.

By 31st July, the British had reached Dodoma, on the central railway that extended from Dar es Salaam to Lake Tanganyika, and roughly two-thirds of East Africa was in British hands. South and east was the push, and if it continued the Germans would be forced into the sea somewhere between Lindi and Kionga at the extreme southeast point of the colony, bordered by neutral Mozambique and the Indian Ocean.

Back moved the Germans and the gun, to Mpapua, Kidete, Kilossa. At this rate it would not be long before the British reached the coastal town of Bagamoyo and then moved against Dar es Salaam. Lieutenant Colonel von Lettow-Vorbeck did not abandon the railway, however; he remained at his headquarters at Morogoro and continued to fight. The defence of Dar es Salaam was left in the hands of Captain Looff, his troops from the *Königsberg*, and the Askaris under his command.

For defence of the capital Captain Looff had precious little at his disposal. One by one his 105-mm guns were taken away from him – one, two, three they went, along with scores of his Askaris to the front on the north and west to fight and delay the advance of the British. By the late summer of 1916 Captain Looff had but two of *Königsberg*'s guns left for the defence of Dar es Salaam, one of them commanded by Lieutenant Wenig, who had lost his left leg in the last fight of the *Königsberg*, but who now was quite capable of moving about on the artificial leg that had been given him and who had grown used to endless hours in the saddle. One could not say that Lieutenant Wenig was as good as new, but he was a strong young man and Captain Looff marvelled at his powers of recuperation and his stamina.

It was good that the youthful blond Wenig was strong. The wounded and the weak of *Königsberg* were succumbing rapidly in the terrible climate of East Africa, to say nothing of the havoc wreaked by British shelling of the capital. No fewer than twenty-eight times in the spring and summer of 1916 the British blockaders moved in off the white sands of the beach to lob their death-dealing shells into the city and its environs; Captain Looff counted the shells fired in the thousands. By late summer the town still was not too badly hurt, for the British had sent in aerial observation planes to spot the guns of the *Königsberg*, and these were their usual target. The devastation was largely in the palm forest around the city, and there was one great luxury the British unwittingly brought their enemies: every time a palm tree was felled the messes enjoyed hearts-of-palm salad.

Captain Looff boasted an imposing title, or rather, three of them; he was Commander of Dar es Salaam, Commander of the Eastern Defence Region, and Director of the Services of Supply. This latter category was one he soon came to detest cordially, for Lieutenant Colonel von Lettow-Vorbeck was constantly calling on him for men and material by summer's end the imposing force he had been given in the beginning existed only on paper. His men and his Askaris, as well as his guns and ammunition, had been drained off for the fighting in the northwest. By summer so severely was the *Königsberg* force reduced that a single cruiser might have made its way into Dar es Salaam harbour, landed its marines, and seized control of the capital of German East Africa with scarcely more than a skirmish, but fortunately for the Germans the British believed firmly that Dar es Salaam harbour was mined, and so no such effort was made from the sea.

Lieutenant Wenig held the key to what defence was possible for Dar es Salaam; he had given the two newly mounted guns of *Königsberg* the greatest possible mobility, moving them to a high point behind Dar es Salaam.

On 16th August at four o'clock in the morning, the black night relieved by the silvery rays of the moon, the shore watchers reported five ships coming towards the beach of the outer harbour. As they moved in towards shore the watchers could see that the decks of the ships were covered with men – a landing was to take place after all.

Lieutenant Wenig was awakened and took charge of his battery, and in a few moments the guns of *Königsberg* opened fire. The first shots went short, but they served to alert the British to the general position of the guns (if they did not know already, through observers and spies). In answer to the two shots of *Königsberg*'s guns came no fewer than thirty-nine replies from the guns of the British squadron.

As dawn broke the British raised a captive balloon above one of their ships, its fat sausage shape climbing rapidly into the air until it stopped several hundred feet above the ship, swaying back and forth in the light breeze. In the growing light it was easy enough for Lieutenant Wenig and his men to see the ships and to fire on them from their position in the forest. But of course, the men of *Königsberg* must take fire in return, too, and it was not long before the air and ground around them were smoking with the results of the British bombardment. The brush in which they were hidden was torn up by dozens of shells and, since it was the dry season, soon the hillside was aflame. The guns had been placed near a planter's bungalow; within a matter of minutes the bungalow was almost totally destroyed by large-calibre shells from the British squadron. So heavy was the fire around the German positions that a constant rain of sand from shell explosions in the earth came down to deluge the men of *Königsberg*'s batteries and every minute or two they had to wash out the barrels of their guns to prevent sand damage. After each shell was fired from his gun Quartermaster Baudach was forced to *pry* loose the used cartridge case from the gun because the sand had wedged it in tight.

The fight lasted a good quarter of an hour, and by the end of that time the Germans manning the guns were nearly deafened from the blasts of their own weapons plus the pounding their position was taking from the British bombardment. But as the daylight strengthened Lieutenant Wenig moved back up on his hill, and there could see, with satisfaction, that his guns had done well. One of the steamers had been hit; she turned and was moving rapidly out to sea, listing heavily. Two other ships were moving to her as if to give her help. A second stricken steamer had lost her smokestack, and a huge gout of black smoke poured out of her amidships, then rose to become a stringy cloud above. What Wenig hoped to do, of course, was put out of commission some of these big guns of the British, but in the hubbub he could tell nothing of what he had accomplished to that end. He saw with satisfaction, however, that the transports had made a half turn and were moving away from the beach: the landing had been repulsed successfully.

Suddenly there was a terrible noise, a cloud of brown and black smoke was raised around one of the guns – the one near Lieutenant Wenig – and he found himself lifted into the air and thrown into a deep ravine fifteen feet from where he was standing a moment earlier. Luckily he landed on a bush, which broke his fall, and after lying there in shock for a moment or two, he scrambled to his feet, bruised, cut, and bleeding, out of the ravine and back to the gun position. A 305-mm shell had burst against the left wheel of the gun, sweeping over the crew, wrecking the gun and throwing up a cloud of sand that covered the position. His men were bowled over like ninepins, and he could not tell for a few moments who was dead, who was wounded, and who was simply knocked down by the concussion. Nearly all were dead.

Luckily, however, the British squadron and the steamers were moving away, not inshore, and the air was silent for a few moments. Lieutenant Wenig and his chief gunner, battered and wounded, examined the gun; it was canted over, but the muzzle was still pointing in the direction of the enemy squadron, and the gun was charged, for it had been ready to fire when its carriage was hit a few moments earlier. Lieutenant Wenig pulled the firing lanyard, and the piece spoke loudly, falling on the recoil so that it would be a long time before that gun ever spoke again – in this case, never.

But that last shell from the *Königsberg* gun flew through the air and landed very close to the leading British ship that was moving out of the harbour. Lieutenant Wenig sighed with pride; at least he had showed them that Germans were still living and still fighting.

A few moments later the lieutenant regretted his burst of enthusiasm, the British warships turned, and for the next two hours they continued to bombard the hillside. But the Germans left alive and unhurt dropped into trenches and waited out the bombardment. At least they were happy to see the enemy wasting his precious ammunition on a broken gun. The wounded Lieutenant Wenig was taken to Captain Looff's own house in Dar es Salaam and there was brought back to health again; and in the interim he became the captain's aide-de-camp.

So that was the story of 16th August 1916 – or part of it. Another part was sadder and less glorious: at Bagamoyo the defence force had been wiped out that same day; Captain Bock von Wulfingen and Captain von Bodecker had been killed, and the city had fallen to the British. The northern flank of Dar es Salaam was opened for direct attacks by the British. There was no need for the British amphibious force to risk lives, as it had appeared they would be doing in going into Dar es Salaam; to British and Germans alike it was apparent that soon Dar es Salaam would be taken.

Two more of the big guns of *Königsberg* were gone now, the gun put out of action in the bombardment of Dar es Salaam and another, a gun sent along with Lieutenant Friedrich and a gun crew from the *Königsberg* to defend Bagamoyo; the lieutenant, his crew, and the gun had fallen with the city. Six guns were now gone, four remained, but only one of them was left at Dar es Salaam for the defence of the capital, and that was the capital city's sole armament.

Coming from land and sea the British had been moving southwards along the coast of German East Africa with a mathematical precision. Tanga, Pangani, Sadani, and now Bagamoyo had fallen to combined land and sea assaults. The pattern was always the same: the warships came in to bombard the port and the town, and they were followed by the troop carriers, surrounded by supply ships and accompanied by airplanes whose observers transmitted their information to the ships. First the bombardment, and then the landing in strength, and soon the defence must crumble against the stronger force.

Now the war had come to Dar es Salaam in earnest. Captain Looff compared the situation to that of Hannibal before the gates of Rome – but unfortunately, he said, with the rueful humour that was his hallmark, he did not have a gate.

Had one no stake in the outcome, the method of the British in approaching Dar es Salaam might have appeared amusing; they were sure the defences of the capital were strong and secure. For many days the British sent observation planes across the city, circling and diving to escape the non-existent anti-aircraft barrage. From the landward side came marching the thousands of troops who had taken Bagamoyo; from the sea came the blockading squadron the troopships, and the dozens of other small vessels of war that added their parts to the whole. Against all these Captain Looff had a hundred and twenty-five men and a gun, the last *Königsberg* gun remaining to him, a hundred of the men deployed on the northern defences against the land invaders and twenty-five men and the gun to protect the city from the sea. The latter group could hardly be called even a fighting force, for these twenty-five men were the sick and wounded, who had been adjudged incompetent to undergo further hardships in the field and so were left in the capital.

Of course the city could not be defended, and Captain Looff, proud as he was to be chief of defence of the largest city of the largest German colony in the world, had no intention of sacrificing his few men, his gun, and his life in a gallant, useless effort. As the British prepared for their assault on the German colonial capital, Captain Looff prepared for his evacuation.

Yet he was not willing to leave the city without giving the British a run for their money; Lieutenant Wenig and the *Königsberg*'s last gun in Dar es Salaam were sent to a position behind the city, on the road that would be used to retreat into the bush. From that point, on the evening of 3rd September, the gun began to fire. After each shot or two Lieutenant Wenig moved the gun to a new position, he and his men travelling as rapidly as they could. The impression they hoped to give was of a number of German guns firing sporadically from different spots. Meanwhile Captain Looff had the searchlights manned, and here and there around the city had men signalling with lanterns, showing to all the world outside that a considerable force still occupied the capital of German East Africa.

The next day, the British began a cautious advance. From the north they came down, eight companies of British and Indian troops. The force facing them, consisting of two platoons of Askaris, fought a bit and then retired a bit, not moving back on the city, but with orders to skirt Dar es Salaam and move back to the south beyond.

From the sea, before the harbour, stood fifteen ships under Rear-Admiral Charlton, who was the successor to Admiral King-Hall as chief of the South African squadron and the blockading force. For an hour the attackers threw everything they had into the city, sparing not even the government hospital – where a hundred of the wounded and seriously ill had to be left behind to the mercies of the enemy and, from where Captain Looff sat, these did not augur to be very tender. The women and children of the Europeans had been gathered together in the neighbourhood of the hospital, assembled under the Red Cross flag of Geneva, and there they waited out the bombardment.

An hour after the bombardment began, the British sent ashore an ultimatum to the 'military governor' of Dar es Salaam.

'You have accomplished admirable things and you have defended yourselves valiantly,' said the ultimatum. 'We now demand that you surrender, under pain of seeing your city bombarded and destroyed. We guarantee the lives of the population on condition that the surrender includes all armed forces and all war materials. No communication by radio may be made. Guarantee must be given that the port is not defended by mines. . . .'

The bearer of the note was directed to the hospital, to the presence of one of Governor Schnee's secretaries, who was the highest (and only) official left in the capital, and he was there only because he was too ill to travel with the rest of the retreating force. The British had occupied the region, including every road out of Dar es Salaam except the coastal road leading south, and it was along this route that the evacuation was made, the soldier-sailors, the remainder of the colonial defence force, and the gun of *Königsberg*. Soon the British entered the city. Captain Looff saw them coming from a vantage point above the town, yet it was several hours before the enemy could raise his flag over Dar es Salaam; Captain Looff had ordered that every halyard on every flagpole in the city be cut away and it had been done. So the battle ended, and the defenders moved on, Captain Looff and his men giving up a position for the second time because they had nothing with which to defend it.

And yet as they retreated there was no thought of defeat; they were simply making a tactical movement to stand another place and fight again.

23

In the Delta

LATE IN AUGUST, as the British took Bagamoyo and threatened Captain Looff at Dar es Salaam, the main land force of South Africans was moving on Lieutenant Colonel von Lettow-Vorbeck's headquarters at Morogoro. Captain Stemmermann and the remaining *Königsberg* gun from Tanga fell back to the Uluguru Mountains and delayed the enemy, while von Lettow-Vorbeck and the headquarters group retreated towards the Rufiji Delta, and on 24th August, as the force retreated, von Lettow-Vorbeck could hear the sounds of explosions coming from the arms depots he had left behind him: the British were blowing up the dump of shells stored there for the guns of the *Königsberg* – the shells brought at such cost and difficulty by the *Kronborg* for the breakout from the delta, which now seemed so long ago.

With the fall of Morogoro, von Lettow-Vorbeck's second headquarters, and the fall of Dar es Salaam, the war in German East Africa took on an entirely different character. The Germans and their Askari allies were becoming hunted creatures, choosing to take to guerrilla tactics rather than surrender the colony to the British. In Dar es Salaam, the women and children had been bidden tearful farewell, and the men had gone off to fight the long struggle, hopeful that they might hold out until such time as the war was decided in Germany's favour in Europe. German missionaries, German civilians, and German women had accompanied the military at New Moshi, and they had lived at Morogoro, but now that Morogoro was evacuated, the women and civilians were left at the Mgeta mission, and the guerrilla nature of the German defence became complete. A handful of nurses were to accompany the German field force, and they were considered to be a part of the military.

The main German force was now in Kissaki in the Rufiji Delta region, and the Germans brought several thousand head of cattle south with them to provide food for the military.

Yet it was not all retreat: Lieutenant Colonel von Lettow-Vorbeck waited with the troops at Kissaki, waiting for the British to make a mistake so he could strike. As he had expected, once he abandoned Morogoro that headquarters ceased to interest the British, for the place itself was of small value. General Smuts sent a few detachments over the Uluguru Mountains to engage the column with the *Königsberg* gun, and the major British force separated into two columns, one moving down the east side of the mountains and the other down the west. Such a split was exactly the move awaited by Lieutenant Colonel von Lettow-Vorbeck.

West of the mountains came General Brits, who had divided his division into two mounted brigade columns and one infantry column. On 7th September, the German force under Captain Otto, encamped at a plantation near Kissaki, was attacked by one of the mounted columns; the British came around the left wing of Otto's force and were pleasantly surprised when he made no attempt to stop them. But there was good reason for Captain Otto's apparent negligence; he knew and the British did not that another German force was protecting his rear. The British came around to the left, behind the Germans, and prepared to launch an assault on the German rear. But instead they found themselves under attack by the German 11th Field Company under Lieutenant Volkwein, who charged with bayonets and routed the column. The Germans were not in position to take or hold prisoners in volume, and the dense bush made a roundup impossible in any event, but the column of British mounted troops was completely disorganised, broken into small units, and destroyed as a fighting force.

Next day, the 2nd British Mounted Brigade marched right into a German trap in the same area, and it, too, was routed. There was more action in this area, but might eventually told, and the German communications were threatened by the sheer number of British units pressing down on two sides, so the retreat began again, and the Germans moved into the Rufiji Delta.

Lieutenant Colonel von Lettow-Vorbeck still had some freedom of movement here with the use of the shallow-draft stern-wheel steamboat *Tomando* which could carry his supplies. Yet he was in constant danger because it was difficult to live off the country – and when one is responsible for the lives of several thousand troops and carriers, as he was, the problem of finding food in a sparsely populated, lightly planted region is most difficult. Indeed, for a time the Delta Force of von Lettow-Vorbeck was largely supported by the shooting of hippos and elephants.

From the Rufiji Delta, the Germans moved out along the perimeter, carrying out patrols and raids on the British who surrounded their refuge. They could not win a war here, but they could keep the British off balance, and that is exactly what Lieutenant Colonel von Lettow-Vorbeck did during the autumn of 1916. Headquarters was established at Makima, and here the soldiers of the north and the sailors from the east met and mingled, and Captain Looff became second in command to Lieutenant Colonel von Lettow-Vorbeck.

In the meantime, the fighting was continuing in other areas, and the crew of *Königsberg* was comporting itself very well indeed. In June a hundred of the *Königsberg* crew had been sent off to join a force of Captain Braunschweig in the west and they fought along the Ruhudje River, joining up with the force under Major Kraut, who kept them in action in the south-west part of the colony.

After Captain Zimmer had sunk the *Graf Götzen* and

scuttled the *Wami* he retired along the railway to Tabora and joined the force of General Wahle there. Wahle was placed by von Lettow-Vorbeck in charge of the entire western area and continued in that capacity as long as the resistance lasted. By the autumn of the year General Wahle's troops, army, navy, and Askari, were grouped around Mahenge in the mountains southwest of the Rufiji Delta. So the Germans were forced south and east as the British had planned. Difficult as their situation was, they held out and tied up huge numbers of British and Belgian troops and British naval forces. Then came another threat in 1916: the Portuguese entered the war on the side of the British and Belgians and moved quickly to occupy the country on the German side of the border between German Southwest Africa and Mozambique, territory the Portuguese long had coveted for their own. A new dimension was added to the war.

24

Captain Looff Goes South

BY AUTUMN, 1916, the effective German force in East Africa was reduced to eleven hundred Europeans, seven thousand three hundred Askaris, some sixteen small field guns, seventy-three machine guns, and the four remaining guns of *Königsberg*. Many Europeans had been killed – perhaps half the scattered force of the men of the *Königsberg* had fallen in actions on land and sea, or, as likely, before the deadly malaria mosquito or the equally dreadful tsetse fly which killed cattle and man alike. The British had occupied the entire coastal area, taking Kilwa, Lindi, and Mikindani, and so the German defence now was limited to a corridor in the interior, well away from the coast and extending down the east centre of the colony to the Portuguese East Africa or Mozambique border.

Lieutenant Colonel von Lettow-Vorbeck decided to hold in the Rufiji Delta as long as possible, but it soon became apparent that he must move from that area because of the food shortage, and he cast his eyes south on the unknown territory in Mozambique. The heavy agricultural areas of Lupembe, Iringa, and Kissaki had been lost to the British and so had the lower Rufiji region. Yet the eastern part of the Lindi area was still in German hands, and here as well as south of the Rovuma was the area chosen by von Lettow-Vorbeck for the next scene of operations. An expeditionary force of some five hundred men under Major von Stümer was sent to cross the Rovuma, scout, and report on the condition of the land east of Lake Nyasa. The Germans were living now on captured stores; the supply of wheat flour from the colony and the store ships was coming to an end. They secured their salt from captured supplies, their fat from elephants and hippo, and sugar gave way to wild honey. In the beginning the Germans had quinine tablets, but soon they were reduced to the use of Peruvian cinchona bark. They boiled the bark and drank the liquid, which came to be known derisively as Lettow-schnapps; it tasted terrible but it did the job and controlled the men's malaria.

Soon Captain Looff was named commander of the south, and sent to the area west of Lindi to strengthen the German position there and keep the southern part of the colony free so the Rufiji force could pass through his organisation when the time came. He had five hundred rifles to begin with, to oppose a force of several thousand British troops in the area, but the situation was not as desperate as the number indicated, for the Germans were to fight a guerrilla war and to refrain from engaging the enemy in force.

The war in the south, one might say, was a naval war; that is, both companies were under the command of officers of the *Königsberg* and Captain Looff was in overall command. Lieutenant Hinrichs had one company, and Lieutenant Sprockhoff had another. Before Captain Looff arrived Hinrich's force consisted of one hundred rifles and Sprockhoff's of eighty, but this was soon remedied. For some months Lieutenant Hinrichs had been facing seven thousand Portuguese troops along the sixty-mile Rovuma front, but both he and Sprockhoff had been driven slowly back as the Portuguese advanced. It was to be expected; here were two companies to guard an area as large as all Bavaria.

Captain Looff went south in October, in response to an order that awaited him one day when he returned from inspection of a steamboat on the Rufiji to his post as commander of Utete in the delta. The manner of the giving of the order was indicative of the relationship of Looff and Lieutenant Colonel von Lettow-Vorbeck; there was no question about the strained quality of the relationship, and von Lettow-Vorbeck was determined to keep Looff at arm's length. So in October Captain Looff headed south, to pick up his men of *Königsberg*. He was to have reinforcements, two new companies. Captain Rothe, the former minister of posts and telegraphs, was to bring them down, and he, Looff, was also to have the gun of *Königsberg* that had been brought south from Dar es Salaam. Lieutenant Wenig would command the gun. Altogether, he would have six hundred men with which to fight the Portuguese and British.

Looff headed south, marching at the head of his column, marching through areas that showed completely white on the map – unknown territory which the Germans had not yet got round to exploring after twenty years of occupation of the colony. For three weeks they travelled through the bush, pushing their way along animal trails and places where there were no trails. Fortunately, Captain Looff had the services of Major Schlobach, an old African hand who knew the tricks of tracking, hunting, and travel in the wilds. And wild it was, this country. One night, a few miles from the Rufiji Delta which seemed like home to the men of *Königsberg*, they were sitting around their campfires in the headquarters company when a lion began roaring not thirty yards away. They could see his eyes staring unwinkingly at them out of the darkness. The campfires kept him at a respectful distance, but woe to any man who chose to go outside the protected zone. And one did, an Askari, Captain Looff's personal servant. The lion was not alone; the next morning they found the Askari's bloody turban and his bayonet. That was all that remained after the lions had done their work and the hyenas had followed them.

Somewhat subdued, not by the British but by the peril of their position in the bush, Captain Looff and his men moved on. It was some time before they learned, from Major Schlobach and the Askaris, that the little beasts of the jungle and the bush were far more dangerous than the large ones: the real threats to their safety were the mosquitoes, ticks, and flies that carried the germs that would kill them far less humanely than the lion. Captain Looff became a hard taskmaster, forcing the men to sleep under netting no matter how far they had marched or how tired they might be when it came time to establish camp, forcing them to stop along the route and examine their legs and arms for ticks.

Now on land, the men of *Königsberg* learned to eat foods they would have scorned when aboard their ship. Indeed, in earlier days the natives had told them how good was the taste of hippopotamus fat, and they had laughed sickly and turned away, the steel decks under their feet. Now, given no alternatives, they came to appreciate hippo fat and Captain Looff even pronounced it tasty – a sign of his development as a 'true colonial'.

Hard as the long trek was, it toughened Looff and his men, and before they were finished they came to appreciate the bush. Under Major Schlobach's patient, good-humoured tutelage, they gained a new joy of living that was intensified by the knowledge that they were heading into battle, from which most of them did not expect to emerge alive.

In the third week they came to the danger zone, the area where British and Portuguese troops were operating, south of the Matumbi Mountains, in the back country behind Kilwa. Danger zone? Captain Looff did not know it, but when he left the Utete country the old Africa hands among the defenders there gave him less than one chance in a hundred even to reach the south without being captured. They knew, and he did not, the territory through which he would be travelling for three weeks, and they quite expected him to give up and go to the coast, where his column would be easy picking for the enemy. His friend, Major Stemmerman, who had succeeded him in command of the Utete force, did not tell him all this, but on their leavetaking Stemmerman had been most solicitous and most grave – it was only much later that Captain Looff learned why. It was this underestimation of Looff's abilities and adaptability which caused in part the conflict between the land and the naval forces in East Africa; Lieutenant Colonel von Lettow-Vorbeck was a fine military commander but he resented Looff's superiority of rank. It was only at Christmas time when he received a welcome personal letter informing him that he, von Lettow-Vorbeck, had been awarded the Kaiser's highest decoration, the Pour le Merite, that he began to unbend a bit. Yet the relationship between the military commander on the one hand and Captain Looff and Governor Schnee, on the other, continued to be strained.

Near the end of their journey, south of the Memkuru River, Captain Looff's column nearly came to disaster, not through any agency of the enemy, but through an attack of quite another kind. At noon on this particular day the column halted in a clearing for the noon break. Major Schlobach had been calling Captain Looff's attention for some time to the presence of some strange small birds in the area through which they were passing. These were called 'honey guides' because they had a habit of guiding men to the hives of bees, certain that the men would leave them a part of the honey for the service. The blacks stopped and went for the honey, and the bees chose this time to attack in force. In a moment the entire column was dispersed, the whites were running for cover, slapping the bees away from their heads and shoulders. For three hours the bees kept after them without stopping, the whites reduced to hiding under their mosquito netting and the blacks hiding where they could. The mules and donkeys of the expedition fled, kicking as they went, and Captain Looff quite despaired of ever bringing his force together again. It was not until nearly nightfall that the bees let up and returned to their hives, and the officers could begin trying to round up the stragglers. Captain Looff could have embraced each and every Askari, porter, and mule as he found them one by one. Humorous as the recounting of the incident might appear later, it was not at all funny at the time. One mule, which was found in the area where they had stopped and where the bees had first attacked, was so badly covered with stings on the head, neck, and underbelly that he had to be destroyed. The other animals were recovered, more or less intact, but they were all sore and skittish and could not be ridden for several days.

South of the Memkuru the safari lost its carefree, hunting atmosphere, for the Germans now were approaching the area in which the British and Portuguese were known to be operating in strength. They moved more slowly and they did not allow themselves to straggle, but kept bunched up, weapons of the fighting men ready for action at any moment.

But also the column was approaching the area where Captain Looff would take command of the southern region, and it was not long before he was met by a young seaman from the ship *Khalif*, a boy who had escaped from internment in Mozambique and made his way across the border to join the fighting force in East Africa. Captain Looff learned with surprise, and then with pleasure as he thought about it, that Lieutenant Hinrichs had known of the column's coming for several days and had sent the youngster out to meet them. The commander was pleased to see that his force had so excellent an intelligence service and his hopes for the future rose.

Soon Captain Looff and his officers were in camp, sitting around a long table under the stars, examining maps and determining the course of the future. The Portuguese had taken a strong series of positions on the high plateau of Makonde and the Germans were in the valley below them. The Portuguese had the advantage of the heights, but the Germans had the advantage of a constant water supply. They did not, however, have the Portuguese completely shut off from the water – and that was the source of Captain Looff's plan: he would move to push the Portuguese high atop the plateau where there was no water and dry them out, hopefully to the point of surrender or evacuation. This plan was easier to lay out than to put into effect, because the British in Lindi were making ready to link up with Portuguese on the plateau and present a solid front in the south. As it stood, the Portuguese were south of the German position, and off to an angle on the left were the British, who held the coastal regions. So it was to be a miniature war on two fronts for the tiny German force. Most important of all, Captain Looff was to carry out his war and still protect the supply ship *Marie*, which had been moved. For months, as the fighting raged in East Africa, Lieutenant Hinrichs had fought with one hand and supervised the movement of those small packs of goods – porter loads – which had been so carefully prepared to order in Germany. They were moved to a secret dump on the Noto plateau; if the British knew of the existence of this mound of supplies they at least did not know where to find them, and it was Captain Looff's primary job to protect them, for they held the key to the continuation of the battle in East Africa. If all else was lost a small body of men could hold out for a long time with these supplies.

Following the principle of attacking the strongest enemy first, Captain Looff concentrated his forces against the Portuguese and left only a platoon of Askaris pitted against the British. Their mission was to make an appearance and begin a skirmish here, then disappear and reappear there, miles away, and to repeat the performance, showing themselves frequently in many different places, giving the enemy the indication of a force ten times as strong, with the sole purpose of preventing the British from launching an attack to link up with the Portuguese.

Headquarters for the German force was established at the plantation of Mtama in the Lindi district, where the retired Captain Kaiser turned over all his provisions and equipment to the force. As for himself, Captain Kaiser went into the field as leader of the Askari platoon against the English, for he knew the countryside intimately and could travel faster than any other European in the force.

Early in November the main force began a forced march against the Portuguese – forced march because anywhere in the African bush the news of the coming of foreigners could not be long concealed. The jungle telegraph too soon would inform the Portuguese Askaris of the coming of the Germans, so when an attack was planned the forced march was *de rigueur*. On 14th November Captain Looff and his footsore men arrived at Massassi, the jumping-off point for the campaign. Lieutenant Colonel von Lettow-Vorbeck had been as good as his word and had sent reinforcements. He had not wanted to do so, but Governor Schnee had insisted. From the west had come Major Kraut with the large force gathered by the compression of Belgians and British from the south, west, and north, and of this force three more companies were sent to Captain Looff. Lieutenant Colonel von Lettow-Vorbeck had wanted to send these companies down to the southeast corner of the colony where the blacks were rebelling against German rule. The commander felt a few hangings would solve the problem (hanging the offenders in rows was not an unusual Germanic custom in treating with the natives). But Governor Schnee insisted that the reinforcements go to Captain Looff, and the commander yielded, so Captain Rothe with one gun of the *Königsberg* under Lieutenant Hauser was sent to reinforce the southern command.

The objective assigned to Captain Rothe was the water supply point at Newalla, situated at the bottom of the canyon. Just before sending off his fighting force, on 22nd November, Captain Looff stopped and gave the men a brief speech, much as he was accustomed to doing aboard his ship just before going into action. It was an unusual gesture among soldiering men, and one that improved the morale of the troops considerably, for they knew what was expected of them and what they were fighting for in this coming battle — and why. The leaders of the two companies under Captain Rothe were Lieutenant Methner, civil counsellor to the governor in peacetime, and Lieutenant Grundmann, head of the post office in Tanga – strange occupations for civil servants, but this was a war to the finish so far as the Germans were concerned, and these officers knew that if they were defeated there would be no civil jobs for them in Africa.

Captain Rothe then barked a few short orders and the two companies set out for the position, where Lieutenant Hinrichs was already established, waiting. They moved out and soon were in position for the assault.

The attack was made under cover of rifle fire and then by bayonet; the charge was repelled once and the Germans and Askaris suffered heavily in dead and wounded, but they rallied and came back again and finally won the day by driving the Portuguese back on to the plateau, away from their water supply, to a strong position on the heights.

After the successful move against the Portuguese water supply, one column of the German force headed south in the direction of the Rovuma River, cutting the Portuguese off from easy access to water in that direction. So the enemy then was threatened by a pincers movement between plateau and the water supply. Was he to die of thirst on the bone-dry plateau? Otherwise he must retreat. The Portuguese holed up in the settlement at Boma on the plateau, where they had established very nearly a fortress, but the cistern was soon dry and they had to make their decision. The siege was laid down by the Looff force.

After several days of siege Captain Looff decided it had come time to make an assault. One of the big guns from *Königsberg* (Wenig's, which seemed much larger and much more important here in the bush than ever aboard the ship) was pushed, heaved, and hauled up the steep trail to the Makonde plateau, having been broken down into pieces, and soon it was in position to open fire on the Portuguese, so secure in their fortified position. For the first time in his long career Captain Looff became an artillery observer, directing the fire from a point a hundred yards from the fort and seeing the marvellous effect (from his viewpoint) of the shells on the Portuguese position.

Soon the Portuguese were calling by radio for reinforcements. The reinforcements came up from the east, passing by a narrow cut where Lieutenant Methner had concealed himself and his company. As the relieving column came to the cut, Lieutenant Methner's men met them with enfilading fire from both sides and so completely demoralised the relief force that it turned and broke and became disorganised, leaving scores of dead and wounded on the field.

With this serious defeat, troubled by lack of water and a shortage of provisions, the Portuguese stole out that very night in a dense fog which enveloped the plateau, through a pass unknown to the Germans, and made their retreat safely. They left behind all their horses, all their mules, and all their sick and wounded, who were half-dead from thirst.

Had the Germans known the Portuguese were fleeing, it probably would have made no difference, for the Askaris would not fight at night; night was the time when the evil spirits of Africa were abroad and the Askaris kept to their fires and sleeping places.

The next morning, as dawn rose over the plateau, Captain Looff and his men moved to the fortress to examine their harvest – for they had learned to live like guerrillas and accept any fruits of victory that came their way – and Captain Looff sent two forces after the retreating Portuguese, one column to follow directly behind them at forced march, attempting to catch up and give the enemy battle, the other column to sweep round in front of the Portuguese and cut them off at the Rovuma River before they could cross back into enemy territory. The latter group included the second gun from *Königsberg* and a number of mortars, and it was hoped that the Portuguese could be cut off and totally destroyed as a fighting force. But the Portuguese knew the territory and Captain Looff's men did not, and the enemy managed to reach the Rovuma and begin the crossing well before the gun and mortars arrived. Finally they did arrive, and then were able to open fire – but only on the last groups of Portuguese, the stragglers, who were making their way across the river.

Not content, the Germans and their Askaris crossed the river into Portuguese territory and followed the retreating troops for twenty miles along the bank before pulling back and returning to their base, satisfied that they had driven the enemy out of East Africa.

Back at the Boma fort Captain Looff, with the happy air of a successful burglar, was counting the loot captured from the Portuguese. Guns, ammunition, clothing, and field supplies, cooking equipment, horses, mules, and harnesses, and, above all, field rations had fallen into their hands in good supply. The Portuguese had planned to use this place as a base and had supplied it accordingly. It was still to be a base, but a German base, so Captain Looff left the supplies in the hands of a small force and went on, following the principle that it is never a good idea for guerrilla forces to remain too long at the scene of battle.

For two or three days the Europeans and the Askaris ate their fill in this camp, the Europeans taking such delicacies as sausages, sardines, and corned beef, and the Askaris having flour and meat, sugar and European salt rather than salt taken from sea water or various African plants as they were used to eating. All the loot was British – the product of the best British factories – and the Germans, not without a touch of envy, sneered at the Portuguese 'satellites' who would fight the war of their hated cousins.

Throughout the conflict in East Africa, each side charged the other endlessly with the use of dumdum bullets – bullets whose points had been hollowed or broken with cross cuts so that the slugs would expand, creating a killing or crippling wound no matter where they struck a man. Captain Looff charged the Portuguese with the use of dumdums and said that in the loot they found numberless examples of these vile weapons. The British made a similar charge against the Germans after the capture of Morogoro.

Throughout, there was little love lost among the enemies. A Portuguese prisoner killed a German sailor, a quarter-master who stopped to give aid on the battlefield – shot him from behind. General Gil of the Portuguese forces sent a messenger under a flag of truce to ask how many dead Portuguese soldiers the Germans had buried and how many prisoners they had taken. He renewed these questions several times, to the German astonishment after they once had answered. Finally Captain Looff learned the answer:

218

General Gil was missing several hundred of his soldiers. Since it was impossible to desert (he said) in a country where there was no water, and since the number of prisoners was so small, the Portuguese began to believe that the Germans had murdered their prisoners on the battlefield and buried them. In consequence, the Portuguese put a price of four thousand gold marks on Captain Looff's head. Also, they put a price of two thousand marks on the head of Lieutenant Angel, the captain's aide, because, they said, he was Looff's principal adviser and just as guilty as the captain.

The placement of prices on heads, however, did not win battles, and when the British at Lindi learned of the defeat of their gallant allies in the west, they began to build up their forces in preparation for an attack of their own. This preparation was no joke: the British brought in load after load of supplies, big guns, and ammunition for them. Captain Looff moved closer to the east coast to give support to the force there, and when he linked forces with them found they were well and strong. The enemy was stronger, of course. The ratio was twelve hundred British troops, with many mortars and field guns, to four Germans and forty-six Askaris on the German perimeter. Naturally enough, the Germans could not have withstood any kind of assault from the British, but they did manage to persuade their enemies, by the usual tactic, that there were many more of them surrounding the Lindi area and thus to keep the British from venturing into the countryside indiscriminately, where they might have learned the true story of German weakness in the field.

Moving in on Lindi, Captain Looff established the headquarters of the German southern command at Mrovoueka plantation and began planning an attack against Lindi, twelve miles away. Lieutenant Hinrichs and Captain Rothe pressed Looff to let them attack as soon as the guns from *Königsberg* could be brought up along with the smaller field guns captured from the Portuguese. The attack was ready to be launched on 24th December 1916, along both banks of the Lukuledi River, and was aimed to drive the British completely away from the Lindi Bay.

Then, however, came interference from the highest quarter. Lieutenant Colonel von Lettow-Vorbeck ordered Captain Rothe to move north – or at least that was what he said he was ordered to do, and Captain Looff confirmed it. Von Lettow-Vorbeck later claimed that Captain Rothe had marched into the country northeast of Lindi without orders, searching for supplies, and that his foray there seriously threatened the future plans of the German high command in the Rufiji Delta, because von Lettow-Vorbeck was working out a strategy of long-time defence which would call for the use of the supplies available in this fertile region, and he did not want the countryside laid waste.

In any event, just before Christmas Eve off went Captain Rothe, one gun from *Königsberg*, and his men marching north instead of east towards Lindi and the sea, and Captain Looff's brave plan was forcibly abandoned. Captain Looff then established positions around the perimeter of the British holdings, close enough to the Lindi area to keep the British uneasy, and fought several engagements there during the next seven months. It was stalemate: he had not the strength to take Lindi and there was no way of getting it, given the strategic views of von Lettow-Vorbeck, and the British had not the strength to drive the guerrilla force out of the region.

Every day the British attacked Captain Looff's headquarters from the air; every morning at the same time an airplane flew over the plantation bungalows and dropped its bombs. But air attack was all; the army under the field commander General O'Grady did not receive enough reinforcements to launch the ground attack that Lieutenant Colonel von Lettow-Vorbeck expected at any moment. To the aerial attacks Captain Looff had one answer: from the depths of the brush, so well concealed that the British could not find it, Wenig's gun from *Königsberg* spoke back every day, so frequently in spite of the perennial shortage of

ammunition for the 105-mm gun that land and sea commanders both became nervous. On the morning of Palm
Sunday, 1917, Captain Looff delivered several dozen
'Easter eggs' to his cousins in Lindi, and only wished he
had a thousand more – for out in Lindi Bay were the ships
of the blockade force, his old enemies who had sunk
Königsberg, or caused him to destroy his ship, and whom he
would like to present with the same fate.

On their part, the British were becoming quite exas-
perated by the continual bombardment by the *Königsberg*
gun. The reason was simple enough; Captain Looff did not
often waste more than two or three shells a day, but just
about every day those two or three shells were fired, either
at some ship or some installation ashore, and the 105-mm
shells were large enough to constitute a constant danger to
the British.

In Lindi a grand war council was held in the spring
aboard the flagship of Rear-Admiral Charlton, a most
unhappy war council, with the navy and army each trying
to blame the other for the continued existence of the
Königsberg's guns in East Africa. Had the navy been able
to use its observation planes properly, said the army, the
gun would have been silenced long ago. (Also, had the navy
taken proper precautions in the first place, the gun never
would have been salvaged from *Königsberg*'s wreck in the
Rufiji.) Had the British army any initiative, said the navy
men with some heat, the gun would have been captured
long ago; had the army been about its business the gun
never would have left Dar es Salaam.

So it went with General O'Grady and Admiral Charlton
and their staffs – and absolutely nothing was resolved,
except that it was agreed that the present situation was
intolerable and that the Germans 'besieging' Lindi in their
small way must be wiped out. A general attack was planned
for 19th May 1917; a landing corps of more than a thousand
men was added to the army force by the fleet, and Captain
Looff and his men in the hills watched them come in in their
small boats, making ready for the attack.

The main attack was directed by General O'Grady, the very experienced and very competent general who had led the march against von Lettow-Vorbeck in the northeast. O'Grady was a perfectionist. From time to time he went aloft in an observation plane himself to survey the enemy positions around him, and when he began this clean-up operation he did it very thoroughly. First the airplanes came over and bombed the German positions, not so much because of the physical effect, but more because of the effect they had on the blacks, who lived in mortal fear of these great birds. When the planes came over, the blacks always grew very excited and the German officers had considerable difficulty in quieting them.

Yet with all its trappings, aerial bombardment, field guns barrage, and frontal attack by the troops, the British assault had little effect. Two Indian regiments led the way, and the Germans fired for a while, then simply vanished in the bush; there were that few of them and they could move quite rapidly, even with the big gun from *Königsberg*. The naval contingent followed and spent much of the day moving through the heat, tiring the sailors, who were not accustomed to land warfare and certainly not to bush warfare in tropical Africa. At the end of the day the exhausted navy men returned to their ships, with nothing to boast about. The Indian regiments searched all day, too, and they also returned to Lindi – and then the Germans returned to their positions. It had been a busy day and not a very constructive one for the British; Captain Looff's one regret was that he was unable to go into Lindi and listen in on the next conference between Admiral Charlton and General O'Grady.

After this British disaster, Captain Looff's men staged a daring attack of their own. Lieutenant Hinrichs and his men moved in on the south. Unfortunately Captain Looff could not give Hinrichs any artillery and the attack nearly was stopped by the British barbed wire entanglements – which the Askaris had never before encountered. To break through they had only their mortars, and mortaring the wire was a slow and difficult job. The result was not very satisfactory: Lieutenant Hinrichs was gravely wounded, the Askaris simply could not penetrate the wire in depth, and Captain Looff lost many men that day.

The failure of this attack was a serious setback to the Germans – and it apparently provided exactly the opportunity Lieutenant Colonel von Lettow-Vorbeck wanted to replace Captain Looff in command of the forces in the south. In the period since Captain Looff had left the Rufiji Delta, Lieutenant Colonel von Lettow-Vorbeck finally had received the promotion he wanted and deserved, to major general in the German army. For two and a half years he had been carrying out the functions of a general without the authority or the honour; finally his Kaiser saw fit to honour him properly. One of General von Lettow-Vorbeck's early acts was to bring General Wahle from the west and to entrust him with the operations in the south, giving as his reason the development of a major offensive there. The real reason, of course, was that he wanted men in charge who were personally responsible to him, and he had never liked or appreciated the efforts of Captain Looff or the captain's strong ties to Governor Schnee.

So in June 1917 General Wahle came from Mahenge in the west and took charge of the southern region. At least by this action much of the crew of *Königsberg* – or those left of it – were reunited. From the west came the men who had been assigned to Captain Zimmer's lake force and the remnants of Commander Koch's *Königsberg* company. The company had long since fallen so far below strength that it had been incorporated into another unit under Koch's command. Georg Koch had left Looff a young and ebullient officer; he returned looking very old. Why, asked his old commander – was it the result of a misspent youth? Whereupon Commander Koch told a story of one terrible night in a forest village.

He and Major Fritsche, the doctor for his unit, had gone to a village in their operational area in response to a plea from the natives, who were badly frightened by a wild bull elephant who had been lurking near the village, rampaging through their crops for several days. They went to destroy the beast. That evening, they had waited on the edge of the village and the elephant had appeared as expected. Major Fritsche fancied himself with an elephant gun, and took a quick shot at the beast, missed his brain, and the elephant wheeled, impaled him with a tusk, and then trampled him to death. Commander Koch had run to a native hut and climbed up on the roof, where the elephant could see him but could not reach him.

All that night the elephant charged and pushed at the hut, trying to knock him off the roof and get at him, and all that night Commander Koch clung to the rooftop for dear life, until finally in the morning the old bull had tired of the sport and wandered away for his daily bath in the mudholes of the nearby river. Then and only then had Commander Koch been able to think about going back to his war against the British; his hair had turned white that night.

25

The Ring Closes

THERE WAS NO possible way in which the German forces in
East Africa could win their war. Major General von Lettow-
Vorbeck realised this from the beginning and that was the
secret of his success as a master strategist; von Lettow-
Vorbeck and Captain Looff never could agree because Looff
wanted to fight battles and win them while the commander
wanted to cause the British as much pain as possible for as
long a period as possible.

In this campaign, General von Lettow-Vorbeck certainly
succeeded. The blockade squadron of ships never could be
released; General von Lettow-Vorbeck and his handful of
Europeans and Askaris tied up thousands of British troops.
Indeed, in his reminiscences of the war the general declared
that at various times one hundred and thirty different
British generals were in the field against him and the
total strength of British and Belgian troops pitted against
East Africa numbered three hundred thousand. The
British figures are not nearly so high, but General Smuts
always looked upon General von Lettow-Vorbeck as a
great commander and admitted the great disparity in
German and British strengths. From his vantage point in
the south, calling for more troops and having troops taken
away from him instead, trying to win battles, and being
superseded in command, Captain Looff had no such lofty
opinion of the commander of the German forces in East
Africa, and his attitude obviously showed. He was reduced
to holding the line on the west of Lindi while General
Wahle conducted operations around the town; the one

solace was that most of the old comrades of the *Königsberg* gravitated to the Looff command, worming their way in by one means or another.

On the British side, General Smuts was relieved by General Hoskins, and then General Hoskins was relieved by General van Devanter. The Germans were reduced to nine companies of Europeans and Askaris in the south, and pitted against them were three full brigades of British troops. The worst of the fighting was that one by one the German officers were falling, for they led their men into battle and were always in the forefront. Not only the officers, but the guns of *Königsberg*, too, were disappearing rapidly. One of the last four guns had been lost in the west, and then two more were sacrificed – destroyed when the supply of ammunition was gone. Finally, in the fall of 1917, only one gun was left, the single 105-mm gun under the command of Lieutenant Wenig, who had been detached from Captain Looff's force when General Wahle took over and had been kept on to harry Lindi.

In the autumn of 1917, Major General von Lettow-Vorbeck left the Rufiji country where he was suffering increasingly from a shortage of food and supplies and moved down to the Lindi region, knowing that there existed the supplies from *Marie* plus the rich resources of the agricultural countryside. In October von Lettow-Vorbeck led an attack in the Mahiwa area that was strikingly successful. Fourteen companies of Germans and Askaris, some fifteen hundred men in all, had defeated a British force at least three times as large, and while the German casualties were fourteen Europeans and eighty-one Askaris killed, fifty-five Europeans and three hundred and sixty-seven Askaris wounded, one European and one Askari missing, the British casualties were estimated at fifteen hundred men; the Germans also captured a small field gun, nine machine guns, and two hundred thousand rounds of ammunition. It was a victory, but it was immediately followed by another British attack from the north – thus emphasising the Germans' problem: they were so completely outnumbered by the British that no matter how many battles they won, they could not win the war. Further, in three years of fighting the Germans had received exactly two shiploads of supplies from home, no other communication was received, and they could not hope for supply or leadership other than that they provided for themselves, while the British were in constant resupply, constant reinforcement, constant touch with London.

Major General von Lettow-Vorbeck bounced back from the counterattack in October, and on 19th October launched a new attack on Lukuledi, but here again the impossibility of the war was brought home: the Germans lost half a dozen officers; they captured three hundred and fifty horses and much other equipment and inflicted serious casualties on the enemy, but the British seemed to have an inexhaustible supply of men and the Germans lost three company commanders.

It was 24th October when Major General von Lettow-Vorbeck first enunciated what had been in his mind for a long time: the war must be carried on, but it could be fought only by evacuating German East Africa and invading Portuguese East Africa. The crux was not even the manpower problem, but the supply problem. Von Lettow-Vorbeck estimated that he had eleven hundred thousand pounds of supplies available to him – which meant six weeks' more fighting. The Germans had one *Königsberg* gun and one Portuguese mountain gun and fifty machine guns. There were shortages of food and medical supplies, and altogether von Lettow-Vorbeck had only four hundred thousand rounds of rifle ammunition.

Considering these facts, he decided that his only course was to reduce the number of soldiers under his command to a force that he could control and keep supplied without difficulty. The reduction would be drastic: he would keep with him three hundred Europeans, perhaps two thousand Askaris, and so perhaps five hundred Europeans and six hundred Askaris would have to be left behind at the hospital at Nambindinga. The general knew well enough that his decision would be unpopular, but he made it nonetheless.

Captain Looff called the move, 'the battle against the wolves', for he said it reminded him of an occurrence in Germany when he was a child; that he had been on a journey by sledge when the sledge was attacked by wolves, and that a child was thrown from the sledge to the wolves in order to stop their progress. The wolves stopped to attack the child, and all the others were saved. Captain Looff's story was perhaps too pat to be literal truth, but such events did occur then in Eastern Europe, and the principle was certainly recognisable: Captain Looff was the first to be thrown to the wolves; General von Lettow-Vorbeck ordered him to lead the sick, the wounded, and all those not selected for the long march and to surrender them in a body to the British enemy.

Every fibre of Captain Looff's being resented the order, but he was an officer in the Kaiser's navy and he was trained to absolute obedience to orders. Without a whimper he accepted his fate and prepared to surrender. Major General von Lettow-Vorbeck would fight on. Governor Schnee would go with the troops, lending authority and dignity to the operation. As for Captain Looff, on 26th November 1917, he led a long, sad column of men dressed in rags that could have been parts of all the uniforms of all the armies in the world, down the Makonde Plateau and into the British camp to surrender to the spit-and-polish soldiers of the King's African Rifles. And as they came, the British Askaris whispered among themselves:

'*Houyou, houyou, bwana unguyu*' – 'Look, look, here comes Mr Zanzibar' – for Captain Looff was known to the Africans among his enemies by the name of the place of his victory over *Pegasus*.

At the British camp, Captain Looff was separated from his officers and men and taken to a British general who began interrogating him. What had happened to the guns of *Königsberg*? the officer wanted to know. How many were still left? How much ammunition was there for them, and where was it located?

Captain Looff, of course, had no intention of giving his enemies any information that would help them. Knowing that there was but one gun left, that it was in charge of Lieutenant Wenig, and that Wenig was even then moving south by mule to cross the Mozambique border, Captain Looff put on his most innocent expression and said he thought there were three or four of the guns with von Lettow-Vorbeck and that they had plenty of ammunition.

The interrogator asked Captain Looff another question: Could he show them the spot where the zeppelin would land?

Zeppelin?

It was true, although Captain Looff knew nothing about the affair. The navy had assigned one of its ships of the air to make a trip to Africa bearing a cargo of guns, ammunition, and above all medical supplies for the German East Africa defenders. The Zeppelin L-56 had set out and had made several abortive attempts to fly across the Mediterranean and the Sahara to reach von Lettow-Vorbeck but, alas, the attempt had come too late, and eventually it was abandoned.

Captain Looff knew nothing, but he put up a brave front. Confidentially, he said, he could tell the general that not one but two zeppelins were coming – one to bomb Tabora and the other to bomb Lindi.

The general did not think it was funny.

It was only later that Captain Looff learned that the zeppelin really was on its way at that time, and that it was setting out for East Africa when Lieutenant Bockholt, its commander, received a message from Berlin to turn around, because the colony was lost and Major General von Lettow-Vorbeck was moving into Portuguese Africa.

Captain Looff gave his captors – were they really captors when he had been ordered to sacrifice himself? – no cause for pleasure and soon the interrogation was ended. He was kept in confinement in Lindi for a time, and then moved back to Dar es Salaam, a British base. The bread of captivity was hard to swallow, particularly the attitude of the

Indians of Dar es Salaam and the half-castes, who sneered at the former masters of the colony, so far fallen.

It was an unhappy fact that the prisoners of the *Königsberg* and the colonial troops were kept at Dar es Salaam, for the climate was anything but salubrious, and faced with prison rations and prison life, without the hope of victory, illness set in among the prisoners and many began to sicken and die. The dreaded influenza attacked the weakened men, and more died, until on the eve of their departure for prison camps in Egypt they were but a pitiful remainder of the once proud crew of *Königsberg* and the troops of the defence force.

In Egypt the officers were lodged in a camp at Sidi Bishr, near Alexandria, while the men were taken to Toura, near Cairo. And here the officers were fairly comfortable, but the conditions of the men were terrible. Soon dysentery appeared, along with typhus, scrofula, and other diseases. As conditions deteriorated in the officers' camp Captain Looff came down with typhus and dysentery, and soon the doctors were despairing for his life, but his will to live was greater than his ailments, and he did survive, a shadow of himself, thin and yellow and shaking for many months.

In the spring of 1918 the Duke of Connaught visited the British prisoner-of-war camp at Sidi Bishr and Captain Looff was presented to him. The duke received the captain with full military honours, before a hundred British officers, and praised him, telling the captain that he often reminded his officers of the gallant manner in which the Germans of *Königsberg* had fought until the last.

Then, and only then, all the officers of the Duke's command came to give Captain Looff the honours due a gallant enemy.

26

The Last Battle

CAPTAIN LOOFF AND his men had held back the enemy at
Nambindinga until the main force of Major General von
Lettow-Vorbeck made his way south to Kitangara, picked
up the ten days' supplies that were available there, headed
south, and then began marching up the Rovuma River.
Some minor changes had been made in the command. It
now consisted of three hundred Europeans, seventeen
hundred Askaris, and three thousand bearers, every man
loaded to capacity.

As the column wended its way south and west, con-
suming supplies, the empty-handed bearers were dropped
off. On 25th November 1917, the force crossed the Rovuma,
and for the first time German East Africa was deserted to
the enemy, while the fighters lived on, to fight again.
They fought first at Ngomano, routing a force of one
thousand Portuguese and Askaris, buried two hundred
dead, and released a hundred and fifty European prisoners
after securing their promise not to fight again – it was
either that or kill the conquered, for they had no place for
prisoners. They marched on, to the confluence of the
Chiulezi, and soon received a summons from General van
Devanter to surrender, which General von Lettow-Vorbeck
cordially ignored. The general was less than cordial to those
around him, however; for the first time, outside German
territory, he could abuse Governor Schnee when Schnee
interfered with his orders, and he did so. He also raged and
insulted and infuriated his men; he drove them and used

every cruelty, yet the men remained loyal and continued the fight. Perhaps this very cruelty was necessary for the task undertaken, but while Major General von Lettow-Vorbeck would go down in history as a fine field commander, touched with genius, he would never go down as a favourite among his men.

In December, German headquarters moved to Chirumba (Mtarika), an outpost of the Portuguese Nyasa Company, a handsome settlement with European houses for shelter and plenty of supplies. They remained there for several weeks, but in January 1918, the British began to march against them, and although they wanted to remain through the harvest in February, they had to move. They marched east to Nanungu, and then towards Mtenda. Late in March they learned by radio of the diehard German offensive in the Amiens area of Europe. They hoped, hoped, hoped that a German victory would come in Europe and solve all their problems. The problems were many: General von Lettow-Vorbeck came down with malaria; he was bitten by a sandfly, the bite became infected and one of his toenails had to be removed; a sharp blade of grass struck him in the right eye, damaged his vision, and endangered the eye, a serious matter because his left eye had already been seriously injured in the Hottentot rebellion in southwest Africa some years before. But he fought on.

Lieutenant Commander Wunderlich of the *Möwe* was shot in the abdomen in a fight with the British around an enormous anthill at Koriwa. He was taken back to the hospital at Nanungu and died there.

In May the Germans fought a battle with the British at Kireka Mountain south of Mahua; sixty-two Germans and three hundred and forty-two Askaris were involved, and they defeated a British force of nearly a thousand. The British lost seventeen Europeans and ninety-four Askaris were killed or taken prisoner and a hundred wounded; the Germans lost sixteen Europeans and ninety-one Askaris were killed or wounded; the Germans captured the territory, but the casualty figures were misleading. Every German casualty counted, and the enemy always had new men to throw into the struggle.

Late in May the British cut off a German detachment at Timbani Mountain and very nearly captured Governor Schnee. Much as General von Lettow-Vorbeck might have liked personally to be rid of the governor, from the standpoint of morale and international politics it was most unwise to lose him, and the entire force moved out from headquarters at Koroma to save the day. Here was the most serious defeat of the southern campaign: the Germans lost seventy thousand rounds of ammunition and thirty thousand rupees – the paper money had been used by the Germans as promissory notes for the supplies they requisitioned from natives and Portuguese settlers as they went along.

Following this defeat, General von Lettow-Vorbeck burned the rest of the paper money and moved into the Kwiri district south of Mahua, and then on to the Lurio River. All the way they were losing officers; Surgeon Meixner was left behind with sick and wounded at Kwiri; Lieutenant Schäfer was left behind with blackwater fever.

They captured Alto-Moloque, an important Portuguese centre, and relieved their supply problem for a time. They marched to Kokosani and captured a Portuguese supply depot, six hundred and sixty pounds of food, three hundred and fifty modern rifles, three hundred cases of ammunition – and suddenly they were as well armed as they had been when they set out for the south, better in that their guns were more modern and more accurate.

Early in July the wandering German force had been heading for the Zambesi River, but they captured British orders which indicated an offensive would be launched against them in that region and so headed for the Likugo River again. They marched to Oriva, towards the territory east of the Ligonja. There was a fight at Namirrue in this region, and the British were routed, though many of the British casualties were Askaris from the old German defence force, conscripted now into the British service to fight against their old masters.

In August the Germans marched to Chalau. General von Lettow-Vorbeck's strategy was to march west and turn either into the rich Blantyre district or east of Lake Nyasa, where there were plenty of crops to be taken from the natives. He marched to Ili and captured an English telegraph station there. From this he discovered that there were stores in the region and captured those. Among his troops were naval Lieutenants Freund and Wenig of the *Königsberg*, Freund in command of an infantry detachment and Wenig with his gun. Freund became famous in the the group as a forager. He could always find some butter or a bit of jam, while others were searching for bits of hippopotamus fat.

As the days went on the number of Germans decreased day by day. Some were shot, some fell ill with fever, but the rest moved on, keeping the British off balance. The course they followed marked a huge rough square in the heart of Portuguese Africa, south, then west, then north, then east again. In September they headed north to move back into German East Africa and surprise the enemy. Lieutenant Freund was killed in a fight near Lioma, where the Germans had gone to raid a supply dump. They moved north, winning battles and losing battles, but moving on, Lieutenant Wenig supervising the incredible transportation of the *Königsberg*'s one remaining gun, hauling it up mountains, across rocky trails, down again, through desert and marsh and across dirty swollen streams. On 5th September, the German column was near Mpuera heading for a waterhole on Mount Hulua when a battalion of the 2nd King's African Rifles attacked; soon two more battalions were in action against the Germans and a major engagement was in process. General von Lettow-Vorbeck considered the idea of throwing his reserves into the action, but did not, because he was sure that by the next day the British would bring in reinforcements. So he contented himself with a holding action at Mpuera. In this fight,

Lieutenant Wenig and his gun played a major role, and indeed Wenig was forced to assume command of the detachment known as Göring's detachment, because Captain Göring and his other officers were all killed or wounded.

By September, the German force was reduced to a hundred and seventy-six Europeans and fifteen hundred Askaris. In this battle the Germans suffered a loss of sixteen Europeans and sixty Askaris killed or wounded, but the entire column of the King's African Rifles, three battalions in all, was put out of action for a time.

All during September the Germans marched north to the Rovuma, and on 28th September, they crossed the river and were once again back on German soil, moving towards Ssongea, passing it on 4th October, and moving north again. Two weeks later General Wahle dropped out of the march, sick with fever, but the main force moved on. Along this route Major General von Lettow-Vorbeck captured English newspapers and learned of the worsening of the war in Europe, the capture of Cambrai, the capture of Armentières, the fall of Bulgaria. At the end of October they were in the far west of the colony between Mbozi and Fife in Rhodesia, at Mwenzo. The Germans captured enough quinine to last them until June 1919, but they were short of artillery, and their one Stokes mortar exploded that day when a shell burst in the barrel.

On 6th November, the Germans arrived at Kajambi, well inside the Rhodesian border. They were ready for a fight, strong and well supplied except for artillery, and the farther they moved into British territory, the better supplied they found the warehouses and depots. Major General von Lettow-Vorbeck was well pleased and hoped for more loot, so he could continue his war indefinitely.

On 11th November 1918, he bicycled to Kasama and sent a detachment south in the direction of the Chambezi ferry. On 12th November the main body of German troops reached Kasama, was attacked in the rear by a British force, and prepared for a major battle, confident that they would rout the British. Von Lettow-Vorbeck wanted to continue his movement south and to resupply from enemy dumps until the Germans could move back into East Africa, there picking up some of their old Askaris who had been demobilised by necessity, maintaining strength by capturing enemy supplies in this region and thus beginning the war all over gain.

But on 13th November, when Major General von Lettow-Vorbeck was bicycling ahead of his main body, behind the scouting detachment, to find a suitable camp, an aide reported that an armistice had been concluded. The German government in Berlin had agreed to the unconditional surrender of all German troops in East Africa. They were to give up their prisoners, disarm their Askaris, and to march to Abercorn, the British headquarters, where they would give up their own arms. There were at that moment a hundred and fifty-five Europeans, including thirty officers, plus eleven hundred and sixty-eight Askaris and three thousand carriers in the German force. Among these was included Lieutenant Richard Wenig in charge of one gun from the *Königsberg*, and *Königsberg*'s Lieutenant Apel in charge of a detachment of Europeans which included twelve sailors from the *Königsberg*.

When the word came that the German weapons must be surrendered to an enemy that the Germans were confidently preparing to defeat in battle that very day, Lieutenant Wenig blew up his gun rather than let it fall into the hands of the British. Then came the final surrender: one Portuguese gun, thirty-seven machine guns, one thousand and seventy rifles, two hundred and eight thousand rounds of ammunition and forty rounds of artillery ammunition – not a single German rifle among the lot.

The Germans felt they were winning the war even at this moment of surrender. Colonel Dickinson of the 4th King's African Rifles told General von Lettow-Vorbeck that he would have to stop the chase because he, Dickinson, was running out of supplies and because von Lettow-Vorbeck was in no position to say he had every belief that before the British could have 'stopped the chase', the Germans would have defeated them at Chambezi and changed the course of the campaign.

But surrender it was. The Germans laid down their arms. They were taken to Lake Tanganyika and up the lake on the steamer *St George* and three other ships. They were put ashore at Kigoma, which had fallen long before to the Belgians. Then it was on to Tabora by rail, and then to Dar es Salaam. They were kept at Dar es Salaam until 17th January 1919, and then sent by way of Cape Town to Rotterdam, where they arrived at the end of February. On the way, General von Lettow-Vorbeck added up the results of their war in East Africa. He found that against his small force, the enemy had put three hundred thousand men and had lost sixty thousand in casualties from fighting and disease, twenty thousand of them Europeans and Indians. The war had cost the British one hundred and forty thousand horses and mules, and at the end, when the surrender was forced on the Germans, the fourteen hundred Germans and Askaris still believed they could defeat the British army and hold out indefinitely, awaiting a German victory at home.

At Hull, where Captain Looff was being held prisoner during these last days, the news arrived that the heroic Germans of East Africa were going home, and someone high in British official circles decided that Captain Looff should go with them. Consequently, he was put aboard a Danish ship at Hull and sent to Rotterdam to join his old companions. At Rotterdam they were united, Captain Looff and his two officers and the dozen men of the *Königsberg*'s crew, plus Governor Schnee. By this time the governor and General von Lettow-Vorbeck were scarcely on speaking terms. Their dislike had blossomed so that even the British were aware of it, but a good front was put up by all, for how could it be otherwise with the welcoming reception they received from the German colony of Rotterdam? The Germans were feasted as heroes there for two days, and then given a special train which carried the crew of *Königsberg* – what was left of it – and the colonial defenders of German East Africa. The train was decorated with greenery and flags and bunting, and at every station hundreds and thousands of people turned out to see the returning heroes. At Berlin they were all taken through the Brandenburg Gate, which was decorated for the occasion; they were specially saluted by Vice Admiral Rogge, the navy's chief of staff; and the mayor gave them a banquet. Most of all they were cheered by Germans everywhere, and not alone by Germans but by all lovers of the fair fight and the underdog who paid homage to true heroes no matter their nationality. For indeed, these were the most spectacular heroes of the great war, men who had fought long and hard without hope of ever winning; especially the fifteen men, the five per cent of the crew of *Königsberg*, all who were left of that novel ship. These were indeed the heroes of the day – The Germans Who Never Lost.

Notes and Acknowledgements

I am indebted to the Yale University Library for the lengthy use of a number of books and documents on which this book is based, and especially to Harry Harrison, the chief of the library's circulation department. The book is based largely on German sources, including the authoritative *Der Krieg zur See* 1914–1918, *Kreuzerkrieg* Bd 2 bearbeitet von C Raeder, Kontre-admiral (Berlin: Verlag von E S Mittler & Sohn, 1923). Other works are *Heia Safari, Deutschlands Kampf in Ostafrika*, General von Lettow-Vorbeck (Leipzig: Hafe & Kohler, 1920); *Deutsch-Ostafrika im Weltkriege*, von Gouverneur H Schnee (Leipzig: Verlag Queele & Meyer, 1919); *With the Nigerians in German East Africa*, W D Downes (London: Methuen & Co Ltd, 1919); *Um Ostafrika*, von Charlotte and Ludwig Deppe (Dresden: Verlag E Beutelspacher & Co, 1925); *Kreuzerfahrt und Buschkampf, mit SMS Könisgberg in Deutsch-Ostafrika* von Vizeadmiral A D Max Looff (Berlin: Anton Bertinetti, 1929); *SMS Königsberg in Monsun und Pori*, von Richard Wenig (Berlin: Safari Verlag); *Marineblau und Khaki, der Helden-kampf des Kreuzers Königsberg*, von Peter Eckart (Stuttgart: Franckh'sche Verlagshandlung, 1939); *L'Aventure du Königs-berg*, Août 1914–Juillet 1915, Keble Chatteron (Paris: Payot, 1932); *Durch! Mit Kriegsmaterial zu Lettow-Vorbeck*, von Kapitënleutnant d R Carl Christiansen (Stuttgart: Verlag fur Volkskinst, Rich Keutel, 1918); *Mit Lettow-Vorbeck im Busch*, von Josef Viera (Stuttgart: Loewes Verlag, Ferdinand Carl, 1943); *Was mir die Engländer über Ostafrika erzahlten*, General von Lettow-Vorbeck (Leipzig: Verlag von K F Koehler, 1932).